THE CATECHISM OF THE CRISIS IN THE CHURCH

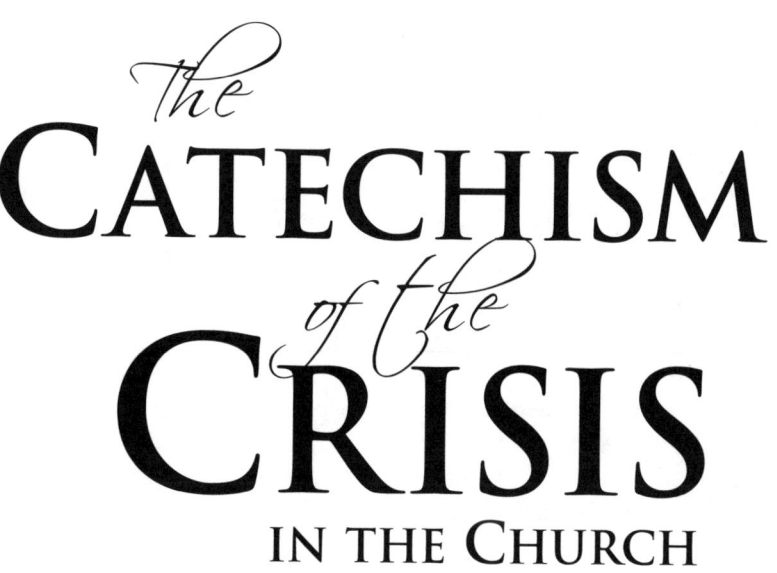

The Catechism of the Crisis in the Church

FR. MATTHIAS GAUDRON

ANGELUS PRESS
2915 FOREST AVENUE
KANSAS CITY, MISSOURI 64109

Title of the German original: *Katholischer Katechismus zur kirchlichen Kriese*
©1997, Rex Regum Verlag, Schloß Jaidhof, Austria

This English version was translated from the second edition (Rex Regum Verlag, 1999) as translated, revised, and edited by the Dominican Fathers of Avrillé in collaboration with the author, with their added subdivisions. After serialization in *The Angelus*, it was revised and updated in accordance with the third French edition published in September 2009.

Library of Congress Cataloging-in-Publication Data

Gaudron, Matthias.
 [Katholischer Katechismus zur kirchlichen Krise. English]
 The catechism of the crisis in the church / Matthias Gaudron.
   p. cm.
 ISBN 978-1-892331-79-3
 1. Catholic Church--Controversial literature--Miscellanea. 2. Catholic traditionalist movement--Miscellanea. I. Title.
 BX1779.5.G3813 2010
 282.09'045--dc22
             2010022331

©2010 by Angelus Press
All rights reserved. No part of this book may be reproduced or transmitted in any form or by any means, electronic or mechanical, including photocopying, recording, or by any information storage and retrieval systems without permission in writing from the publisher, except by a reviewer, who may quote brief passages in a review.

ANGELUS PRESS
2915 FOREST AVENUE
KANSAS CITY, MISSOURI 64109
PHONE (816) 753-3150
FAX (816) 753-3557
ORDER LINE 1-800-966-7337
www.angeluspress.org

ISBN 978-1-892331-79-3
FIRST PRINTING–July 2010

Printed in the United States of America

Contents

Abbreviations vi
   I. The Crisis in the Church 1
  II. The Faith 9
 III. The Church's Magisterium 21
 IV. The Second Vatican Council. 41
  V. Religious Liberty 57
 VI. Ecumenism 87
 VII. The New Mass 123
VIII. The Catholic Priesthood. 163
 IX. The Sacraments 183
  X. Archbishop Lefebvre and
     The Society of St. Pius X. 211

ABBREVIATIONS

AAA   *Acta Apostolicæ Sedis.*

DC   *La Documentation Catholique.*

DS   H. Denzinger and A. Schönmetzer. *Enchiridion Symbolorum, Definitionum et Declarationum de Rebus Fidei et Morum*, 36th ed. Herder, 1976.

Dz.   Denzinger. *The Sources of Catholic Dogma,* tr. Roy J. Deferrari. Loreto Publications, n.d. (1955).

PG   Migne. *Patrologia Graeca.*

PL   Migne. *Patrologia Latina.*

ST   St. Thomas Aquinas. *Summa Theologica.*

I

THE CRISIS IN THE CHURCH

1) Is there a crisis in the Church today?

One would have to close one's eyes not to see that the Catholic Church is suffering a grave crisis. In the 1960's, at the time of the Second Vatican Council, there were hopes for a new springtime in the Church; exactly the opposite has come to pass. Thousands of priests have abandoned their office, and thousands of monks and religious have returned to secular life. There are very few vocations in Europe and not many in North America either; countless seminaries, convents, and religious houses have closed their doors. Many parishes lack priests, and religious congregations are obliged to abandon schools, hospitals, and homes for the aged. As Pope Paul VI lamented on June 29, 1972, "Through some crack, the smoke of Satan has entered the temple of God."[1]

- **Do we know how many priests abandoned the priesthood in the 1960's?**

According to an article by Fabrizio de Santis in the *Corriere della Sera* of September 25, 1971, somewhere between 7,000 to 8,000 priests had abandoned the priesthood in Italy alone over the previous eight years. In the Church as a whole 21,320 priests were reduced to lay status between 1962 and 1972. Not included in this number are those who didn't bother to seek official reduction to lay status.[2] From 1967 to 1974, 30,000 to 40,000 priests abandoned their vocation. These catastrophic events can be compared with the effects of the so-called Protestant Reformation of the sixteenth century.

---

[1] *Der Fels,* No. 10, 1972, p. 313; *DC,* No. 1613, 1972, p. 658.
[2] Georg May, *Die Krise der nachkonziliaren Kirche und Wir* (Vienna: Mediatrix Verlag), pp. 50ff.

● Has there been a comparable disaster in the congregations of nuns?

Some comments by Cardinal Ratzinger illustrate what has happened by a single example. In the early 1960's, Quebec was the region that counted, proportionally speaking, the most nuns in the world. "Between 1961 and 1981, because of departures, deaths, and the end of new vocations, the number of nuns fell from 46,933 to 26,294, a decline of 44 percent, and there is still no end in sight. During the same period new vocations fell by at least 98.5 percent. A large part of the remaining 1.5 percent is composed, not of young women, but of late vocations. As a result, sociologists agree on a grim but objective conclusion: "Soon (unless there is a reversal of the trend, which is wholly improbable, at least viewed humanly) women's religious life as we have known it will be only a memory in Canada."[3]

● Is not the situation improving today, and can we not now consider that the crisis has past?

In America in 1960, there were 1,527 men ordained to the priesthood. In 1998, only 460 were ordained–a decline of over 1,000 per year. In France in the 1950's there were about 1,000 priestly ordinations per year. In the 1990's there were no more than 100 per year; the number of entries into seminaries continues to decrease. In Germany, 1996 represented a new record low of candidates for the priesthood: German seminaries and religious orders had only 232 entries; as recently as 1986 there were 727 entries.[4] The number of religious in the world continues to decline.[5]

● Does this crisis also affect the faithful?

In the 1950's, Mass attendance in America was often higher than 70 percent among Catholics; some studies show that in 2000, this number had fallen to under 30 percent. In 1958, 35 percent of the French attended Mass every Sunday; today fewer than 5 percent do so, and these are often old people. In 1950 more than 90 percent of the French were baptized as children; today fewer than 60 percent are.

---

[3] Joseph Cardinal Ratzinger with Vittorio Messori, *The Ratzinger Report* (1985; San Francisco: Ignatius Press, 1985), p. 101.
[4] *Osterhofener Zeitung,* April 19, 1996.
[5] *Deutsche Tagespost,* August 13, 1998.

- **Is there not, however, an increase of adult baptisms in some countries?**

Several thousand adult baptisms cannot compensate for the loss of hundreds of thousands of infant baptisms (all the more since the perseverance of the late baptized often leaves something to be desired). Infant baptisms in America averaged over 1.3 million in the 1960's, yet has only recently come back over 1 million baptisms a year, notably on account of the increase in the general population. Almost 150,000 adults converted to the Faith in America in 1960; in 2002, this number was under 80,000.

- **Is the case of France or America really typical?**

Everywhere interest in the Church is declining. Now only a minority of Catholics fulfill their Sunday obligations, and thousands leave the Church every year. It is especially disquieting that it is above all young people who turn their backs on the Church. Of the 93,000 who left the Church in Germany in 1989, 70 percent were under 35 years old. Between 1970 and 1993, 1.9 million Germans officially left the Catholic Church. Hatred or anger are not the most frequent causes, but simply indifference. The Church no longer speaks to people, she no longer has importance in their lives and thus people go their own way, sometimes simply to avoid the German church tax. Catholicism is on course to become the religion of a small minority. Germany is in danger, as Karl Rahner put it, of becoming a "pagan land with a Christian past and some vestiges of Christianity." The same holds true for most formerly Christian countries.

- **Can it not be said that this terrible crisis is merely local, affecting Western Europe and North America, but sparing Latin America, Africa, and Asia, where, on the contrary, Catholicism seems especially dynamic?**

Some statistics may suggest that the crisis is merely local. The Pontifical Annuary, for example, stresses that the increase in seminarians and ordinations in the Third World compensates for the decline observed in Western countries. In fact, the crisis is universal, even if it does not appear everywhere in the same way. (Poor countries, where the priesthood can represent social advancement, recruit new vocations relatively easily–but of what quality?) Latin America, for example, passes for a bastion of Catholicism, but it is in fact becoming Protestant at a more rapid pace than Germany did in the sixteenth century. In 1900, just 3 percent of the population of Brazil were Protestants; they are now 18 percent, and the number continues to increase. Five new Pentecostal churches are built in Rio de Janeiro every week.

Fr. Franc Rodé, secretary of the Pontifical Council for Dialogue with Non-believers, estimated in 1993 that the Church was losing 600,000 Latin American faithful every year. Other sources provide even graver indications: 8,000 Catholics a day pass over to sects.[6] In Chile it is believed that 20 percent of the population has joined Protestant sects since 1960, and 30 percent in Guatemala. In the latter country, the number of Protestants increased sevenfold from 1960 to 1985.

2) Is this crisis a crisis of faith?

The Catholic Faith is dwindling away. Fundamental Christian truths such as belief in God, the divinity of Jesus Christ, heaven, purgatory, and hell are less and less believed in. Most disturbingly, these articles of faith are denied even by people who call themselves Catholic and regularly attend Mass.

• Are there any statistics to illustrate this crisis of faith?

Without being altogether reliable, polls do represent general tendencies in society. Many statistics for the United States can be found in Kenneth C. Jones's *Index of Leading Catholic Indicators*. For example, 77 percent of American Catholics in 1999 did not believe one must attend Mass on Sunday to be a good Catholic. Only 17 percent of young Catholics in America believe the priesthood should be restricted to males. Only 10 percent of Catholic elementary school religion teachers agree with the Church's teaching on artificial birth control.[7] A 1992 poll in *Der Spiegel* showed that only 56 percent of Germans believe in the existence of God, 38 percent in His omnipotence, 30 percent in original sin, 29 percent that Jesus is the Son of God, and 24 percent in the existence of hell.[8] Likewise catastrophic is the situation among Catholics. Only 43 percent of them believe in the fundamental dogma of the Resurrection of Christ. Of those who attend Mass on Sundays, only 55 percent believe in the Virgin Birth and only 44 percent recognize papal infallibility. Among all Catholics, only 32 percent believe in papal infallibility. In France a recent poll showed that only 58 percent of the French consider the existence of God certain or probable (compared with 61 percent in 1994); 65 percent (and 80 percent of those eighteen to twenty-four years old) say that they do not believe in the Holy Trinity, and 67 percent (compared with 48 percent in 1994) do not believe in the existence of hell. Only 12 percent of Catholics say they definitely believe in hell (16 percent have some belief in hell, 72 percent deny its existence). Even among regularly practicing Catholics

---

[6] *Présent*, May 22, 1993.
[7] Kenneth C. Jones, *Index of Leading Catholic Indicators* (Roman Catholic Books, 2003), pp. 77-79.
[8] *Der Spiegel*, 25/1992, pp. 36ff.

the statistics are catastrophic: only 23 percent of them firmly believe in hell, while 54 percent deny its existence. Thirty-four percent of these same practicing Catholics are firmly convinced that Mohammed was a prophet, while only 28 percent deny it (35 percent believe it "up to a point," the others are not sure).[9] In 2006, only 7 percent of French Catholics believed that Catholicism is the only true religion.[10] "We can measure the depth of the change by noting that in 1952 most Catholics believed that there was but one true religion," observed the sociologist Yves Lambert.[11] In Valais, the conservative canton of Switzerland that is home to the International Society of Saint Pius X (SSPX) seminary at Ecône, 81.3 percent of Catholics maintain that all religions lead to eternal salvation.[12]

- **What lesson can we draw from these statistics?**

They show the true extent of the crisis. It is *first and foremost* a crisis of faith. Not only is the number of those who consider themselves to belong to the Church diminishing, but even the majority of those who are officially members of the Church no longer hold the Catholic faith! Someone who denies a truth of the Faith has lost the Faith, for the Faith must be held as a whole. If 72 percent of Catholics reject belief in hell, not even one Catholic in three still has the Faith.

3) Is the crisis also a moral one?

A crisis of morality goes hand in hand with the crisis of faith. Whereas St. Paul reminded Christians that they should by their way of life shine in the eyes of a corrupt generation like the stars in the firmament (Phil. 2:15), the way of life of contemporary Christians differs little from that of the children of this world, unbelievers, and others. Their weak faith, emptied of substance, no longer has the strength to influence their life, still less to shape it.

- **What is the connection between faith and morality?**

Man, weakened by original sin, is always inclined to give his passions free rein and thus to lose mastery over himself. The Christian Faith shows man what God expects of him and how he ought to conduct his life in accordance with the will of God. By the Faith

---

[9] CSA poll, *La Vie–Le Monde,* taken in March 2003.
[10] CSA poll, *Le monde des religions,* October 2006.
[11] Report of INSEE, *Données sociales: La société française* (2002-2003 ed.), study by Yves Lambert (CNRS) on "La religion en France des années soixantes à nos jours" [Religion in France from the 1960's to Our Day]. The author notes that the great rupture goes back to the mid-1960's, marked by a decline in religious practice and belief. Formal adherence to religious confessions persisted somewhat longer, showing its first notable decline in 1975-76.
[12] Poll taken by the Link Institute, September 1990.

man knows the promises of what he can hope for if he keeps the commandments of God, and also the punishments he will suffer if he turns away from God. The Faith and the sacraments give man the power to overcome his bad inclinations and to give himself entirely to the good and to the love of God.

- **What are the moral consequences of a crisis of faith?**

When he loses faith man no longer believes that he is called to moral perfection and eternal life in God's presence. He will inevitably yield himself more and more to the unregulated pleasures of this life.

- **Does the contemporary crisis of morality also affect Catholics?**

We are today experiencing this reality. Fidelity, purity, justice, and the spirit of sacrifice are no longer uncontested goods, even for Christians. These days one marriage in three ends in divorce after five to ten years, and ever more Catholics seek Church recognition of separation and "remarriage" after divorce. In 1984 the review *Herderkorrespondenz* showed that, in the very Catholic region of Austria called the Tyrol, 88 percent of the population rejected the Catholic teaching on birth control, and that among the population aged eighteen to thirty full adhesion to Catholic teaching in this regard was practically non-existent (1.8 percent). In the Valais 81.5 percent of Catholics believe that divorced and "remarried" Catholics should be able to receive Communion.[13] In France in 2003 one quarter of practicing Catholics stated that, for them, the idea of sin had little importance. The number of annulments in America jumped from 338 in 1968 to over 50,000 in 1998.

4) Is there also a crisis of the clergy today?

The lack of vocations to the priesthood and the religious life together with the large numbers of priests and religious who abandon their duties show the profound crisis that is ravaging the clergy as well. Many of her members have lost the Faith, and the clergy in general is no longer capable of communicating and inflaming people with the Faith.

- **What is the connection between the crisis of faith and the crisis of the clergy?**

The crisis of the clergy is the *cause* of the crisis of faith amongst Catholics. If the faith of Catholics who attend Sunday Mass regularly

---

[13] *Ibid.*

is so weak, the cause must have its origins in defective preaching. If priests were regularly teaching the Catholic Faith the situation would be very different. Men have not lost belief in the articles of Faith on their own; it has been taken from them through catechism and from the pulpit. When over the course of years sermons put the truths of faith in question, relativize them, or even openly deny them, it is no wonder that simple believers lose the Faith. Often the young have never even known it.

● Can you give an example of this bad teaching dispensed by the clergy?

These days it is not unusual for a child making his First Holy Communion to be unaware that Jesus Christ is truly, really, and substantially present in the Eucharist. He doesn't know this because the parish priest himself no longer believes in this mystery. In *How We Live,* a book of religious instruction used in Germany, one reads that: "When Christians share their meal with Jesus, they go to the altar. The priest gives them a little piece of bread. They eat the bread."[14] This book of religious instruction received an imprimatur and has been authorized by the German bishops!

● Is the situation better in France?

If 34 percent of regularly practicing Catholics believe "completely" that Mohammed is a prophet, and another 35 percent believe it to some degree (giving a total of 69 percent), we note that the statistic is much lower among non-practicing Catholics (21 percent and 22 percent, giving a total of 43 percent). On this question non-practicing Catholics are more Catholic than those who practice. This is evidence of the kind of teaching being dispensed at church. In fact, many French bishops have given churches to the Muslims, and Pope John Paul II kissed the Koran on May 14, 1999.[15]

● Is the crisis of the clergy also a moral crisis?

The crisis is above all a crisis of faith, but a clergy of such weak faith cannot have the strength to observe celibacy, for this is possible only for someone animated by living faith and great love for our Lord. It surprises no one that many priests today maintain sinful relationships with a woman, and do so more and more publicly. It is common to hear that a priest has abandoned his post, admitting that he had not been celibate for years prior. And, in this regard, the situation

---

[14] *Wie Wir Menschen Leben: Ein Religionsbuch* (Herder, 1972), p. 78. The imprimatur was given on January 17, 1972, by the General Vicar of the Diocese of Freiburg, Dr. Schlund.
[15] See *Sel de la Terre,* No. 31, p. 186.

of the clergy in the Third World (whose numbers are increasing) is unfortunately no better.

- **Are not these departures of priests deliberately brought to public attention in order to win the suppression of priestly celibacy?**

It is clear that celibacy keeps many young people away from the priesthood. But rather than entering into polemics on this question, it would be better to ask why there used to be so many men who gladly made this sacrifice, and why this is no longer the case today.

5) How does the current crisis differ from Church crises in the past?

The current crisis in the Church is distinct from those of the past above all in the fact that it is the highest authorities in the Church themselves who have unleashed this crisis, who maintain it, and who prevent the implementation of effective measures for its resolution.

- **Have there not been very grave crises in the Church in the past?**

There have always been crises in the Church. Priests, bishops, and even popes have not always lived their lives in accordance with the Gospel. Immorality and indiscipline among the clergy have often led to decline in the Church. From time to time priests and bishops have departed from the true Faith. But never, as in our times, have errors and the public negation of truths of the Faith been spread abroad thanks to the tolerance, approbation, and even the active efforts of the Roman authorities and the episcopate throughout the world. This is the peculiar characteristic of the current crisis: the fact that it is favored by the highest authorities in the Church, including the pope.

- **Has this singular character of the current crisis been recognized by the authorities in the Church?**

Pope Paul VI himself in 1968 made his famous declaration that the Church finds herself in a state of "self-destruction": "The Church today finds herself in a state of disquiet, self-criticism, one might even say of self-destruction. It is like an interior upheaval, acute and complex, which no one expected after the Council....as though the Church were striking herself."[16]

---

[16] Speech on December 7, 1968; *DC*, No. 1531 (1969), p. 12.

II

THE FAITH

6) What is faith?

Faith is a supernatural virtue through which, relying on the authority of God Himself and moved by His grace, we hold everything He has revealed as absolutely true.[1]

- **Does faith presuppose divine revelation?**

Yes, faith is the response of man to the revelation of God.

- **How did God reveal Himself to men?**

God spoke to men through Moses, the prophets, and above all through His only-begotten Son, our Lord Jesus Christ.

- **What are the truths that man knows thanks to divine Revelation?**

Thanks to Revelation, we know the attributes of God and His Trinitarian essence. We also know our own eternal destiny, which is the vision of God in heaven. Revelation shows us the path we must follow to arrive at this end: observance of the commandments of God and reception of the sacraments, the means of salvation instituted by God.

---

[1] The Council of Trent teaches that faith is "a supernatural virtue by which we, with the aid and inspiration of the grace of God, believe that the things revealed by Him are true, not because the intrinsic truth of the revealed things has been perceived by the natural light of reason, but because of the authority of God Himself who reveals them, who can neither deceive nor be deceived" (Dz. 1789).

- **Why is faith called supernatural?**

The truths revealed by God, which are the object of faith, exceed the natural capacity of our intelligence. It is thus not possible to adhere to them without the supernatural help of God, which is called grace.

- **On what grounds do we adhere to the truths revealed by God?**

The reason for faith is uniquely the authority of God who reveals Himself. We believe the truths of faith because God has affirmed them and not because we had knowledge of them through our own efforts. We believe, for example, in the Holy Trinity or the divinity of Jesus Christ, not because we have discovered these truths by our reason, but because God has revealed them to us.

7) How is the Faith communicated to us?

One source of the Faith is Sacred Scripture or the Bible. It is divided into two parts: the Old Testament, containing the Revelation of God to the Hebrews before the advent of Christ, and the New Testament, which explicitly transmits Christian Revelation.

- **How is Sacred Scripture distinct from other religious writings?**

Sacred Scripture is inspired by the Holy Ghost. This means that it is not a merely human text, but that behind the human author stands God Himself, who has guided the men who composed it in a mysterious way. For this reason Sacred Scripture is really and truly the Word of God.

8) Is Sacred Scripture the only source of Revelation?

To say that Sacred Scripture is the only source of Revelation is a Protestant error. The teaching *orally* transmitted by the Apostles, called Apostolic *Tradition*, is also, next to Sacred Scripture, a true source of Revelation.[2]

---

[2] The Council of Trent teaches that Revelation is "contained in the written books and in the unwritten traditions, which have been received by the apostles from the mouth of Christ Himself, or from the apostles themselves, at the dictation of the Holy Spirit, and ha[s] thus come to us..." (Dz. 783). This teaching was reiterated by Vatican I (Dz. 1787).

- **Is there any mention in Sacred Scripture itself of another source of Revelation?**

  Everything Jesus Christ said and ordained is not found in Sacred Scripture. Scripture itself says so: "But there are also many other things which Jesus did; which, if they were written every one, the world itself, I think, would not be able to contain the books that should be written" (Jn. 21:25). In those days, less was committed to writing than today, and thus oral tradition had a higher status.

- **What other reason can be invoked to show the necessity of Tradition?**

  It is only by Tradition that we know certain truths revealed by God, notably, *what books* belong to Sacred Scripture. There are in fact other "Gospels" and pretended letters of the Apostles which are not authentic Biblical writings. Protestants, who would recognize only the Bible as a source of Faith, are obliged to have recourse to Tradition at least in this respect, for it is their only basis for receiving Sacred Scripture.

- **Which is the first of the two sources of Revelation, Sacred Scripture or Apostolic Tradition?**

  Tradition is the first of the two sources of Revelation by virtue of its *antiquity* (the Apostles began by preaching), its *fullness* (being itself the source of Scripture, Tradition contains all the truths revealed by God), and by its *sufficiency* (Tradition has no need of Scripture as the basis of its divine authority; on the contrary, it is Tradition that gives us the list of the books inspired by God and permits us to know its authentic meaning).

9) Who can authoritatively tell us what belongs to Revelation?

Only the Magisterium of the Church, which resides first of all in the pope, can tell us with certitude what is to be believed and what is erroneous in regard to disputed matters. It was to Peter and his successors that Christ said: "Thou art Peter; and upon this rock I will build my church, and the gates of hell shall not prevail against it" (Mt. 16:18). He likewise gave Peter the mission of confirming his brothers in the faith: "But I have prayed for thee, that thy faith fail not: and thou, being once converted, confirm thy brethren" (Lk. 22:32).

A doctrine that the Church has defined as belonging definitively to divine Revelation is called a *dogma*.

- **What does Sacred Scripture say about the manner in which it should be interpreted?**

St. Peter says in his second epistle: "...no prophecy of scripture is made by private interpretation. For prophecy came not by the will of man at any time: but the holy men of God spoke, inspired by the Holy Ghost" (II Pet. 1:20-21). This passage shows both the inspiration of Sacred Scripture by the Holy Ghost and the fact that we cannot interpret it as we please. This, however, is exactly what the Protestants do: everyone interprets the Bible, and, naturally, everyone understands it in a different way.

- **Can the existence of an infallible magisterium in the Church be proven in a different way?**

Simple reflection suffices to show the necessity of an infallible magisterium. Christ did not intend to speak to His contemporaries in Palestine alone, but to all men of all times to come and of all regions of the earth. But His doctrine could not have been preserved unchanged over the course of centuries had He not instituted a competent authority to resolve the disputes that would arise. Thus this authority was established.

- **Are there other indications of the necessity of this institution?**

The example of the Protestants shows in practice what we have just explained. Among them there is no magisterium, but each individual is in a certain way his own pope. This is why the Protestants are divided into a multitude of groupings, each believing differently from the others. The Catholic Church, on the contrary, has preserved intact the faith of the first Christians.

10) What is the consequence of denying a dogma?

Whoever denies *a single dogma* has lost the Faith, for he does not receive the Revelation of God but sets himself up as judge of what is to be believed.

- **Can one not deny one dogma while continuing to believe in the others and thus conserve the Faith, at least partially?**

As we saw above, the Faith does not depend on our personal judgment, but on the authority of God who reveals Himself and who can neither deceive nor be deceived. Thus it is necessary to receive everything that God has revealed and not take only that which seems good to us. Therefore someone who makes a choice about the revealed deposit of faith and does not want to accept it as a whole imposes a limit on God, for he lets his reason have the last word. He who acts in this way no longer has supernatural faith, but only a *human* faith, however numerous the points on which it may be in accord with supernatural faith.

• Can papal teachings be cited on this point?

When Pope Pius IX defined the dogma of the Immaculate Conception of the Virgin Mary in 1854 he said: "Hence, if anyone shall dare–which God forbid!–to think otherwise than as has been defined by us, let him know and understand that he is condemned by his own judgment; that he has suffered shipwreck in the faith; that he has separated from the unity of the Church."[3]

Leo XIII taught the same thing: "He who denies one of the truths of the faith, even in a single point, in reality loses the whole of the faith, for he refuses to respect God as supreme Truth and formal grounds of the faith."[4] The pope further cites St. Augustine who said, with regard to heretics:

> They are in agreement with me on many things, and we disagree on but a few things. But *because of those few things* in which they are not in agreement with me, the many points of agreement are of no value to them.[5]

• In matters of faith then, is it all or nothing?

One cannot be 70 or 99 percent Catholic; one accepts the whole of Revelation or one does not, in which case one possesses only a *human* faith which one has fabricated for oneself. To choose some truths out of the ensemble of the truths of the Faith is called *heresy* (in Greek, *choice*).

• What should one make of the now popular slogan to the effect that, in our relations with "separated Christians," we should look to what unites rather than to what divides us?

It is altogether false and contrary to the traditional teaching of the Church to say, with regard to non-Catholics, that one must look to what unites rather than to what divides us. This creates the impression that differences relate only to details without importance, when in fact the fullness of revealed truth is at stake.

---

[3] Bull *Ineffabilis Deus*, December 8, 1854. [Except where otherwise noted, English versions of papal writings are taken from the Vatican Web site.–*Tr.*]
[4] Encyclical *Satis Cognitum*, June 29, 1896.
[5] St. Augustine, *Commentary on Psalm 54*, No. 19 (*PL*, 36, 641).

11) Is not faith primarily a sentiment?

It is one of the errors of modernism, condemned by St. Pius X in 1907 in the Encyclical *Pascendi*, to say that faith is a sentiment issued from the subconscious, arising from some need for the divine. In fact, the act of faith is not a sentiment, but a form of understanding, the conscious and voluntary reception of divine Revelation as it is has been presented to man in Sacred Scripture and Tradition.

- **What is Revelation for the modernists?**

For the modernists revelation is created when the religious sentiment passes from the realm of the subconscious to the conscious mind. Faith would thus be something sentimental and subjective. Revelation would not come from the outside (from on high) but would arise from the interior of man.

- **What then is the role of Christ in Revelation for the modernists?**

Modernists believe that, at the origins of Christianity, there was the religious experience of Jesus Christ (who, to be sure, is not thought of as true God). He shared His experience with others, who lived it themselves and communicated it to others in turn. From this need of the faithful to communicate their religious experiences to others and to form a community was born the Church. The Church is thus not a divine institution; she, like the sacraments, the papacy, the dogmas, is only the result of the religious needs of believers.

- **Is is not true that man naturally has a religious sentiment?**

The *natural* religious sentiment must be carefully distinguished from the *supernatural* faith of the Catholic. There is certainly a need for God in the human heart, but if God does not really respond to this need, it remains an empty sentiment. Furthermore, like everything that is natural in us, the religious sentiment is wounded by original sin: it can easily lead to error and even to sin (superstition, idolatry, *etc.*).

- **Is faith not linked to the religious sentiment all the same?**

It is true that a sentiment of security and well-being is linked to the virtue of faith, but this is not the essence of faith. This sentiment, like all other sentiments, is changeable, sometimes waxing and sometimes waning; at times it can even disappear altogether. Great saints, like St. Vincent de Paul or St. Theresa of the Child Jesus, have sometimes been deprived of this sensible certainty without, however, becoming hesitant in their belief in the truth and the certitude of the Faith.

- **Where can one find the certain teaching of the Church on this matter?**

In the Anti-modernist Oath that, until 1967, all priests were obliged to pronounce before their ordination:

> I hold with certainty and sincerely confess that faith is not a blind sentiment of religion welling up from the depths of the subconscious under the impulse of the heart and the motion of a will trained to morality; but faith is a genuine assent of the intellect to truth received by hearing from an external source. By this assent, because of the authority of the supremely truthful God, we believe to be true that which has been revealed and attested to by a personal God, our Creator and Lord.

12) Can the Faith change?

According to modernist doctrine the Faith can change, for dogmas are only the expression of a sentiment of interior faith and of a religious need. They thus need to be adapted and formulated in a new manner when religious sentiments and needs change.

If, however, as the Church teaches, dogmas express the truths of the Faith in an infallible manner, it is evident that they cannot be changed, for what was true yesterday cannot be false today and vice versa. As truth is immutable, so is the true Faith. Thus St. Paul writes: "But though we, or an angel from heaven, preach a gospel to you besides that which we have preached to you, let him be anathema" (Gal. 1:8). "*Jesus Christus heri et hodie ipse et in saecula*–Jesus Christ yesterday, and today, and the same for ever" (Heb. 13:8).

- **Isn't there progress in the Faith?**

Progress in the doctrine of the Faith is possible only in the sense that the truths of faith are better understood and explicated. Such a development was predicted by Jesus Christ for His Church when He said: "But the Paraclete, the Holy Ghost, whom the Father will send in my name, He will teach you all things, and bring all things to your mind, whatsoever I shall have said to you" (Jn. 14:26).

- **Doesn't the Holy Ghost teach new truths to the Church?**

Revelation ended with the death of the last Apostle.[6] Since then, the Holy Ghost does not teach new truths, but rather makes the Church enter ever more profoundly into the truth brought by Christ. Thus revealed truths that played only a secondary role in the life of

---

[6] Among the modernist errors condemned in 1907 by St. Pius X is the following: "Revelation, constituting the object of the Catholic faith, was not completed with the Apostles." *Lamentabile Sane*, proposition 21.

the Church at a certain period may assume a primary importance in another age. The controversies that opposed the Church to heretics also forced her to set forth the truths of the Faith in a more precise and clear manner, making *explicit* truths that till then were *implicitly* held, but never adding to the deposit of faith [*depositum fidei*] as revealed to the Apostles.

- **What are the rules of this development of the Faith?**

The development of doctrine can *elaborate* that which was taught in the past, but it can never *contradict* or *modify* it. There can be no opposition to what has been taught. Once a dogma has been defined it cannot later become false, void, or take on a new meaning.

- **When she teaches a new dogma, doesn't the Church reveal new truths?**

When the Church defines a new dogma, she does not reveal new truths, but she explains and puts the accent in a new manner on that which, fundamentally, has always been believed. It is always "the same dogma, with the same sense and the same understanding."[7] The First Vatican Council clearly teaches: "The Holy Ghost has not been promised to the successors of Peter that under His revelation they should reveal new doctrine, but that with His assistance they might in a holy manner guard and faithfully set forth Revelation as transmitted by the apostles, that is to say the deposit of the faith."[8]

13) Can several religions possess the true Faith?

From the fact that different religions contradict themselves on fundamental points it follows that several of them cannot be true. Only one religion can be true, and that is the Catholic religion. God revealed Himself in Jesus Christ, not in Buddha or Mohammed; and Christ founded only one Church which must communicate His teaching and His grace until the end of the world. Faith in a trinitarian God, in Christ, and in the Church thus forms an indivisible unity.

- **Do the different religions really contradict one another?**

God is either the Trinity, or He is not. If He is the Trinity, all non-Christian religions are false. But Christian confessions also contradict one another: some do not believe in the divinity of Christ, many

---

[7] "*In eodem scilicet dogmate, eodem sensu eademque sententia.*" Vatican I, Dz. 1800, quoting St. Vincent of Lerins, *Commonitorium Primum* 23, 3; *PL* 50, 668A.
[8] Dogmatic Constitution I on the Church of Christ, Dz. 1836.

do not believe in the real presence of the Body and Blood of Christ in the sacrament of the Eucharist, *etc.* Such opposite beliefs are not compatible.

14) How can we recognize that the Catholic Faith is true?

Christ proved the truth of His mission by the miracles that He worked. This is why He says: "Believe you not that I am in the Father, and the Father in me? Otherwise believe me for the very works' sake" (Jn. 14:11-12). The Apostles also established themselves by their miracles: "But they going forth preached everywhere: the Lord working withal, and confirming the word with signs that followed" (Mk. 16:20). Miracles are the proof of the divine mission of the Church.

• Can we be sure of the existence of miracles?

There have always been miracles in the Church. In fact, the existence of these miracles has never been more certain than today when, thanks to scientific knowledge and tools of investigation, we can rule out natural explanations more easily than in the past. Self-suggestion and hallucination have no place here. The multiplication of food observed by numerous persons who have in no way been influenced in advance, the resurrection of a dead man, or the sudden cure of an organ which has been almost completely destroyed can scarcely be explained in this way. The Church never recognizes a miracle so long as the slightest possibility of a natural explanation exists.

• Are all miracles of a physical nature?

Next to so-called "physical" miracles (facts that cannot be physically explained by natural processes alone) there are also what can be called "moral" miracles (facts that cannot be morally explained by the forces of nature alone.)

• Give some examples of moral miracles.

The diffusion of Christianity is a moral miracle, for no natural explanation can account for the fact that twelve uninstructed fishermen lacking any influence could convert a great part of the world in a short period of time, notwithstanding the opposition of the rich and powerful. The multifaceted sanctity that has flourished uninterruptedly in the Church for the last two thousand years is also a moral miracle.

• Do miracles prove the truths of the Faith?

Miracles cannot directly prove the truths of the Faith nor oblige anyone to believe, for then it would no longer be faith but science.

They nevertheless show that faith is not blind confidence lacking foundation, that it is not opposed to reason, and that on the contrary it is unreasonable not to believe!

• Apart from the proofs of the truth of Catholicism, are there direct proofs of the falsehood of Protestantism?

The fact that the Protestant factions of Christianity cannot possess the truth is apparent from the simple fact that they are relatively recent separations from the Church of Christ. Luther did not reform the Church, as he pretended, but on the contrary invented new doctrines opposed to those that Christians had always believed until then. Christians have always been convinced, for example, that the Eucharist can only be celebrated by a man ordained priest and that the holy Mass is a true sacrifice: how could it be truthful to suddenly proclaim something different fifteen hundred years later? How could the Anglican Church be the true Church when it only owes its existence to the adultery of Henry VIII?

• Is it then easy to find the true religion?

As Pope Leo XIII observed:

> To recognize what is the true religion is not difficult for whomever would judge the matter in prudence and sincerity. In fact very numerous and striking proofs, the truth of the prophecies, the multitude of miracles, the prodigious speed of the propagation of the Faith, even amongst its enemies and in spite of the greatest obstacles, the testimony of the martyrs and other similar arguments prove clearly that the only true religion is that which Jesus Christ Himself instituted, and which He charged the Church to guard and propagate.[9]

• If it is easy to find the true religion, how is it that so many people do not find it?

If so many people are unaware of the true religion, it is above all because so many sin *out of negligence* in this regard. They are unconcerned to know the truth about God but content themselves with the pleasures of this world or with the habits and superstitions prevalent where they live, which suffice to satisfy their religious sentiment. They lack thirst for the truth. Furthermore, many foresee that the true religion would demand sacrifices of them, which they do not want to make. Lastly, man is by nature a social animal: he needs help in every domain (physical, technical, intellectual, and moral) and depends a great deal on the society in which he lives. If that society is Islamic or atheist (like our own), if school and the media turn him away from

---

[9] Leo XIII, Encyclical *Immortale Dei*, November 1, 1885.

Christianity (and even stupefy him so as to keep him from thinking) it will be very difficult for him to swim against the tide.

15) Is faith necessary for salvation?

Sacred Scripture teaches that faith is absolutely necessary to obtain eternal salvation. "He that believeth and is baptized, shall be saved: but he that believeth not shall be condemned" (Mk. 16:16). St. Paul teaches: "But without faith it is impossible to please God" (Heb. 11:6).

• What is this faith that is necessary for salvation?

The faith necessary for salvation is not any faith whatsoever, but the true faith, which adheres in a supernatural manner to the true doctrine revealed by God.

• Is the necessity of true doctrine apparent in Sacred Scripture?

The necessity of keeping true doctrine is manifest in the repeated warnings of the Apostles in regard to heretics and disbelievers:

> For there shall be a time, when they will not endure sound doctrine; but, according to their own desires, they will heap to themselves teachers, having itching ears: And will indeed turn away their hearing from the truth, but will be turned unto fables. (II Tim. 4:3-4)

• Are those who, through no fault of their own, do not adhere to revealed truths necessarily damned?

God gives everyone the possibility of saving himself. He who is ignorant of the truths of faith *without any fault on his part* will obtain from God, at one time or another, if he does everything possible to live well, the possibility of receiving sanctifying grace. But it is evident that anyone who does not profess the true religion *by his own fault* will be eternally damned.

• Is the true Faith thus of sovereign importance?

Indeed it is. This is not a matter of vain controversy among theologians, but of the eternal salvation or misery of immortal souls.

III

THE CHURCH'S MAGISTERIUM

16) In the Church, who holds the power to teach with authority (the magisterial authority, or magisterium)?

The holders of the ecclesiastical magisterium are, by divine right, the pope for the universal Church, and the bishops for their dioceses.

- **How do the pope and the bishops receive this authority?**

The pope is the successor of St. Peter, and the bishops are the successors of the Apostles, whom our Lord Jesus Christ Himself instituted as supreme doctors of the faith. They received from God the mandate to preach Christian doctrine to their subjects and to safeguard its purity. In this way they continue the work of our Lord Jesus Christ, who, since His Ascension, no longer remains visibly among us.

- **Did our Lord clearly mention the teaching authority transmitted to the bishops?**

Jesus said to His Apostles: "He that heareth you, heareth me; and he that despiseth you, despiseth me" (Lk. 10:16). The same pertains for the bishops, who are the successors of the Apostles.

17) Is the ecclesiastical magisterium infallible?

Yes, the ecclesiastical magisterium, or teaching authority of the Church, is infallible. But for this to be true, precise conditions must be met. If they are not fulfilled, the bishops and the pope can err. A declaration or a homily and even a papal encyclical or a conciliar document are not necessarily infallible. They are only infallible when infallibility is claimed.

18) When is the pope infallible?

The pope is infallible when he speaks *ex cathedra*, that is, when as supreme teacher of the nations, he elevates a truth to the rank of a dogma that must be believed by the faithful. In this case, the assistance of the Holy Ghost is promised to the pope so that he cannot err. Theologians generally attribute the privilege of infallibility to the pope in a few other cases, for example, canonizations,[1] the general laws of the Church, and when he echoes the teaching of his predecessors.

- **Where are the conditions in which the pope is infallible clearly set forth?**

The conditions in which the pope speaks infallibly are very clearly set out by the First Vatican Council, which precisely defined papal infallibility. The Council teaches:

> When the Roman Pontiff speaks *ex cathedra,* that is, when, in the exercise of his office as shepherd and teacher of all Christians, in virtue of his supreme apostolic authority, he defines a doctrine concerning faith or morals to be held by the whole Church, he possesses, by the divine assistance promised to him in blessed Peter, that infallibility which the divine Redeemer willed his Church to enjoy in defining doctrine concerning faith or morals.[2]

- **What can we learn from this text of Vatican Council I?**

By attentively reading this text of Vatican I, we learn that there are four conditions for papal infallibility: **1)** the pope must speak "in the exercise of his office as shepherd and teacher of all Christians," that is, not as a private theologian but as head of the Church explicitly engaging "his supreme apostolic authority" received directly from Christ; **2)** the subject on which he pronounces must be "a doctrine concerning faith or morals"; **3)** the doctrine must not only be taught, but the pope must declare it obligatory by an authoritative act ("a doctrine...*to be held*"); **4)** this will to oblige the faithful to assent must be addressed to "the universal Church."

---

[1] At least the canonizations prior to 1983. The simplification of the procedures implemented at that date as well as the veritable explosion in the number of canonizations allow the existence of a serious doubt as to whether John Paul II ha[d] the same intention as his predecessors when he carrie[d] out canonizations.)

[2] Vatican I, Dogmatic Constitution *Pastor Aeternus*, Dz. 1839.

- **Is the manifestation of the pope's will to oblige the universal Church essential for a papal act to be infallible?**

Yes, the pope's manifestation of his will to oblige the universal Church to hold a point of doctrine or morals is necessary for infallibility to be engaged: this act of authority is even the essential element of the *ex cathedra* definition.

- **How does the pope manifest this will to oblige?**

The pope manifests his will to make a doctrine obligatory in the Church by clearly declaring that those who refuse it no longer have the Catholic faith and are henceforth outside the Church.

- **Can the pope use his infallibility to impose novelties?**

Papal infallibility is entirely at the service of the conservation of the faith, which, as we have seen, is immutable and necessary for salvation.[3] Vatican I teaches: "For the Holy Spirit was promised to the successors of Peter not so that they might, by His revelation, make known some new doctrine, but that, by His assistance, they might religiously guard and faithfully expound the revelation or deposit of faith transmitted by the Apostles."[4]

- **Does the solemn (infallible) definition of a truth of faith occur frequently?**

The solemn definition of a truth of faith does not occur often; numerous popes have never used this power. There was only one instance of this in the twentieth century: the definition of the dogma of the Assumption of the Virgin Mary into heaven by Pope Pius XII on November 1, 1950.

- **How did Pope Pius XII manifest his will to oblige the Church during the definition of the dogma of the Assumption?**

Pius XII proclaimed the dogma of the Assumption of our Lady by declaring, in the Apostolic Constitution *Munificentissimus Deus*:

> by the authority of our Lord Jesus Christ, of the Blessed Apostles Peter and Paul, and by Our own authority We pronounce, declare, and define that the dogma was revealed by God, that the Immaculate Mother of God, the ever Virgin Mary, after completing her course of life upon earth, was assumed to the glory of heaven both in body and soul. Therefore, if anyone, which may God forbid, should dare either to deny this, or

---

[3] *Ibid.*
[4] *Ibid.*

voluntarily call into doubt what has been defined by Us, he should realize that he has cut himself off entirely from the divine and Catholic faith.[5]

19) When are the bishops infallible?

The bishops are infallible in two cases: **1)** When they solemnly proclaim a truth of faith in an ecumenical council in union with the pope, their supreme head. All the ancient ecumenical councils proclaimed the truths of faith in this manner. It is important, then, that the pope approve these decisions, even if it is not necessary that he be present at the council himself. A council the decrees of which were not ratified by the pope could not be considered infallible. **2)** The bishops are equally infallible when, dispersed throughout the world, they unanimously teach a truth as belonging to the deposit of faith. This is the case for the articles of faith in general which have for a long time been taught everywhere in the Church without having been subject to doubt.

• How are these two modes of episcopal infallibility designated?

1) An infallible affirmation made by the pope or a council is called a solemn judgment; it is an act of the Church's *extraordinary magisterium*; **2)** the infallible transmission of the faith by the bishops dispersed throughout the world is called, on the contrary, the *ordinary and universal magisterium* (sometimes abbreviated OUM).

• Is not one mode of infallibility sufficient? Why are there two?

Normally, the common teaching of the bishops (the OUM) is sufficient for knowing with certitude the truths of faith. But in times of crisis, when the bishops disagree among themselves or simply fail to use their authority to reiterate revealed truth, then it is no longer possible to have recourse to this criterion. To resolve the crisis, an extraordinary act of the magisterium is required, that is, a solemn judgment pronounced by a council or by the pope.

• Can you give us an example?

All Christians firmly believed in the real presence of the Body and Blood of our Lord in the sacrament of the Eucharist long before it was solemnly defined. It was taught throughout the whole Church as a truth of faith. Nevertheless, the denial of this truth by the Protestants made its solemn definition by the Council of Trent necessary. In fact, the attacks of heretics are often the occasion for the Church to solemnly define a truth.

---

[5] Dz. 2333.

- **What is the advantage of having a solemn judgment over and above the teaching of the ordinary and universal magisterium?**

A solemn judgment delivered by the pope or a council has the advantage of resolving a doctrinal difficulty with a single judgment of incontestable authority, whereas the ordinary and universal magisterium refers to a multitude of acts posed in divers terms and contexts by different bishops; thus it is more difficult to discern.

- **What precisely is the ordinary and universal magisterium?**

Pius IX gave the following definition: "[It is] those matters which are handed down as divinely revealed by the ordinary teaching power of the whole Church spread throughout the world, and therefore, by universal and common consent are held by Catholic theologians to belong to the faith."[6]

- **What does this definition show?**

This definition shows that, like the pope's teaching, the universal teaching of the bishops (the ordinary and universal magisterium) is only infallible under certain conditions.

- **For a doctrine to be infallibly certain by virtue of the ordinary and universal magisterium of the Church, isn't it enough for all the bishops of the world to be unanimously in agreement at a given moment?**

No, it is not enough for all the bishops to adopt simultaneously some new theory for it to become infallible. The infallibility of the ordinary and universal magisterium can only apply to: **1)** a *truth* touching faith or morals that **2)** the bishops teach *with authority* **3)** in a universally unanimous way **4)** as divinely revealed to the Apostles or necessary to safeguard the deposit of faith, and thus as immutable and obligatory. If these four conditions are not met, there is no infallibility.

- **Then only a doctrine the bishops teach as having been revealed to the Apostles and transmitted to us by Tradition can enjoy the infallibility of the ordinary and universal magisterium?**

Yes, only a truth the bishops are unanimous in teaching with authority as belonging to the deposit of faith (or necessarily linked to

---

[6] Letter of Pius IX to the Archbishop of Munich dated December 21, 1863 (Dz. 1683).

it) can be guaranteed by the infallibility of the ordinary and universal magisterium.

- **What is the reason for this condition?**

The magisterium was not instituted to reveal new doctrines, but only to transmit the truths already revealed to the Apostles. It is this transmission, and not subsequent extraneous accretions, that infallibility protects.

20) What responsibility do the bishops have for the current crisis in the Church?

"The crisis in the Church is a crisis of bishops," Cardinal Seper said.[7] Among the four thousand bishops of the Catholic Church, there are certainly some who want to be Catholic and to serve the faith, but by most of them, the faith is maltreated. Instead of defending it, they allow free rein to the priests and professors who openly deny truths of faith; moreover, they encourage them. Many bishops even personally support positions incompatible with Catholic faith and morals.

- **Can you give some examples?**

In France, Cardinal Lustiger, Archbishop of Paris, publicly teaches that the Jews need not convert to Christianity. Proselytism aimed at them would make no sense. Similarly, Archbishop Doré of Strasbourg (and former dean of the theology faculty of the Catholic Institute of Paris) denies that the Jews, having rejected Jesus Christ, can be considered as "perfidious" and "blind": it is not they who would be in need of conversion, but rather the Catholics, who usurped their place by claiming to be the "new Israel."[8]

- **Can you give other examples of bishops betraying the Catholic faith?**

They are unfortunately superabundant. In 2001, the doctrinal commission of the French episcopate publicly encouraged the reading of the Bayard edition of the Bible, underscoring its "profound fidelity to divine revelation." Yet this version of the Bible denies the historicity of

---

[7] Quoted by Dr. Georg May, *Gefahren, die der Kirche drohen* (St. Andrä-Wörden: Mediatrix, 1990), p. 27.
[8] Most Reverend Joseph Doré, Address to the Jewish Lodge René Hirschler of B'nai B'rith and published in the diocesan bulletin, July-August 2003, pp. 1-3. [Archbishop Doré's address as well as an open letter to him from Fr. Stephen Abraham, FSSPX, were published in *The Angelus*, February 2004.]

the facts reported in the Gospels.[9] In 2003, Bishop Dufour of Limoges declared from the pulpit: "We do not know whether God exists. We do not know it with scientific certitude, but we know it by faith."[10] But St. Paul and the Church teach that the existence of God can be known with certitude by reason, even without faith.[11]

On November 6, 1997, during a conference at Berlin, the president of the German Episcopal Conference, Bishop Karl Lehmann, called Luther "the common Doctor," a title customarily given by the Church to St. Thomas Aquinas! The list of abuses could easily be extended. It is a sad fact that many bishops contradict basic articles of faith.

21) Does the pope also share the responsibility for the current crisis in the Church?

As we related, one of the characteristics of the current crisis in the Church is that it is encouraged by the highest authorities in the Church. The conciliar popes have encouraged this crisis: **1)** by giving modernist theologians their support; **2)** by their defending opinions and acting in ways incompatible with the Catholic faith; and **3)** by erecting obstacles to the work of defenders of the Faith.

• Can you prove these assertions?

We shall give some illustrations here; others will appear further on in our study.

• Does Pope John XXIII have a share in the responsibility for the current crisis?

John XXIII (1958-63) is the pope who made the crisis, which had been simmering for several decades, erupt. Despite warning voices, he convoked the Second Vatican Council, and his *aggiornamento* became the marching order for an unlimited upheaval as well as for the entrance of the spirit of the world into the Church.

---

[9] "The first Christians are more interested in the Christ of faith than in the Jesus of history" (p. 2988). See *Sel de la Terre*, No. 39, pp. 6-26.
[10] Most Reverend Dufour, Confirmation homily, published in the *Courrier Français*, Limoges edition, July 25, 2003, p. 4.
[11] "If anyone shall have said that the one true God, our Creator and our Lord, cannot be known with certitude by those things which have been made, by the natural light of human reason: let him be anathema." Vatican Council I, Constitution *Dei Filius* (Dz. 1806).

- **Can John XXIII really be blamed for convoking Vatican II?**

Even more than for convoking the Council, John XXIII should be blamed for the goal and the spirit of the convocation. In his opening discourse at the Council, after recalling that the Church had never failed to condemn errors, Pope John XXIII continued:

> Nowadays, however, the Spouse of Christ prefers to make use of the medicine of mercy rather than that of severity. She considers that she meets the needs of the present day by demonstrating the validity of her teaching rather than by condemnations. Not, certainly, that there is a lack of fallacious teaching, opinions, and dangerous concepts to be guarded against and dissipated. But these are so obviously in contrast with the right norm of honesty, and have produced such lethal fruits that by now it would seem that men of themselves are inclined to condemn them.[12]

The Pope was also against the "prophets of gloom" and thought that the errors would vanish by themselves "like fog before the sun."

- **What is blameworthy in these statements?**

Its naive viewpoint has no connection with reality. Buddhism, Islam, and Protestantism are errors that have existed for centuries and have scarcely vanished by themselves. On the contrary, they are spreading even more because the Church nowadays refuses to condemn them. In the Church itself, despite the optimistic expectations of Pope John, the truth has not shone, but on the contrary a multitude of errors have spread.

- **Are there other examples of John XXIII's eirenism?**

Even worse is the episode witnessed by Archbishop Lefebvre while a member of the Council's Preparatory Commission. At one of the meetings during which experts for the Council were being chosen, he was astonished to discover on the lists, contrary to the rules, the names of at least three experts who had been condemned by Rome for their heterodoxy. At the end of the meeting, Cardinal Ottaviani approached Archbishop Lefebvre and explained to him that this was at the Pope's express wish. Thus the Pope wanted at the Council experts the integrity of whose faith was questionable!

- **What was the attitude of John XXIII's successor, Pope Paul VI?**

Pope Paul VI (1963-78), who continued the Council after John XXIII's death, clearly supported the liberals. He appointed the four Cardinals Döpfner, Suenens, Lercaro, and Agagianian to be the

---

[12] John XXIII, Opening discourse, *The Documents of Vatican II*, Abbott ed.

moderators of the Council. The first three were well-known liberals, and the fourth was not an outstanding personality.

- **During the Council, didn't Paul VI oppose the liberal bishops (especially during what came to be called "the black week" in November 1964)?**

Even if Paul VI sometimes acted against the extremist liberals, it is certain that the situation of the conservatives among the Council Fathers was practically blocked because the liberals visibly enjoyed the Pope's favor.

On December 7, 1965, Pope Paul declared to the bishops assembled for the Council's cloture:

> The religion of the God who became man has met the religion (for such it is) of man who makes himself God. And what happened? Was there a clash, a battle, a condemnation? There could have been, but there was none. The old story of the Samaritan has been the model of the spirituality of the Council. A feeling of boundless sympathy has permeated the whole of it. The attention of our Council has been absorbed by the discovery of human needs (and these needs grow in proportion to the greatness which the son of the earth claims for himself). But we call upon those who term themselves modern humanists, and who have renounced the transcendent value of the highest realities, to give the Council credit at least for one quality and to recognise our own new type of humanism: we, too, in fact, we more than any others, honour mankind [literally: have the cult or worship of man].[13]

- **What should we make of this declaration?**

It can be contrasted with the advice given by St. Pius X in his first encyclical: "We must use every means and exert all our energy to bring about the utter disappearance of the enormous and detestable wickedness so characteristic of our time–the substitution of man for God."[14]

Freemasonry, the goal of which is the destruction of the Catholic Church, has the cult of man, but not the Catholic Church. Hearing Paul VI promote the cult of man, the Freemasons must have savored their triumph. Is it not the achievement of the plans they forged in the nineteenth century?

---

[13] Paul VI, Public Session, December 7, 1965 [English version: Xavier Rynne, *The Fourth Session* (London, 1966)].

[14] Pope St. Pius X, Encyclical *E Supremi Apostolatus* (§9). The holy Pope identified as "the distinguishing mark of Antichrist" the fact that "man has with infinite temerity put himself in the place of God, raising himself above all that is called God; in such wise that although he cannot utterly extinguish in himself all knowledge of God, he has contemned God's majesty and, as it were, made of the universe a temple wherein he himself is to be adored" (§5).

- **How can one learn about the plans elaborated by Freemasonry against the Church?**

One way the plans of Freemasonry were made known was through the secret correspondence of the heads of the Italian *Alta Vendita* that fell into the hands of the Vatican police in 1846, which Pope Gregory XVI ordered to be published.[15]

- **What do the Masonic plans foretell?**

The correspondence that was seized and published shows that the Freemasons wanted to do everything so that "a Pope according to our wants" could ascend the throne of Peter. They explained:

> [T]hat Pontiff, like the greater part of his contemporaries, will be necessarily imbued with the...humanitarian principles which we are about to put in circulation....You will have fished up a Revolution in Tiara and Cope, marching with Cross and banner–a Revolution which needs only to be spurred on a little to put the four quarters of the world on fire.[16]

- **Can it truly be said that Paul VI was this Pope imbued with humanitarian principles?**

The following hymn, which Paul VI intoned when man walked on the moon, would be suitably placed on the lips of a Freemason: "Hail to man; hail to thought and science, to technology and work; hail to the boldness of man....Hail to man, king of the earth and now prince of the heavens."[17]

- **Is Paul VI responsible for other aspects of the current crisis?**

Paul VI is also the pope who introduced the new rite of Mass, the harmfulness of which we shall examine.

- **What else should be pointed out about Paul VI?**

It was during Paul VI's reign that the persecution of priests who wanted to stay Catholic and who refused to abandon the faithful to Protestantism, modernism, and apostasy began.

---

[15] The publication was done by Jacques Crétineau-Joly (1803-75) in his work *L'Église romaine en face de la Révolution* (1859). The work was honored by a brief of approbation from Pius IX (February 25, 1861), who implicitly guaranteed the authenticity of the documents. (All the documents were reproduced by Msgr. Delassus in an appendix to his work *The Anti-Christian Conspiracy* [French]).

[16] *Ibid.* The texts cited by Crétineau-Joly were published by Msgr. George Dillon in *Grand Orient Freemasonry Unmasked* (1885; reprint in Palmdale, CA: Christian Book Club of America [Omni Publications], 1999), pp. 91, 95.

[17] Paul VI, February 7, 1971, *DC*, February 21, 1971, p. 156.

● Didn't Pope John Paul II turn things around?

Endowed with a stronger personality than Paul VI, John Paul II was able to seem firmer on certain points, but he also committed himself more resolutely to the course of novelties. He performed actions to which the note of apostasy or suspect of heresy would formerly have been attached.

● Can you give us an example?

On May 29, 1982, John Paul II recited the Creed with the so-called Archbishop of Canterbury, Lord Runcie, in Canterbury Cathedral, and then gave the benediction with him. The Primate of the Anglican Church was vested in all his pontifical regalia, whereas he is just a layman by reason of the invalidity of Anglican orders.[18]

● Are there any similar examples?

There is worse: participation in idolatrous rites. In August of 1985, John Paul II participated in an animist rite in the sacred forest of Togo. On February 2, 1986, at Bombay, he received on his forehead the *Tilac*, which symbolizes the Hindu deity Shiva's third eye.[19] On February 5, at Madras, he received the *Vibhuti* (sacred ashes), sign of the adorers of Shiva and Vishnu.[20]

● How far did the Pope's participation in false worship go?

The sad climax of these activities was reached with the prayer meeting of religions at Assisi on October 27, 1986. The Pope invited all the religions of the world to come and pray for peace at Assisi, with the representatives of each religion praying according to their own rite. Catholic churches were placed at their disposition for the celebration of pagan rites. In San Pietro's Church, they even placed a statue of Buddha on the tabernacle.

● Isn't it a good thing to promote peace and elicit prayers for this intention?

It is not peace, but idolatry and superstition that are bad, for they seriously impinge on the honor due to God. A good intention can never justify committing or encouraging inherently evil acts.

---

[18] The invalidity of Anglican ordinations was solemnly pronounced by Leo XIII in the Letter *Apostolicæ Curæ* of September 13, 1896.

[19] *La Croix*, February 6, 1986; and *L'Express*, February 7, 1986, with photograph.

[20] *Indian Express*, February 6, 1986.

● Did John Paul II stop there?

After 1986, John Paul II continued to sponsor annually interreligious meetings like the one at Assisi. He also continued the spectacular gestures in support of false religions. On May 14, 1999, he publicly kissed the Koran. The diffusion of the photograph of this act, widely broadcast in Muslim countries, could only confirm the Mohammedans in their false religion.

● Hasn't Benedict XVI initiated a return to Tradition?

Benedict XVI is undoubtedly more favorable to liturgical tradition than was John Paul II. By his motu proprio of July 7, 2007, *Summorum Pontificum*, he gave more freedom to the traditional liturgy in spite of the opposition of numerous bishops (notably in France and Germany). On January 24, 2009, he also lifted the official excommunication that, since 1988, had weighed upon the bishops consecrated by Archbishop Lefebvre (though without acknowledgment that this excommunication had been null).[21]

But though his heart may be traditional, he also received a modernist formation. In the books he wrote as a young theologian, one finds numerous affirmations contrary to the faith, sometimes bordering on heresy. Even if he seems to have changed his mind on certain points, he has not disavowed his former errors. His book *Introduction to Christianity*, for instance, is still in print even though it calls in question, among other things, the divinity of Jesus Christ.[22]

Benedict XVI absolutely intends to save Vatican II. That is why he is trying to situate it in continuity with Tradition. We are going to see that this is impossible.

● Has Benedict XVI done anything as scandalous as John Paul II?

The pontificate of Benedict XVI comes across as more serious than that of his predecessor. Nevertheless, he has already done some things that are incompatible with the Catholic Faith:

- At John Paul II's funeral Mass, eleven days before being elected to the papacy, Cardinal Ratzinger gave Communion in the hand to Brother Roger Schutz of Taizé, whom he knew to be a Protes-

---

[21] See below, Question 98.
[22] The latest English version was published by Ignatius Press in 2004, with a new preface by then Cardinal Ratzinger dated April 2000.

tant.²³ One might, however, suppose that he was caught off guard, because this incident was not repeated at his enthronement Mass.

- During the same Mass, he spoke of John Paul II as "standing at the window of the Father's house," thereby indicating that, having by-passed purgatory, John Paul II was already in heaven, and proceeded to a kind of instantaneous canonization.²⁴

- In his first papal homily, Benedict XVI promised to pursue the ecumenical dialogue championed by Pope John Paul II.

- Just four months after his election, he visited the Cologne synagogue (August 19, 2005), implying that the worship rendered there is pleasing to God (it was obviously not a matter of private tourism, but rather a highly symbolic public act, which Benedict XVI added on his own initiative to the itinerary of his trip to Germany.)

- On November 30, 2006, Benedict XVI took off his shoes (and put on a pair of white slippers) before entering the Blue Mosque in Istanbul. There, after turning towards Mecca, he paused for a few moments of reflection. Once again, his attitude gave the impression that the worship rendered in the mosque was also legitimate and pleasing to God.²⁵

- On February 4, 2008, Benedict XVI modified the traditional missal by suppressing every mention of the blindness of the Jews in the Good Friday prayer for them.²⁶

22) Why do these popes pass for conservatives?

The conciliar popes generally pass for conservatives because they continue to defend certain principles of the natural law that the modern world rejects, and because, in doctrinal matters, they seek to restrain the more radical of the modernist theologians.

---

[23] Contrary to what has sometimes been said, Brother Roger Schutz never converted to Catholicism. His successor at the head of the Taizé community, Brother Aloïs, in an article in *La Croix* of September 7, 2006, objected to "statements...alleging the conversion of the founder of Taizé to Catholicism. 'No,' declared Brother Aloïs, 'Brother Roger never formally "converted" to Catholicism.'"

[24] "Cardinal Ratzinger's Homily at John Paul II's Funeral Mass," *Zenit*, April 8, 2005.

[25] Benedict XVI visited two more mosques during his trip to the Holy Land in May 2009. On May 12, after a moment of recollection before the Wailing Wall at Jerusalem and having inserted in it a prayer addressed to "the God of all the ages" without any mention of our Lord Jesus Christ, the Pope once again took off his shoes to enter the Dome of the Rock mosque.

[26] See below, Question 47, p. 106.

- **Is there any other explanation for this mistaken reputation as "conservative"?**

One characteristic of the current crisis is the great confusion of ideas and viewpoints which holds sway even in the Catholic Church. It is sufficient to defend some point of Catholic doctrine to be labeled *conservative*. The expression no longer signifies very much.

- **Why does Pope Paul VI have the reputation of being a conservative pope in matters of morals?**

Pope Paul VI passes for a conservative because of the Encyclical *Humanae Vitae* (July 25, 1968), which reaffirmed the Church's opposition to contraception. This encyclical aroused much hatred against him, and many bishops were more or less openly against it.

- **Given the circumstances, wasn't Paul VI's promulgation of the Encyclical *Humanae Vitae* a courageous act?**

Promulgating *Humanae Vitae* undoubtedly required a certain courage on his part, and it certainly is proof of the divine assistance afforded the Church even in the midst of the current crisis. But it should not be forgotten that Pope Paul VI was chiefly responsible for the prevailing circumstances since he had refused to allow a clear condemnation of contraception by the Council. The door would not have been so difficult to shut had it not been left ajar during the Council.

- **Isn't John Paul II a great herald of Christian morality to the modern world?**

John Paul II is decried as a hard-core conservative because of his clear position on the questions of conjugal morality and celibacy. Yet let us not deceive ourselves: even in these matters, there has been some doctrinal slackening.

- **Can you give an example of a relaxation in John Paul II's teaching on morals?**

The Pope's declarations give the impression that, if artificial birth control is indeed forbidden, the natural regulation of births is authorized without restriction. But according to Catholic teaching, it is only authorized under certain conditions: when, whether temporarily or permanently, a couple can no longer have children for grave reasons.

• Does the moral teaching of John Paul II deviate from Tradition on other points?

In the justifications John Paul II gives for Christian morals, the accent is shifted: the dignity of man is always given as the primary reason. The new Catechism of the Catholic Church, for instance, affirms: "The murder of a human being is gravely contrary to the dignity of the person and the holiness of the Creator" (§2320). Such an inversion of the order of those two things shows just how far the humanism of churchmen has gone. It echoes Paul VI's affirmation that the Church also "has the cult of man."

• As regards doctrine, didn't Paul VI defend traditional doctrine in his "Credo of the People of God," as did John Paul II in his Apostolic Letter *Ordinatio Sacerdotalis* of May 22, 1994, clearly declaring that the ordination of women is absolutely out of the question?

The current popes are not (and, thank God, they cannot be) deficient in everything. But it is enough for them to be deficient in some things for the consequences to be tragic for the whole Church. And in fact, these popes have in numerous cases upheld the modernists and abandoned or even condemned the defenders of Catholic truth.

• Can examples be cited in which John Paul II supported modernists?

John Paul II named cardinal four neo-modernist leaders: the French theologians Henri de Lubac and Yves Congar, and the German-language theologians Hans Urs von Balthasar and Walter Kaspar.

• Who is Henri de Lubac?

Henri de Lubac (Jesuit, 1896-1991) was the principal leader in France of what is called the "new theology." After World War II, the "new theology" adopted the modernist theses condemned by St. Pius X in 1907 (confounding of the natural and the supernatural, doctrinal evolutionism, *etc.*), but more cleverly. The Jesuit Teilhard de Chardin (1881-1955) said of St. Augustine: "Don't mention that unfortunate man; he spoiled everything by introducing the supernatural."[27] His confrere and friend Henri de Lubac, who always defended him (not hesitating to abridge his correspondence while claiming to publish it

---

[27] Teilhard de Chardin to Dietrich von Hildebrand in March 1948, published in the appendix of *The Trojan Horse in the City of God* (London: Sands & Co., 1969), p. 227.

in its entirety),[28] was much more subtle: he admitted in principle the distinction between "natural" and "supernatural," but then in his books deliberately worked to make it lose all meaning. Without denying anything too categorically, the "new theology" excels at making everything hazy by systematically putting forward the least precise authors. It invokes the Fathers of the Church against St. Thomas, the Greek Fathers against the Latin Fathers, and even, when useful, St. Thomas himself against his most exact commentators.

Pius XII condemned the principal theses of the "new theology" in the Encyclical *Humani Generis* in 1950, but the Encyclical was hardly obeyed. Henri de Lubac, who had been suspended from teaching by his Roman superiors, was a theologian at Vatican Council II and named cardinal by John Paul II in February 1983.

• Who is Yves Congar?

Yves Congar (Dominican, 1904-95) was the father of the "new ecclesiology," that is, the new way of conceiving the Church. A disciple of Fr. Marie-Dominique Chenu, he took classes at the Protestant Faculty of Strasbourg just after being ordained to the priesthood. He decided to consecrate his whole life to the rapprochement of the Church with the heretics and schismatics, going so far as to claim:

> Luther is one of the greatest religious geniuses of all history. In this regard I put him on the same level as St. Augustine, St. Thomas Aquinas, or Pascal. In a certain way, he is even greater. He entirely rethought Christianity....I studied Luther a lot. Scarcely a month goes by without my revisiting his writings.[29]

Subject to strict surveillance after 1947, (he would later say: "From the beginning of 1947 until the end of 1956, I experienced nothing but an uninterrupted series of denunciations, warnings, restrictive or discriminatory measures, and mistrustful interventions"[30]) he cleaved to the same ideas (in his intimate diary, he relates that twice while at Rome he went to urinate against the door of the Holy Office as a sign of revolt![31]). Nevertheless, Yves Congar was summoned as an expert to Vatican II by John XXIII and greatly influenced the Council. John Paul II named him cardinal in October 1994.

---

[28] See Henri Rambaud, "The Trickeries of Father de Lubac," [French] *Itinéraires*, No. 168, pp. 69-109.
[29] Congar, *Une Vie pour la Vérité* (Paris: Centurion, 1975), p. 59. Pope Adrian VII, in the Bull *Satis et Plus*, designated Luther as "the apostle of the Antichrist," and St. Alphonsus Liguori called him "a baneful monster from hell."
[30] *Informations Catholiques Internationales*, June 1, 1964, p. 28.
[31] On May 17, 1946, and then on November 27, 1954. See Yves Congar, *Journal d'un théologien (1946-56)*, presented and annotated by Étienne Fouilloux (Paris: Cerf, 2001), pp. 88, 293.

• Who is Hans Urs von Balthasar?

In keeping with the "new theology," Hans Urs von Balthasar (Swiss, 1905-88) devoted himself to reconstructing theology around modern philosophers and poets. Highly influenced by the fake mystic Adrienne von Speyr (1902-67),[32] he also developed the thesis of an empty hell. Named cardinal by John Paul II in 1988, his sudden death prevented him from receiving the cardinal's hat.

• Who is Walter Kasper?

President (since 2001) of the Pontifical Council for Promoting Christian Unity, Walter Kasper is notwithstanding a declared enemy of the Catholic Faith. In his book *Jesus the Christ*, he openly denies many miracles recounted in the Gospels: "We must count as legendary many of the stories of miracles contained in the Gospels. In these legends one must seek not so much their historical content as their theological aim."[33] He doubts the historicity of the Resurrection: "This observation of the existence of an historical core in the accounts concerning the tomb in no way implies a proof in favor of the resurrection."[34] He also goes so far as to put in doubt our Lord's divinity, writing pages and pages to relativize all the scriptural passages that mention it. Nevertheless, Kasper was named cardinal by John Paul II in 2001 without having retracted any of his theses.

• Does Benedict XVI also back these modernist theologians

On September 24, 2005, Benedict XVI received in a private audience for several hours the heretical theologian Hans Küng, whom John Paul II had always refused to receive because of his revolt against the Church's magisterium. In October 2005, he praised Hans Urs von Balthasar at a conference honoring this modernist theologian.[35] In May 2007, he authorized the International Theological Commission to publish a document calling in question the Church's doctrine on purgatory.

• Hasn't Benedict XVI been trying to appoint conservative bishops?

Several of Benedict XVI's appointments are disastrous.

---

[32] The Italian daily *Avvenire* (affiliated with the Italian episcopate) published on August 15, 1992, some damning testimonies about the alleged mystic, in which she comes across as proud, domineering, lazy, gluttonous, choleric, and little inclined to devotion. See *Le Courrier de Rome*, December 1992, p. 7.
[33] Walter Kasper, *Jesus the Christ* [5th French ed.] (Paris: Cerf, 1996), p. 130.
[34] *Ibid.*, p. 193.
[35] *Zenit*, October 10, 2005.

- Archbishop William Levada, appointed prefect of the Congregation for the Doctrine of the Faith in May 2005, used to cover up homosexual priests in his successive dioceses in the United States. He is one of the most ecumenical prelates of that country. He was the first American bishop to visit a synagogue, and he hosted events in his cathedral in "the spirit of Assisi," in which Jews, Muslims, Buddhists, Hindus, *etc.*, participated.[36] He also declared that transubstantiation is "a long and difficult word" that "we no longer use."[37]
- Msgr. George Niederauer, named archbishop of San Francisco, is openly a friend of homosexuals. He was publicly praised for this by Sam Sinnet and Francis DeBernardo, presidents of homosexual groups.[38]
- Msgr. Odilo Pedro Scherer, named archbishop of Sao Paulo on March 21, 2007, was previously the secretary general of the very progressive Brazilian Episcopal Conference.

23) Are the post-conciliar popes then heretics?

A heretic, in the precise meaning of the word, is someone who expressly denies a dogma. Now, Popes Paul VI and John Paul II have done and said many things that have seriously harmed the Church and the faith and that could have confirmed the heretics in their way of acting, but it cannot be proven that they knowingly and willingly denied a dogma. Rather, they must be counted among the number of liberal Catholics, who on the one hand want to remain Catholics, but on the other desire to please the world and do everything to accommodate it.

- **Isn't it possible for a liberal Catholic to push his conciliation with the world to the point of heresy?**

One of the characteristics of Catholics of this kind is that they never want to commit themselves; for this reason alone, it is very difficult for them to maintain a heresy with pertinacity.

---

[36] John Vennari, "Ecumenical Archbishop Levada to Head Sacred Congregation for the Doctrine of the Faith," *Catholic Family News*, June 2005. See also, "New San Francisco Archbishop thinks propaganda film *Brokeback Mountain* is 'very powerful,'" Lifesite, February 13, 2005.
[37] *Priest, Where Is Thy Mass? Mass, Where Is Thy Priest?* (Kansas City: Angelus Press, 2004), p. 64.
[38] Dale Vree, "Homosexuals in the Seminary: Why the Priesthood Will Continue to Become a 'Gay' Profession," *New Oxford Review*, February 2006, p. 4.

• Is pertinacity in error absolutely necessary for someone to be a heretic?

It suffices to contradict a single dogma to be *materially* heretical. But to really commit the sin of heresy (to be *formally* heretical) this negation must be conscious and deliberate. A child who, having badly learned his catechism, attributes two persons to our Lord Jesus Christ has committed a sin of laziness but not the sin of heresy (he proffers a heresy without being conscious of it; he is not *formally* a heretic). A liberal Catholic multiplying ambiguities and concessions to please the world may even arrive at uttering heresies without being really conscious of it: he is not *formally* a heretic.

• What is the Church's teaching on these liberal Catholics?

About the liberal Catholic, Pius IX said: "These are more deadly and dangerous than declared enemies....Because [by remaining just outside the bounds] of formally condemned opinions, they show a certain sign of apparent integrity and irreproachable doctrine, convincing thereby imprudent amateurs who support conciliation and misleading honest souls who would have revolted against a declared error."[39]

24) In the Church's history, are there analogous examples of papal deficiencies?

If there have been, unfortunately, a certain number of popes whose moral lives were not exemplary, yet in doctrinal matters, they were almost always irreproachable. There are, however, some examples of popes who fell into error or who, at least, upheld error instead of fighting it. These were the Popes Liberius, Honorius I, and John XXII.

• How did Pope Liberius uphold error?

Pope Liberius (352-66) succumbed to the pressure of the Arians, who denied the divinity of Christ. In 357, he excommunicated Bishop Athanasius, the valiant defender of Catholic doctrine, and subscribed to an ambiguous profession of faith.[40]

---

[39] Pius IX, Brief to the Catholic Circle of Milan (1873), cited in Rev. A. Roussel, *Liberalism and Catholicism* (1926; Kansas City: Angelus Press, 1998), pp. 120-21.

[40] Letter *Studens Pacis* addressed by Pope Liberius to the Bishops of the Orient in the spring of 357:
> ...By this letter, which I composed with a concern for unanimity with you, know that I am in peace with all of you and with all the Bishops of the Catholic Church, but the aforementioned Athanasius is excluded from communion with me, that is to say, from communion with the Roman Church, and from the exchange of ecclesiastical letters. (DS 138)

• How did Pope Honorius I uphold error?

In the seventh century, Sergius, the Patriarch of Constantinople, invented the heresy of monothelitism. This error teaches that in Christ there is only one will, while in fact Christ possesses two wills, the divine will and a human will. Sergius succeeded in deceiving Honorius I (625-38) and winning him to his cause.

• Did Pope Honorius really adhere to the error of monothelitism?

It seems that Honorius did not really share the Patriarch of Constantinople's error, but, not understanding thoroughly the whole matter and seeing in it nothing but a theologians' quarrel, he still took Sergius's side and silenced St. Sophronius, who defended the Catholic cause. For this reason, Honorius was posthumously condemned by Pope Leo II.[41]

• How did Pope John XXII uphold error?

John XXII (1316-34) supported the false doctrine according to which the souls of the faithful departed do not obtain the beatific vision and thus full beatitude until after the general judgment. Beforehand, they simply enjoy the vision of Christ's humanity. Similarly, the demons and damned men do not undergo the eternal pains of hell until after the last judgment. However, he had the humility to allow himself to be corrected and retracted his error on December 3, 1334, the day before he died.[42]

• What lesson can be learned from these three examples?

From these examples, and especially from that of St. Athanasius, we see that it can happen that a lone bishop may be in the right in his principled stand against the pope.

Pope Liberius confirms this excommunication of St. Athanasius in the Letters *Pro Deifico* (DS 140), *Quia Scio* (DS 142), and *Non Doceo* (DS 143).

[41] John IV (pope 641-642) took up the defense of his predecessor Honorius in the Letter *Dominus Qui Dixit* (DS 496-498), showing that the ambiguous texts of Honorius can be interpreted in an orthodox sense. But the Third Council of Constantinople (680-681) and Pope Leo II (682-683) pronounced an anathema against Honorius, who had in fact favored heresy (DS 552 and 563).

[42] John XXII retracted his errors in the Bull *Ne Super His* (DS 990-991), which was published by his successor, Benedict XII.

IV

THE SECOND VATICAN COUNCIL

25) When did the Second Vatican Council take place?

Vatican Council II was opened by Pope John XXIII on October 11, 1962. John XXIII died the following year, but his successor, Paul VI, continued the Council and brought it to a close on December 8, 1965.

- **Did the Council last more than three years without interruption?**

The Vatican Council II comprised four sessions lasting fewer than three months, between which the bishops returned to their dioceses. The first session (October 11 to December 3, 1962), the only one to occur during the pontificate of John XXIII, promulgated no document; it was essentially used to discard the documents prepared by the Preparatory Commission.

- **How does Vatican II rank among the other Councils?**

The Second Vatican Council was the twenty-first ecumenical council. It was the biggest in terms of the number of participants: two thousand bishops attended.

26) How does Vatican II differ from previous Councils?

Vatican Council II was declared to be no more than a "pastoral" council, one that does not resolve questions of faith, but which gives pastoral directives for the life of the Church. The authorities renounced defining dogmas, and so they renounced the infallibility which appertains to a council. Thus its documents are not infallible.

- **What are the usual ends of a council?**

In his letter convoking the First Vatican Council, Pius IX indicates that general councils were especially convoked "during epochs of great perturbations, when calamities of every sort befell the Church and nations." All the ecumenical councils of the past were convoked to rout heresy (this is notably the case of the first seven), or to correct a prevailing evil (simony, schism, corruption of the clergy, *etc.*). Pius IX summarizes the principal aims of a council: "To decide with prudence and wisdom all that might contribute to *define* dogmas of faith; to *condemn the errors* being insidiously spread; to *defend*, clarify, and explain Catholic doctrine; to preserve and restore ecclesiastical *discipline*; and to *strengthen the lax mores* of the people."[1]

- **Was there never, then, a "pastoral" council before Vatican II?**

All the Church's councils have been pastoral, but they were so by defining dogmas, exposing errors, defending Catholic doctrine, and by fighting against disciplinary and moral disorders. The originality of Vatican II was to seek to be "pastoral" *in a new way*, by refusing to define dogmas, to condemn errors, and even to present Catholic dogma defensively.

- **Didn't Vatican II promulgate dogmatic documents?**

Vatican II promulgated sixteen documents: nine decrees, three declarations, and four constitutions. Among these, two are called "dogmatic constitutions": *Lumen Gentium* (on the Church) and *Dei Verbum* (on Revelation). That does not mean that they proclaimed dogmas or that they were infallible, but only that they treat of a matter bearing on dogma. Vatican II refused to define anything infallibly; Paul VI explicitly stated this on January 12, 1966, a few weeks after the Council's cloture: "Given the Council's pastoral character, it avoided pronouncing, in an extraordinary manner, dogmas endowed with the note of infallibility."[2]

---

[1] "*Ea omnia provide sapienterque constituerent quae ad fidei potissimum dogmata definienda, ad grassantes errores profligandos, ad catholicam propugnandam, illustrandam et evolvendam doctrinam, ad ecclesiasticam tuendam ac reparandam disciplinam, ad corruptos populorum mores corrigendos possent conducere.*" Pius IX, Bull of Convocation of the First Vatican Council, June 29, 1868, *AAS*, IV, 5.

[2] Paul VI, General Audience of January 12, 1966, in *Insegnamenti di Paolo VI*, IV, 700.

• Is the "pastorality" of Vatican II characterized by the adaptation of the Church to our time?

All the councils have adapted the Church to their time, but they did it by anathematizing the errors of the day, by sanctioning the disciplinary or moral deviations of their time, by arming the Church against its enemies. The adaptation did not aim at conforming the Church to the world, but in resisting it. It was not question of pleasing the world, but of confronting it and vanquishing it so as to please God. John XXIII and Paul VI, on the contrary, sought to make the Church appealing to modern man.

• Did John XXIII and Paul VI express this intention?

On February 14, 1960, John XXIII declared: "The main goal of the Council is to present to the world the Church of God in its perpetual vigor of life and truth, and with its legislation adapted to the present circumstances in such a way as to be ever more in keeping with its divine mission and ready for the needs of today and tomorrow."[3]

Cardinal Montini, the future Paul VI, declared in April 1962: "By means of the next council, the Church proposes to enter into contact with the world....It will try to be...amiable in its language and conduct." And during the Council, Paul VI affirmed in the Encyclical *Ecclesiam Suam*: "The Church...might content itself with conducting an inquiry into the evils current in secular society, condemning them publicly, and fighting a crusade against them....But it seems to Us that the sort of relationship for the Church to establish with the world should be more in the nature of a dialogue" (§78).

• Then Vatican II was meant to be from the beginning a council of opening and dialogue?

Actually, the members of the Preparatory Commission established by John XXIII thought they were supposed to organize a normal council. They did an enormous amount of work to draft schemata that could serve as the basis for the conciliar debates. But, meanwhile, the Secretariat for the Unity of Christians, also established by John XXIII (in June 1960), was working at cross-purposes. Finally, John XXIII's real intention prevailed: at the beginning of the Council, the preparatory schemata were discarded, being adjudged too "doctrinal," and the Council set off in the direction prepared by the Secretariat for Unity.

---

[3] "*Scopo primo ed immediato del Concilio è di ripresentare al mondo la Chiesa di Dio nel suo perenne vigore di vita e di verità, e con la sua legislazione aggiornata....*"Jean XXIII, speech to the General Council of Italian Catholic Action, February 14, 1960. *Acta et Documenta Concilio Oecumenico Vaticano II Apparendo*, Series I (antepræparatoria), Vol. I (*Acta Summi Pontificis Joannis XXIII*), p. 74. See also his speech of August 3, 1959, *DC*, No. 1311 (1959), col. 1099.

• How did the Secretariat for Unity prepare the Council?

Under the presidency of Cardinal Bea, the Secretariat for Unity prepared the Council by asking non-Catholics what they expected from the Church. They established contacts with the Orthodox, the Protestants, the Jews, the Communists, and the Freemasons, and even went so far as to assure them that certain of their desiderata would be satisfied.

• What were the demands of the Orthodox and the Communists?

To obtain the presence of Orthodox observers at the Council, John XXIII promised that Communism would not be condemned there. Monsignor Roche, a friend and confidant of Cardinal Tisserant, testified: "Cardinal Tisserant received formal orders both to negotiate the agreement and to supervise its exact execution during the Council. That is why each time a bishop wanted to broach the question of Communism, the Cardinal, from his table as adviser to the Council moderators, intervened."[4]

• What were the Jews' demands?

In No. 1001 of the *Tribune Juive* (December 25-31, 1987), Lazare Landau recounted:

> On a foggy, frigid winter's evening 1962-63, I attended an extraordinary event at the Strasbourg Community Center for Peace. The Jewish directors secretly received a papal delegate in the basement. At the conclusion of the Sabbath, we were about a dozen to welcome a Dominican dressed in white, the Reverend Fr. Yves Congar, tasked by Cardinal Bea, in John XXIII's name, with asking us, at the threshold of the Council, what we expected of the Catholic Church....
>
> The Jews, for nearly twenty centuries kept on the margin of Christian society, often treated as inferiors, enemies, and deicides, asked for their complete rehabilitation. As direct descendants of Abraham, whence came Christianity, they asked to be considered as brothers, partners of equal dignity, of the Christian Church....
>
> The white-robed messenger, not wearing any symbol or ornament, returned to Rome the bearer of the innumerable requests that reinforced our own people. After difficult debates..., the Council did justice to our wishes. The Declaration *Nostra Aetate* No. 4 constituted–Father Congar and the three drafters of the text confirmed it to me–a veritable revolution in the Church's doctrine on the Jews....
>
> Within a few years, sermons and catechisms had changed....Since the secret visit of Father Congar to a hidden room of the synagogue on a cold

---

[4] *Itinéraires*, No. 285, p. 157. Concerning this agreement, see also *France Nouvelle* (the French Communist party weekly), No. 900, January 16-22, 1963, p. 15; *La Croix*, February 15, 1963, p. 5; *Itinéraires*, No. 280, pp. 1-15; P. Floridi, S.J., *Moscow and the Vatican* [French] (Paris: France-Empire, 1979), pp. 142-48; *etc.*

winter's night, the doctrine of the Church had indeed undergone a total mutation.[5]

- **What were the demands of the Protestants and Freemasons?**

In September 1961 at Milan, Cardinal Bea secretly met the Pastor William A. Visser't Hooft, secretary general of the Ecumenical Council of Churches (an organization of Protestant origin and Masonic tendencies). Religious liberty was one of the major themes of the meeting. Later, on July 22, 1965, on the eve of the last conciliar session, the same Ecumenical Council of Churches published the list of its seven fundamental exigencies regarding religious liberty. All were satisfied by the Council in the document *Dignitatis Humanae*.[6]

- **What conclusions can be drawn from the politics of openness followed by Vatican Council II?**

It becomes clear that Vatican II was not a council like the others. The documents it promulgated, fruit of a "dialogue" with the world, are more in the nature of diplomatic or "public relations" communications (destined to foster a good image of the Church) than magisterial texts (teaching clearly and authoritatively the truths of faith). None of these documents is, of itself, infallible.

27) What was the influence of the Council on the crisis in the Church?

The liberal and modernist forces that were already undermining the Church succeeded in taking control of the Council. Thus one can say that Vatican II was the spark that ignited a crisis that had been building for a long time in the Church.

- **How far back do the origins of this crisis go?**

St. Pius X already observed in his Encyclical *Pascendi* that modernism was no longer an enemy outside the Church, but that it had penetrated within, although its adepts still hid their real intentions.

---

[5] See also on this subject *Le Sel de la Terre*, No. 34, pp. 196-217 (and, notably, the account of the secret visit Cardinal Bea made to the American Jewish Committee on March 31, 1963).–Note of the Dominican Fathers.

[6] "During the last conciliar session, the bishop of Monaco, Msgr. Rupp, in a widely listened to speech, asked the Council to content itself with adopting these seven requests and to confirm them by its own authority....In reality, the Council did more. Not only did it adopt, in equivalent terms, the seven demands, but it solidly established them...." Msgr. Willebrands, in *Vatican II: Religious Liberty*, collection *Unam Sanctam* (Paris: Cerf, 1967), pp. 241-42.

- **Didn't Pope St. Pius X vigorously combat these modernists?**

St. Pius X energetically combated modernism; his successors up to Pius XII did likewise, more or less energetically; but they were not really able to vanquish it. The Encyclical *Humani Generis* of Pius XII condemning what was called the "new theology" (in 1950) was outwardly accepted, but in reality it was despised by many. They continued to be interested in the condemned theses, and in houses of formation, future priests were encouraged to do likewise.

- **Can it be said that Vatican II was a revolution in the Church?**

Some of its own defenders themselves proclaim loud and clear that the Council was a revolution in the Church. For instance, Cardinal Suenens made a parallel between the Council and the French Revolution, saying that Vatican II was 1789 in the Church; Fr. Yves Congar, a conciliar theologian, compared the Council to the Bolshevik Revolution: "The Church has peacefully undergone its October Revolution."[7]

28) How did the liberals take over the Council?

Thanks to the support of John XXIII and Paul VI, the liberal and neo-modernist forces were able to introduce a great number of their ideas into the conciliar texts. Before the Council, the Preparatory Commission had carefully prepared the schemata, which were the echo of the Church's faith. The discussion and voting should have been about these schemata, but they were rejected during the first session of the Council and replaced by new schemata prepared by the liberals.

- **Were there no defenders of the traditional doctrine at the Council?**

There was at the Council a group of about 250 to 270 bishops determined to defend the Church's Tradition. They eventually formed the *Coetus Internationalis Patrum*. But they were opposed by an already existing and perfectly organized group of cardinals and bishops that has been called the Rhine alliance.

- **Where does the name "the Rhine alliance" come from?**

The name comes from the fact that the leaders of this liberal group were almost all bishops from dioceses bordering on the Rhine River. Every day this group inundated the Council with typed sheets, in which they told the bishops how they should vote. That is why one

---

[7] Yves Congar, *The Council Day by Day: Second Session* [French] (Paris: 1964), p. 215.

journalist, Fr. Ralph Wiltgen, entitled his book on the Council *The Rhine Flows into the Tiber.*

- **Were the innovators in the majority?**

Like every revolution, Vatican II was not led by the majority, but by an active, well-organized minority. The majority of bishops were undecided and equally ready to follow the conservatives. But when they saw that the leaders of the Rhine alliance were the personal friends of the Pope, and that some of them (the Cardinals Döpfner, Suenens, and Lercaro) had even been appointed the moderators of the Council, they followed them.

- **The texts of Vatican II, then, are not representative of the thinking of the majority of the bishops at the Council's opening?**

A theologian of the progressivist party, Hans Küng, jubilantly asserted that the dream of a small minority had prevailed at the Council: "No one who was here for the Council will go back home as he came. I myself never expected so many bold and explicit statements from the bishops on the Council floor."[8]

- **Who is this theologian Hans Küng?**

Since the Council, Hans Küng has shown his true colors. This churchman denies most Catholic dogmas, including papal infallibility and the divinity of Christ, to such an extent that even conciliar Rome had to withdraw his authorization to teach.

- **Did other heretical theologians exercise an influence at Vatican II?**

The Jesuit Karl Rahner (1904-84), while being more prudent and less explicit, spread analogous theses in his works. As early as 1949, the Holy Office had to impose silence on him regarding certain questions. Yet he enjoyed an immense influence at the Council; Fr. Wiltgen even goes so far as to name him the Council's most influential theologian:

> Since the position of the German-language bishops was regularly adopted by the European [Rhine] alliance, and since the alliance position was generally adopted by the Council, a single theologian might have his views accepted by the whole Council if they had been accepted by the German-speaking bishops. There was such a theologian: Father Karl Rahner, S.J.[9]

---

[8] Quoted by Fr. Ralph Wiltgen, *The Rhine Flows into the Tiber* (1967; Rockford, Ill.: TAN Books & Publishers, 1985), p. 60.
[9] *Ibid.*, p. 80.

- **Is there any other testimony on Rahner's influence at the Council?**

    Fr. Congar related:

    > The atmosphere became: *"Rahner dixit, ergo verum est."*[10] I will give you an example. The Doctrinal Commission was made up of bishops, each with his own expert at his side, but also included certain superior generals (of the Dominicans or the Carmelites, for instance). Now, there were two microphones on the table of the Commission, but Rahner practically had one of them to himself alone. Rahner was a little invasive and, in addition, very often the cardinal from Vienna, Franz König, of whom Rahner was the expert, turned toward him and invited him to intervene by saying: "Rahner, *quid?*" Naturally, Rahner intervened....[11]

- **What was Karl Rahner's line of thinking?**

    Karl Rahner completely rebelled against the Church's traditional teaching, which was for him nothing but "monolithism" and "School theology." A letter he wrote dated February 22, 1962, on the occasion of the publication of the Italian version of his dictionary of theology enlightens us about his feelings toward the magisterium of the Church:

    > An Italian version certainly poses a special problem because of the presence at Rome of the bonzes and guardians of orthodoxy. On the other hand, I am more than ever fortified in my positions. One might also say that this little lexicon has been written in such a way that these people can understand nothing, and hence will not see what is written against their narrow-mindedness.[12]

- **Did Karl Rahner let his rebellion against the Church's Tradition and the Magisterium show during the Council?**

    One day during the Council, Cardinal Ottaviani, the prefect of the Holy Office, was expressing in a speech his disquietude about some innovations. He was speaking without notes since he was nearly blind, and he exceeded the allotted time. The microphone was simply switched off. Rahner commented on the event in a letter written to Vorgrimler on November 5, 1962: "Undoubtedly you have already heard that Alfrink once again cut off Ottaviani because he was talking too long. Everyone began to clap (which wasn't usual). Motto: There's no pleasure like another man's pain."[13]

---

[10] "Rahner has spoken, therefore it is true."
[11] Yves Congar, in *Thirty Days* [French], No. 3, 1993, p. 26. [English version: Fr. Dominic Bourmaud, *One Hundred Years of Modernism* (Kansas City: Angelus Press, 2003), pp. 268-69.]
[12] Herbert Vorgrimler, *Karl Rahner Verstehen* (Fribourg: Herder, 1995), p. 175.
[13] *Deutsche Tagespost*, October 10, 1992, p. 2. In German: "*Schadenfreude ist die reinste Freude.*"

The Second Vatican Council

• Do we find other aspects of Rahner's sentiments in his correspondence during the Council?

The publication in 1994 of the correspondence exchanged between Fr. Karl Rahner and the Austrian poetess Luise Rinser (1911-2002) opened wide a scandal: at the very time he was holding sway at the Council, Karl Rahner was exchanging love letters with this woman, in his passion writing to her as many as three times a day (276 letters during the year 1964 alone).

• Did other bad theologians influence Vatican II?

One can name, among others, Fr. Congar and Fr. Henri de Lubac, previously introduced, Fr. Edward Schillebeeckx, Fr. John Courtney Murray, *etc*.

• What influence did Fr. Congar have at Vatican II?

Archbishop Lefebvre related this incident:

> At the beginning of Vatican II, I would go to the meetings [of the French bishops] at St-Louis-des-Français. But I was amazed to see how things went. The bishops literally behaved themselves like little boys before the Congars and the other experts who came. Fr. Congar would go up to the head table and without the least reticence would say: "Your Excellency So-and-so, you will make this intervention on this subject. Don't worry, we will prepare the text for you, and you will only need to read it." I couldn't believe my eyes or my ears! And I stopped going to these meetings....[14]

• Are there any other testimonies about Fr. Congar's influence?

Msgr. Desmazières, auxiliary bishop of Bordeaux, related:

> In the afternoon, the workshops continue. I go to mine, directed by Fr. Congar, on Scripture and Tradition. There are about a dozen of us. We have to prepare the interventions to be made the next day. I am asked to take the second. I do not refuse, provided that Fr. Congar prepare the text for me. That is agreed. He will pass it to me tomorrow in the bus. I get my first look at the text in the bus; I am decided to change nothing. Getting out at St. Peter's, I go to register: I am the twenty-first....[15]

• What does Fr. Congar have to say about it?

Fr. Congar rather minimized his influence at the Council. Nonetheless, he summarized his action thus: "The preparation of the Council was under the domination...of men from the Curia and the Holy Office....Everything consisted, practically speaking, in putting them

---

[14] Archbishop Marcel Lefebvre, *Fideliter*, No. 59, p. 53.
[15] Msgr. Desmazières, *L'Aquitaine* (the Bordeaux diocesan weekly), December 1962, p. 580.

in the minority."[16] That was a victory for him. Ten years earlier, sanctioned by his superiors, he wrote in his private diary the following resolutions:

> Continue writing in the same vein, taking advantage of every opportunity. My combat is especially there. I know (and "they" know) that sooner or later, everything that I say and write is the negation of the system. Yes, that is my real combat: in my theological, historical, ecclesiological, and pastoral work. The class I am currently teaching, exactly as if nothing had happened, is a true response; it is my real dynamite under the scribes' armchair.[17]

After the Council, he declared:

> The Council liquidated what I would call the "unconditionality" of the system. I mean by *system* the very coherent ensemble of ideas communicated by the teaching of the Roman universities, codified by Canon Law, and protected by a close, fairly effective surveillance under Pius XII, with reports, warnings, submission of writings to Roman censors, *etc.*[18]

● Who is Fr. Murray?

Fr. John Courtney Murray, an American Jesuit (1904-67), had been condemned in 1957 by the Holy Office for his study *The Problem of Religious Freedom*. He was nonetheless invited to the Council as an expert in 1963. During the debates on religious liberty, he offered to draft the interventions of some bishops and thus exercised considerable influence. At the end of his life, he tried to prove that the Church's teaching on contraception could evolve as it had evolved on religious freedom.

● What can be concluded from all this?

That men like Küng, Rahner, Congar, Lubac, Murray, *etc.*, could have influenced the Council does not speak in its favor nor in favor of its reforms. Unfortunately, certain declarations of Pope John Paul II are not to its advantage either, like one that he made in 1963 (while he was still a simple bishop):

> Never before had a Council known such a broad preparation, never before had Catholic opinion been so amply sounded. Not only the bishops, the Catholic universities, and the superior generals of congregations expressed their opinions on the problems examined by the Council, but also a great percentage of Catholic laymen and non-Catholics. Theologians as eminent as Henri de Lubac, J. Danielou, Yves Congar, H. Küng, R.

---

[16] Yves Congar, O.P., *Une vie pour la vérité: Jean Puyo interroge le père Congar* (Paris: Centurion, 1975), p. 140.
[17] Yves Congar, O.P., manuscript notes of February 1954 quoted by François Leprieur, O.P., *Quand Rome Condamne* (Paris: Plon/Cerf, 1989), p. 259.
[18] Congar, *Une vie pour la vérité*, p. 220.

Lombardi, Karl Rahner, and others played an extraordinary role in the preparatory work.[19]

29) Should all of the Vatican II documents be rejected?

The documents of Vatican II can be divided in three groups: **1)** Some are acceptable because they are in conformity with Catholic doctrine, as for example the decree on the formation of priests; **2)** others are equivocal, that is, they can be understood correctly, but can also be interpreted erroneously; and **3)** some cannot be understood in an orthodox way; in their present formulation, they are unacceptable. This is the case for the declaration on religious freedom. The ambiguous texts can be accepted if they are, in Archbishop Lefebvre's words, interpreted in the light of Tradition. The texts of the third group cannot be accepted until they have been rectified.

● What accounts for the ambiguous nature of certain Vatican II documents?

The equivocations were deliberately introduced into the conciliar texts to deceive the conservative Fathers. They could be deluded by insisting on the fact that fundamentally the text did not mean anything else than what the Church had always taught. But afterwards, it was possible to use these passages to defend heterodox theses.

● Is there any proof that these ambiguities were deliberately introduced?

Karl Rahner and Herbert Vorgrimler confirmed this when they wrote, for example, that "a certain number of important theological questions about which no agreement could be reached were left open by choosing formulations that could be interpreted differently by particular groups and theological tendencies at the Council."[20]

● How could such imprecision in the conciliar documents be justified?

This deliberate ambiguity was justified by the fact that the Second Vatican Council was only meant to be a pastoral council, and that it was thus not necessary to draft its documents with the theological rigor required for a dogmatic council.

---

[19] Cited by M. Malinski, *My Friend Karol Wojtyla* [French] (Paris: Le Centurion, 1980), p. 189.
[20] K. Rahner and H. Vorgrimler, *Kleines Konzilskompendium: Sämtliche Texte des Zweiten Vatikanums* (Fribourg: Herder, 1986), p. 21.

- **Can you provide some examples of these calculated ambiguities?**

One example of this ambiguity is the notorious expression "*subsistit in*" introduced in the Dogmatic Constitution *Lumen Gentium*, on the Church (I, 8), which declares that the Church of Christ "subsists in" [*subsistit in*] the Catholic Church.

- **What is the traditional teaching on this subject?**

The traditional teaching expressly says that the Church of Christ *is* the Catholic Church. This word "*est*" is still found in the first drafts of this constitution on the Church. It was subsequently replaced by the expression *subsistit in*. It is evident that this change was not made without a reason.

- **Why is the word "*est*" here important?**

The Catholic Church is not only a certain embodiment of the Church of Christ: it *is* the Church of Christ, which signifies that there is an absolute identity between the Church founded by Christ and the Catholic Church. The other ecclesial communities never belong to the Church of Christ. The expression "*subsistit in*" introduces an ambiguity on this point.

- **Hasn't the Congregation for the Doctrine of the Faith given a good interpretation of the "*subsistit in*" in its documents of August 2000 (*Dominus Jesus*) and July 2007?**

The Congregation for the Doctrine of the Faith rejected the most extreme modernist interpretation of this term, according to which the Catholic Church is but one realization among others of the Church of Christ. But we shall see further on (Question 45) that nonetheless it does not uphold the traditional doctrine, according to which the Catholic Church is purely and simply the Church of Christ. The formula "*subsistit in*" admits of the thesis that "veritable ecclesial realities" exist outside the Catholic Church.

- **Is the identity of the person at the origin of this new expression "*subsistit in*" known?**

The Protestant pastor Wilhelm Schmidt claimed the paternity of this new expression. Here is his testimony:

> At the time I was pastor of the Church of the Holy Cross at Bremen-Horn, and during the third and fourth sessions, an observer at the Council as the representative of the Evangelical Fraternity Michael, at Cardinal Bea's invitation. I submitted in writing the formulation "*Subsistit in*" to

the man who was then the theological adviser of Cardinal Frings: Joseph Ratzinger, who relayed it to the Cardinal.[21]

30) What are the principal errors of Vatican II?

The two most harmful conciliar errors are religious liberty and ecumenism, which shall be treated of in detail in the next two chapters. To these must be added the teaching on episcopal collegiality. Finally, in many conciliar documents one finds a naive belief in progress and wonder at the modern world which are truly frightening.

• What is episcopal collegiality?

The principle of episcopal collegiality rises in opposition to the exercise of authority. The pope and the bishops must no longer use their power, but must direct the Church collegially, or collectively. Today the bishop is the head of his diocese in theory only; in practice, he is bound, at least morally, by the decisions of the bishops' conference, the priests' councils, and different assemblies. Rome no longer dares uphold its own authority over the episcopal conferences, but in general yields to their pressure. The idea of equality propagated by the French Revolution has been imposed. It is based on the false notion of Rousseau, which denied the existence of an authority willed by God and attributed all power to the people. This theory is contrary to the teaching of Holy Scripture: "Let every soul be subject to higher powers: for there is no power but from God: and those that are, are ordained of God. Therefore he that resisteth the power, resisteth the ordinance of God" (Rom. 13:1-2).

• Is there a link between collegiality and the two principal errors of the Council (religious liberty and ecumenism)?

These three errors of the Council–religious liberty, collegiality, and ecumenism–correspond exactly to the principles of the French Revolution: liberty, equality, fraternity. This correlation illustrates Cardinal Suenens's statement that Vatican II was 1789 in the Church.

• In which conciliar texts does one find a naive belief in progress?

The most serious example of a naive belief in progress is found in the Pastoral Constitution on the Church in the Modern World, *Gaudium*

---

[21] Pastor Wilhelm Schmidt (not to be confused with the ethnologist of the same name), letter of August 3, 2000, to the author of this Catechism. (Pastor Schmidt made clear in his letter that "I have no objection to the publication of this information.")

et Spes. It rhapsodizes in an astonishing manner on the progress of the modern world, even though it daily strays farther from God. We read in Section 12: "According to the almost unanimous opinion of believers and unbelievers alike, all things on earth should be related to man as their center and crown." And in Section 57, Christians are exhorted "to work with all men in the building of a more human world." A world in which man is the center and end, and in which all should collaborate in the realization of an earthly paradise corresponds to the Freemasons' idea of the world, and not to that of Catholics.

• What is the Christian teaching on this point?

Catholic doctrine teaches that God alone is the end of all creatures and that there cannot be true peace or happiness on earth unless men give themselves to Jesus Christ and follow His commandments.

• In the final analysis, what judgment can be made of *Gaudium et Spes*?

Cardinal Joseph Ratzinger called *Gaudium et Spes* a countersyllabus,[22] and rightly so. This Vatican II document in effect positively affirms what Pius IX denied and condemned in the catalogue of contemporary errors that he established in 1864 and which bears the name of *Syllabus*.

• Did Cardinal Ratzinger explain why he described *Gaudium et Spes* as a "countersyllabus"?

The Cardinal justified his analogy by explaining that in the 1960's the Church appropriated "the best values of two centuries of liberal culture," values which, he said, "originate outside the Church" but which now have found a place within it.[23]

• Is it a bad thing for the Church to appropriate values that originate outside it?

The real question is, rather, can there be genuine moral values outside the Church? The Church received from Christ the plenitude of religious truth and good. Liberalism is only the corruption of Christian ideas gone mad, as G. K. Chesterton would say. Everything good it might possess was stolen from the Gospel; but everything that belongs to liberalism properly speaking (unbridled liberty, rejection of authority established by God, *etc.*) is, of itself, anti-Christian. That is why Pius

---

[22] Joseph Cardinal Ratzinger, *Principles of Catholic Theology* (1982; San Francisco: Ignatius Press, 1987), p. 381.

[23] Interview of Cardinal Ratzinger by the Italian journalist Vittorio Messori, published in English as *The Ratzinger Report: An Exclusive Interview on the State of the Church* (San Francisco: Ignatius Press, 1985), p. 36.

IX repeatedly condemned liberalism, and in the last proposition of his Syllabus denounced the following error: "The Roman Pontiff can and should reconcile and adapt himself to progress, liberalism, and the modern civilization."[24] It is precisely this reconciliation and this friendship that are advocated by Vatican II in general and *Gaudium et Spes* in particular.

31) Isn't Vatican II infallible insofar as it is an organ of the ordinary magisterium?

Some claim that even if Vatican II did not produce any acts of the extraordinary magisterium, it would possess the note of infallibility as an organ of the ordinary and universal magisterium, since almost all the bishops of the world were present. Moreover, they say, ecumenism and religious liberty are taught nowadays by the bishops of the entire world, which would also be equivalent to the exercise of the ordinary and universal magisterium, which is infallible.

But this argumentation is flawed. Vatican II, a "pastoral" council, refused to invoke its authority to define anything; it did not impose religious liberty and ecumenism as truths of faith, and that is why it escapes the extraordinary magisterium. But, by the same token, it also escapes the infallible ordinary magisterium, for there can be no infallibility if the bishops do not authoritatively certify that the teaching they dispense belongs to the deposit of faith (or is necessarily linked to it), and that it must be held as immutable and obligatory.

- **Are not some Vatican II teachings presented as "based on Revelation," "in conformity with Revelation," "handed down by the Church," or "decreed in the Holy Spirit"?**

Those are pious formulas, but very insufficient to assure infallibility. It would be necessary to impose this teaching authoritatively as necessarily linked to divine Revelation, which is immutable and obligatory. But religious liberty and ecumenism are novelties, contrary to previous Church teaching. In fact, the bishops do not impose them firmly and precisely as immutable truths. In preaching them, they do not invoke their authority as guardians of the deposit revealed to the Apostles, but rather they present them in a liberal ("pastoral") fashion as the fruit of a dialogue with the modern world and as the reflection of what Christians believe today. This is enough to exclude infallibility.[25]

---

[24] Condemned proposition, Dz. 1780.
[25] See on this subject the arguments developed by Fr. Calderon in *Sel de la Terre*, No. 47, pp. 60-69 and 91-95.–Note of the Dominican Fathers.

- **Thus one cannot invoke the Church's ordinary and universal magisterium with regard to ecumenism and religious liberty?**

One cannot invoke the ordinary and universal magisterium *in favor of* ecumenism and religious liberty, but one could justly affirm that it is the condemnations declared over the course of the last two centuries *against* religious liberty and ecumenism that are infallible by reason of the ordinary magisterium.

- **Do the current Church authorities acknowledge the non-infallibility of Vatican II?**

Cardinal Ratzinger expressly stated in 1988 that Vatican II is not infallible: "The truth is that the Council itself did not define any dogma, and limited itself to a more modest level, simply as a pastoral council. In spite of this, numerous are those who interpret it as if it involved a 'super-dogma' that alone has importance."[26]

- **Why does the current hierarchy put so much stock in Vatican II, since they recognize at the same time that it is not infallible?**

In fact, from the beginning, Vatican II has been the object of a ruse. During the Council, its pastoral character was emphasized so that the use of precise theological language could be dispensed with; but afterwards, those who insisted upon its pastoral nature ascribed to conciliar teaching an authority equal, if not superior, to that of previous councils. This trick was denounced by one of the participants at the Council, Archbishop Lefebvre, in 1976:

> It is imperative, therefore, to shatter the myths which have been built up around Vatican II–this Council which they wanted to make a pastoral one, because of their instinctive horror for dogma, to facilitate the introduction of Liberal ideas into an official text of the Church. By the time it was over, however, they had dogmatized the Council, comparing it with that of Nicaea, and claiming that it was equal if not superior to the Councils that had gone before it![27]

---

[26] Cardinal Ratzinger, Allocution to the Bishops' Conference of Chile, July 13, 1988 (quoted in *Itinéraires*, February 1989, p. 4).
[27] Archbishop Marcel Lefebvre, *I Accuse the Council* (1976; Angelus Press, 1982), pp. x-xi.

V

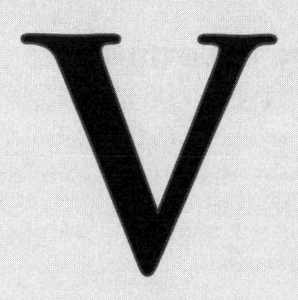

RELIGIOUS LIBERTY
---

32) Is Jesus Christ the king of civil society?

Jesus Christ is not only king of the Church or of the faithful, but also of all men and of all nations. He said so before His Ascension: "All power is given to me in heaven and in earth" (Mt. 28:18). He is king of the whole world; nothing can escape His rule.

- **What are the foundations of Christ's kingship?**

Pope Pius XI teaches in the Encyclical *Quas Primas* that Christ has a twofold claim to kingship: **1)** He is king by nature, by an innate right (He is the Man-God); and **2)** He is king by conquest, by an acquired right (by redeeming the world, He acquired all men by His blood).

- **Doesn't Christ's kingship extend only over the baptized?**

In reply to this objection, Pope Pius XI cites his predecessor Leo XIII: "His empire extends not only over Catholic nations and those who, having been duly washed in the waters of holy baptism, belong of right to the Church...; it comprises also all those who are deprived of the Christian faith, so that the whole human race is most truly under the power of Jesus Christ."[1]

---

[1] Leo XIII, Encyclical *Annum Sacrum* (May 25, 1899), §3, quoted by Pius XI in *Quas Primas* (December 11, 1925).

33) Didn't Jesus Christ say that His kingdom is not of this world?

Christ affirmed before Pilate that His kingdom is not of this world (Jn. 18:36). He meant by this that His kingship does not originate in this world, and that its nature is superior to that of all earthly kingships; but it is exercised on earth. The kingdom of Jesus Christ is not of this world, but it is indeed in this world.

• Is this interpretation certain?

Christ's words are so clear that they scarcely need interpreting. Just as our Lord declared that He was not *of* the world,[2] but that He was sent *into* the world by the Father,[3] He declared before Pilate that His kingdom is not *of* this world, but that, being king, He came *into* the world to give testimony to the truth.[4]

• What do the Fathers of the Church say about it?

The Fathers of the Church point out that our Lord did not say "My kingdom is not here," but rather "My kingdom is not from here."[5] His kingship indeed has its exercise *in* the world.

• Why then did Jesus Christ affirm that His kingdom is not of this world?

Jesus Christ refused to allow Himself to be proclaimed king (Jn. 6:15) in order to dissociate His kingdom from the false messianic pretensions of the Jews (liberation from the Roman yoke and world dominion). Speaking to a Roman governor, He indicates that His kingship, essentially supernatural, does not threaten the emperor; it does not compete against the rulers of the earth, whose limits, vulnerability, and petty ambitions it does not share. Christ's kingdom encompasses all the world's kingdoms, as the second antiphon of the Vespers for the Feast of Christ the King proclaims: "His kingdom is a kingdom of all ages, and all kings shall serve and obey Him."

---

[2] Jn. 17:16–*Ego non sum de mundo.* In Latin, the preposition *de* indicates origin, point of departure.

[3] Jn. 17:18–*Tu me misisti in mundum.* The preposition *in* followed by the accusative indicates the destination of a motion.

[4] Jn. 18:36-37–*Regnum meum non est de hoc mundo....Rex sum ego. Ego in hoc natus sum, et ad hoc veni in mundum, ut testimonium perhibeam veritati.*

[5] Jn. 18:36–*Regnum meum non est hinc.* The Latin adverb *hinc* indicates the provenance (it answers the question *unde*, whence). The adverb *hic* indicates present location. This fact is explicitly underscored by St. Augustine, St. John Chrysostom, and Theophylactus (quoted by St. Thomas in the *Catena Aurea* on Jn. 18).

- **Isn't Christ's kingship essentially spiritual?**

  Indeed, Pius XI teaches in *Quas Primas* that the kingdom of Christ "is spiritual and is concerned with spiritual things" (§15).

- **If it is essentially spiritual, does Christ's kingship extend over temporal affairs?**

  In the same encyclical, Pius XI continues to say: "It would be a grave error, on the other hand, to say that Christ has no authority whatever in civil affairs, since, by virtue of the absolute empire over all creatures committed to Him by the Father, all things are in His power" (§17).

- **Even if He has this power, didn't our Lord manifest that He was not interested in temporal power and desired to reign only over souls?**

  Our Lord desires first and foremost to save souls and to reign in them by His grace. To turn men heavenwards, during His life on earth He refused any exercise of temporal authority. He carefully distinguished the religious society He founded (the holy Catholic Church) from civil society. He left to the kings of the earth their power. But Christ's kingship nonetheless exists, and temporal authorities have the duty to acknowledge it publicly once they become cognizant of it.

- **Why must rulers recognize Christ's kingship?**

  For heads of state, the public recognition of Christ's kingship is first of all a duty in justice *to our Lord* (His kingship is the source of their authority). It is also a duty *to their subjects*, whom they strongly help to save their souls, and upon whom they draw down the Savior's particular blessing. Lastly, it is a duty *to the Church*, which must be sustained in its mission.

- **Why insist so much upon Christ's social kingship? Isn't it enough to be occupied with the main thing: His reign in souls?**

  Man is not a pure spirit. Pope Pius XII teaches: "Souls are affected for better or for worse by the form given to society, depending on whether it is in harmony with divine law or not."[6]

---

[6] Pius XII, Radio Message of June 1, 1941.

34) Does the State, then, have duties in regard to our Lord Jesus Christ and to religion?

Just as all men have the duty to honor God their Creator, and, in order to do so, to embrace the true faith once they know it (their personal salvation depends upon their acceptance or rejection of Jesus Christ), so too does the State. "The happiness of the State flows from no other source than that of individuals, since a city is nothing else than the ensemble of particular individuals living in harmony."[7]

- **Must political society itself honor God publicly? Isn't it enough that individuals do so?**

Leo XIII teaches: "The State, constituted as it is, is clearly bound to act up to the manifold and weighty duties linking it to God, by the public profession of religion."[8]

- **Where does this duty to honor God publicly come from?**

Leo XIII explains:

> For men living together in society are under the power of God no less than individuals are, and society, no less than individuals, owes gratitude to God who gave it being....Since, then, no one is allowed to be remiss in the service due to God, and since the chief duty of all men is to cling to religion in both its teaching and practice (not such religion as they may have a preference for, but the religion which God enjoins, and which certain and most clear marks show to be the only one true religion), it is a public crime to act as though there were no God. So, too, is it a sin for the State not to have care for religion as something beyond its scope, or as of no practical benefit; or out of many forms of religion to adopt that one which chimes in with the fancy.[9]

- **To honor God publicly, must civil society necessarily profess the Catholic religion?**

Jesus Christ, who is the unique mediator between men and God, is never optional. And the Catholic Church, which is the unique Church of Christ, is not any more so. Leo XIII teaches: "We are bound absolutely to worship God in that way which He has shown to be His will."[10]

---

[7] St. Augustine (354-430), Letter 155 to Macedonius, 3, 9, *PL* 33, 670.
[8] Leo XIII, Encyclical *Immortale Dei* (Nov. 1, 1885) on the Christian Constitution of States, §6.
[9] *Ibid.*
[10] *Ibid.*

● But is the State competent in religious matters?

The State is not competent to legislate in religious matters according to its lights. But it is competent to recognize the true religion by certain marks, and to submit to it. Leo XIII affirms: "Since, then, the profession of one religion is necessary in the State, that religion must be professed which alone is true, and which can be recognized without difficulty, especially in Catholic States, because the marks of truth are, as it were, engraved upon it. This religion, therefore, the rulers of the State must preserve and protect...."[11]

● Has the State other religious duties besides the public worship of God?

Yes, the State, while staying within its own domain, must foster its citizens' eternal salvation.

● Isn't it the Church's affair, and not the State's, to aid people to reach eternal happiness?

God willed to create a specifically religious society (the holy Catholic Church), distinct from civil society. Man, then, must belong to both of these societies, yet man has only one last end. He cannot go in two directions simultaneously: his temporal life is given him to prepare his eternity. The State, whose proper domain is the temporal order, cannot organize society independently of its last end. It is not directly responsible for the eternal happiness of its citizens, but it must contribute to that end indirectly. If the State should neglect to do so, it would be ignoring the most important part of the common good. Such is the teaching of the Fathers of the Church, St. Thomas Aquinas, and the popes.

● What do the Fathers of the Church have to say about this?

St. Augustine asserts:

> For a man serves God in one way in that he is man, in another way in that he is also king. In that he is man, he serves Him by living faithfully; but in that he is also king, he serves Him by enforcing with suitable rigor such laws as ordain what is righteous, and punish what is the reverse. Even as Hezekiah served Him by destroying the groves and the temples of the idols... (II Kings 18:4), or even as Josiah served Him by doing the same things in his turn (II Kings 23:4-5)..., or as Darius served Him by giving the idol into the power of Daniel to be broken... (Dan. 3:29). In this way,

---

[11] Leo XIII, Encyclical *Libertas* (June 20, 1888), §21. The same teaching is given in *Immortale Dei*.

therefore, kings can serve the Lord, even in so far as they are kings, when they do in His service what they could not do were they not kings.[12]

Elsewhere he teaches:

It is by acting thus that kings serve God in their royal capacity: if in their kingdom they command the good and prohibit evil, not only in the things pertaining to human society, but also in those that pertain to the true religion.[13]

And elsewhere:

But we say that [rulers] are happy if they rule justly; ...if they make their power the handmaid of His majesty by using it for the greatest possible extension of His worship; if they fear, love, worship God....[14]

• What do the other Fathers of the Church say?

St. Ambrose begins a letter to the Emperor thus: "As all men who live under the Roman sway engage in military service under you, the Emperors and Princes of the world, so too do you yourselves owe service to Almighty God and our holy faith."[15]

St. Leo the Great wrote to the Emperor Leo I: "The kingly power has been conferred on you not for the governance of the world alone but more especially for the guardianship of the Church...."[16]

St. Gregory the Great affirms: "For power over all men has been given from heaven to the piety of my lords to this end, that they who aspire to what is good may be helped, and that the way to heaven may be more widely open, so that an earthly kingdom may wait upon the heavenly kingdom."[17]

St. John Chrysostom explains: "For there are a duller sort, upon whom things to come have not such a hold as things present. He then who by fear and rewards gives the soul of the majority a preparatory turn towards its becoming more suited for the word of doctrine, is with good reason called 'the Minister of God.'"[18]

---

[12] St. Augustine, Letter 185, Chap. 5, §19, *PL* 33, col. 801 [on line at http://www.newadvent.org/fathers].
[13] St. Augustine, "Four Books in Answer to the Grammarian Cresconius," *Retractations*, Chap. 51, §56.
[14] St. Augustine, *The City of God*, Book 5, Chap. 24.
[15] St. Ambrose, Letter 17, *PL*, col. 961 [online at www.newadvent.org/fathers].
[16] St. Leo the Great (Pope 440-61), Letter to Leo Augustus, *PL* 54, col. 1130 [online at www.catholicculture.org/library/fathers].
[17] St. Gregory the Great (Pope 590–604), to Mauricius Augustus, *PL* 77, col. 663, [online at www.catholicculture.org/library/fathers].
[18] St. John Chrysostom, Homily XXIII on the Epistle to the Romans [online at www.newadvent.org/fathers].

● And what did St. Thomas Aquinas teach?

In his treatise on politics, the *De Regno*, he wrote: "Since the beatitude of heaven is the end of that virtuous life which we live at present, it pertains to the king's office to promote the good life of the multitude in such a way as to make it suitable for the attainment of heavenly happiness, that is to say, he should command those things which lead to the happiness of heaven and, as far as possible, forbid the contrary."[19]

● Are the Doctors of the Church unanimous on this point?

Yes, the Doctors of the Church are unanimous on this point. On the brink of the French Revolution of 1789, the great doctor of moral theology St. Alphonsus de Liguori employed the same language as St. Augustine:

> An individual will save his soul by keeping the divine laws; a king, to save his soul, must keep them and make his subjects keep them, that is to say, reform bad morals and uproot scandal. He must fulfill this duty courageously and unflinchingly....He must not hesitate to banish from his realm every preacher of impiety, nor to seize works infected with bad doctrine at the border. This is their imperious duty, and it is for failing to accomplish it that princes have lost their crown.[20]

● Have recent popes dealt with this question?

After the Revolution of 1789, when the temporal powers ceased to fulfill their function, the popes had to treat explicitly of the matter at length. Gregory XVI reminded the princes that

> their power has been given them, not only for the government of the world, but especially for the support and defence of the Church....let them be convinced that the cause of faith should be far dearer to them than that of their kingdom....Set up as fathers and guardians of their nations, they will secure their true and constant happiness, with peace and plenty, if they make it their principal care to make religion flourish with piety towards God, who bears written on His thigh: "King of kings, Lord of lords."[21]

● Did Gregory XVI's successors employ the same language?

All the popes until Vatican II are unanimous. Leo XIII explains:

---

[19] St. Thomas Aquinas, *On Kingship*, tr. by Gerald B. Phelan and revised by I. Th. Eschmann, O.P. (Toronto: Institute of Mediaeval Studies, 1949) [online at www.diafrica.org/kenny/CDtexts/DeRegno.htm#0].

[20] St. Alphonsus de Liguori, *Fedelta dei Vassali* (June 1777), quoted by Augustin Berthe, C.SS.R., *St. Alphonse de Liguori 1696-1787* (Paris: Reteaux), II, 440-41.

[21] Gregory XVI, *Mirari Vos* (Kansas City: Angelus Press, n.d.), §29.

For one and all are we destined by our birth and adoption to enjoy, when this frail and fleeting life is ended, a supreme and final good in heaven....Hence, civil society, established for the common welfare, should not only safeguard the well-being of the community, but have also at heart the interests of its individual members, in such mode as not in any way to hinder, but in every manner to render as easy as may be, the possession of that highest and unchangeable good for which all should seek. Wherefore, for this purpose, care must especially be taken to preserve unharmed and unimpeded the religion whereof the practice is the link connecting man with God.[22]

● So then, Church and State should not be separated?

The Church and the State are two distinct societies, but their strict separation is absurd and unnatural. Man is not divided into a Christian and a citizen. He must be a Christian not only in his private life, but in every facet of his life. Thus he must pursue a Christian politics by striving to bring civil laws into accord with the divine laws.

● Was the separation of Church and State condemned by the popes?

Pius IX condemned the proposition that "the Church ought to be separated from the State, and the State from the Church,"[23] and St. Pius X wrote:

> That the State must be separated from the Church is a thesis absolutely false, a most pernicious error. Based, as it is, on the principle that the State must not recognize any religious cult, it is in the first place guilty of a great injustice to God; for the Creator of man is also the Founder of human societies, and preserves their existence as He preserves our own. We owe Him, therefore, not only a private cult, but a public and social worship to honor Him. Besides, this thesis is an obvious negation of the supernatural order. It limits the action of the State to the pursuit of public prosperity during this life only, which is but the proximate object of political societies; and it occupies itself in no fashion (on the plea that this is foreign to it) with their ultimate object which is man's eternal happiness after this short life shall have run its course.[24]

35) What ought to be the relations between the Church and the State?

In practice, the relations between the Church and the State depend upon the religious composition of the population. Normally, when the population is predominantly Catholic, the State ought to be Catholic

---

[22] *Immortale Dei*, §6. The Pope develops the same idea in *Libertas*.
[23] Condemned Proposition 55 from the Syllabus of Errors (Dec. 8, 1864).
[24] St. Pius X, Encyclical *Vehementer Nos*, on the French Law of Separation (Feb. 11, 1906), §3.

officially. It should then adhere to the Catholic religion and proclaim it the religion of the State, protect and favor it, and make its feast days public holidays. Its representatives should participate in their official capacity in liturgical celebrations. Moreover, it should assist Catholic schools and charitable institutions, and assure that the Commandments of God be expressed in civil laws, such as the observance of Sunday and the prohibition of divorce, contraception, and abortion.

- **Are the normal relations between the Church and the State always applicable?**

The integral application of the normal relations between the Church and the State is not always possible or prudent. It could sometimes even lead to civil war. A nation's circumstances must be prudently taken into account. Yet, at the very least, the government should protect the freedom of the Catholic Church and enforce respect for the tenets of the natural law by forbidding divorce, abortion, and the other immoral practices that were prohibited in most States until recent decades.

- **How might one sum up the normal duties of the State to the Church?**

Leo XIII summarized these duties thus: "All who rule, therefore, would hold in honour the holy name of God, and one of their chief duties must be to favour religion, to protect it, to shield it under the credit and sanction of the laws, and neither to organize nor enact any measure that may compromise its safety. This is the bounden duty of rulers to the people over whom they rule."[25]

36) In a Catholic State, must the citizens be Catholic?

When a very great majority of a people are Catholic, Catholicism ought to be the religion of the State, but this does not mean that all the citizens must be forced to embrace the Catholic Faith. Forced conversions are, to the contrary, strictly forbidden, because the act of faith must be an act of free will and cannot be compelled.

- **Ought a Catholic State to allow its subjects freedom in religious matters?**

In principle, the State is only concerned with what pertains to social life. Hence it has no authority to scrutinize consciences or the

---

[25] Leo XIII, *Immortale Dei*, §6.

private exercise of cult. But it cannot disregard the public exercise of religious activities.

● Ought a Catholic State to forbid the public exercise of false cults?

The false religions are an evil from which the Catholic State must protect its citizens. It ought therefore to prohibit or limit as much as possible their public exercise and propaganda. However, it can (and sometimes must) tolerate them if that results in safeguarding a greater good or avoiding a greater evil.

● What is tolerance?

Tolerance is the patient endurance of an evil.

● Isn't it unjust to bear an evil?

Justice is not the supreme virtue: it must be regulated by prudence and animated by charity. Tolerance is not exercised in the name of justice, but in the name of prudence and charity.

● But isn't the tolerance of an evil an imperfection?

If it is really prudent, the tolerance of evil is in itself good and praiseworthy, but it is the result and sign of imperfection in a society. Leo XIII teaches: "The more a State is driven to tolerate evil, the further is it from perfection."[26]

● What are the limits of this tolerance of false religions?

It is incumbent upon the prudence of the head of state to establish, according to the circumstances, more or less broad limits to the exercise of false religions. The general rule is that evil must be tolerated only in as much as the common good requires. Leo XIII declares: "The tolerance of evil which is dictated by political prudence should be strictly confined to the limits which its justifying cause, the public welfare, requires."[27]

37) Is there a right to the free exercise of any and all religions?

There is an absolute right to develop and to practice freely the *true religion*, for no one can be impeded from serving God in the way He Himself has prescribed. It is an exigency of the natural law. There

---

[26] *Libertas*, §34.
[27] *Ibid.*

is no real right, however, to practice the false religions precisely because they are false and erroneous. Error can never have any right; only the truth has rights. Heads of state, therefore, are not obliged in justice (based upon natural law) to practice tolerance towards the false religions, but they may do so from prudence or Christian charity.

- **Is it certain that error has no rights?**

Leo XIII teaches very clearly that error cannot have any rights: "While not conceding any right to anything save what is true and honest, [the Church] does not forbid public authority to tolerate what is at variance with truth and justice, for the sake of avoiding some greater evil, or of obtaining or preserving some greater good."[28] Pius XII teaches that "what does not correspond to the truth and to the moral standards has, objectively, no right to exist, to be taught, or to be done."[29]

- **Hence the toleration of false religions cannot be guaranteed by law?**

The toleration of false religions may find expression in civil law. A Catholic State may, if so required, guarantee it by law, but that grant would be something completely different from a natural right.

- **Can you expound the difference between natural law and civil law?**

The natural law is founded directly upon the nature of man and the duties that flow from it (an act contrary to the natural law is *per se* morally bad or unjust). But the natural law is not entirely sufficient for the governance of society. It must be completed and particularized by civil law, decreed by the political authority for the sake of the common good of a particular society. The virtue of prudence comes into play in the establishment of the positive civil law (another society might, for particular reasons, establish contrary rules, which would not for that reason be unjust). For prudential reasons (principally for the sake of peace), the free exercise of false religions may in certain cases be guaranteed by the civil law of a Catholic country, but it can never be a natural right.

---

[28] *Ibid.*, §33.
[29] *Ci Riesce*, Discourse to the Convention of Italian Catholic Jurists, Dec. 6, 1953 [English version: Msgr. Joseph C. Fenton, "Pius XII and the Theological Treatise on the Church," *The American Ecclesiastical Review* on line at www.catholicculture.org/library/view.cfm?recnum=5086].

38) What does Vatican II teach about religious liberty?

The Declaration of Vatican II on religious liberty, *Dignitatis Humanae* (§2), affirms:

> This Vatican Synod declares that the human person has a right to religious freedom. This freedom means that all men are to be immune from coercion on the part of individuals or of social groups and of any human power, in such wise that in matters religious no one is to be forced to act in a manner contrary to his own beliefs. Nor is anyone to be restrained from acting in accordance with his own beliefs, whether privately or publicly, whether alone or in association with others, within due limits.[30]

• What is noteworthy in this passage from Vatican II?

1) First, Vatican II not only says that no one should be forced to believe (which the Church has always taught), but also claims that no one can be restrained from practicing the religion of his choice.

2) Then, and this is paramount, Vatican II no longer speaks of tolerance alone, but actually recognizes a real natural right of the adepts of all religions not to be hindered in the practice of their religion.

3) Finally, this right not only concerns practice in private, but also public worship and propagation of the religion. Thus Vatican II promotes something the Church always condemned previously.

• Does Vatican II truly intend to speak of a genuine natural right of man (and not merely of a simple civil right)?

Unfortunately yes, Vatican II presents the right not to be impeded from acting in accordance with one's conscience in matters religious as a genuine natural right. It explains that this right is based on "the very dignity of the human person" (and not on a positive juridical determination); consequently it is only upon this basis that religious liberty must also be recognized as a civil right (*DH* 2).[31]

---

[30] Walter M. Abbott, S.J., Editor, *The Documents of Vatican II* (New York: The America Press, 1966), pp. 678-79.

[31] The new Catechism of the Catholic Church affirms: "The right to religious liberty is neither a moral license to adhere to error, nor a supposed right to error, but rather *a natural right of the human person* to civil liberty, i.e., immunity, within just limits, from external constraint in religious matters by political authorities. This *natural right* ought to be acknowledged in the juridical order of society in such a way that it constitutes a civil right" (§2108, emphasis added).

● Doesn't Vatican II speak of "due limits" on this "right"?

Vatican II does mention "due limits" circumscribing religious liberty, but the nature of the limits is not clearly stated in the document. In paragraph 2, it seems to involve safeguarding public order; further on, paragraph 7 speaks of "the objective moral order," which is better, but illusory and ultimately insufficient.

● Why is this mention of "the objective moral order" illusory?

Taken literally, the implication of limiting religious liberty to "the objective moral order" is that only the Catholic Church could enjoy unrestricted freedom of religion because she alone conserves the natural law in its entirety (Islam authorizes polygamy; the Protestants—and even the Eastern schismatics in some cases—allow divorce; *etc.*). But this conclusion obviously contradicts the rest of the text. For Vatican II, having set aside the obligations of strict natural law, the only restraining limit on religious freedom is public order. As long as the cult is not a cover for terrorist attacks, criminal networks, pedophilia, or some other infringement of "the rights of man," everything must be authorized.

● Why should the mention of "the objective moral order" be considered insufficient?

Even interpreted strictly, this limitation of religious liberty to the "objective moral order" is inadequate because restricted to the natural order of things, thereby omitting consideration of the supernatural order. Such a conception of religious liberty fails to recognize the social kingship of our Lord Jesus Christ, the supernatural rights of His Church, and the supernatural end of man in the common good of the political order. It fails to consider that the false religions, by the mere fact that they keep souls from the Catholic Church, lead souls to hell. In a word, it is naturalism. To it can be applied what St. Pius X said about the separation of Church and State:

> This thesis is an obvious negation of the supernatural order. It limits the action of the State to the pursuit of public prosperity during this life only, which is but the *proximate* object of political societies; and it occupies itself in no fashion (on the plea that this is foreign to it) with their *ultimate* object, which is man's eternal happiness after this short life shall have run its course.[32]

---

[32] St. Pius X, Encyclical *Vehementer Nos* (February 11, 1906), §3.

- **Does the teaching of Vatican II on religious freedom contradict the Church's perennial teaching?**

The religious liberty taught by Vatican II not only contradicts the *teaching* of the Church, but also, and foremost, its constant practice.

- **How does Vatican II contradict the constant practice of the Church?**

The saints have never hesitated to break idols, destroy their temples, or legislate against pagan or heretical practices. The Church—without ever forcing anyone to believe or be baptized—has always recognized its right and duty to protect the faith of her children and to impede, whenever possible, the public exercise and propagation of false cults. To accept the teaching of Vatican II is to grant that, for two millennia, the popes, saints, Fathers and Doctors of the Church, bishops, and Catholic kings have constantly violated the natural rights of men without anyone in the Church noticing. Such a thesis is as absurd as it is impious.

- **Can you name some saints who would have violated the "right of religious freedom" as it is taught by Vatican II?**

One can cite, among many others, St. Polyeuctus, St. Christina, St. Martin, St. Benedict, St. Gall, St. Peter of Verona, St. Louis, St. Vincent Ferrer, St. Casimir, St. Antonine (of Florence), St. Pius V, St. Francis Xavier, St. Louis Bertrand, St. Francis de Sales, *etc.*, not to mention all the Doctors who justified this practice (St. Ambrose, St. Augustine, St. Thomas Aquinas,[33] St. Alphonsus, *etc.*).

- **Might one not say that these saints acted under the influence of the prejudices of their age and that, with the passage of time, subsequent generations have understood the spirit of the Gospel better?**

Such a hypothesis is unsustainable for at least seven reasons:

1) It destroys the infallibility of the Church (which would have erred in a serious matter for more than two millennia).

2) It insults her maternal mildness (the Church would have conducted herself for centuries like a possessive mother or even a cruel stepmother).

3) It ruins her claim to holiness (practically denying the action of the Holy Ghost, who purifies the saints from their too human tendencies or

---

[33] Of St. Thomas, see especially *ST*, II-II, Q. 11, Art. 3.

conceptions, enlightens them on the true meaning of the Gospel, gives them strength and the holy liberty necessary to brave the prejudices of the world).

4) It discredits Christian charity (the natural bent of which should have prevented the violation of one of the fundamental "rights" of the human person for centuries).

5) It distorts history by gratuitously considering as a more or less unconscious prejudice imposed by the time in which they lived what was in fact a serious, solidly argued conviction held by many saints. (St. Augustine debated at length the Donatists, who were partisans of religious liberty, and thought about this question deeply; the same can be said of the thirteenth-century theologians in their encounters with some Cathars).

6) It constitutes what English philosophers call "a self-refuting system." (Why should our century have fewer prejudices than centuries past? If the prejudices linked to those centuries exercised an invincible pressure even on the Popes and Doctors of the Church, why should the non-infallible Vatican II have escaped any better from the [liberal] prejudices of our time than the saints of the past from the prejudices of their day?)

7) Lastly, this thesis accords the enemies of the Church (the Donatists, Cathars, Humanists, Encyclopedists, Freemasons, *etc.*) the extravagant privilege of having penetrated the spirit of the Gospel on this point long before the Catholic Doctors (in this regard, Voltaire would have been a better Catholic than St. Alphonsus de Liguori and the entire episcopate of the time).

● Have there never been any defenders of religious liberty in the Church?

There have always been defenders of *true* religious liberty in the Church (the freedom of the true religion), just as there have been of Christian tolerance, but never of religious liberty as it is preached by Vatican II. The first defenders of liberty for all religions were heretics or enemies of the Church. Its great promoters were the English philosophers of the seventeenth century, then the French philosophers of the Enlightenment in the eighteenth century. The Catholics who later thought it was opportune to demand this liberty in response to persecutions formed what were called the "liberal Catholics," frequently condemned by the popes.

● What popes condemned the "liberal Catholics"?

Several successive waves of "liberal Catholics" were condemned by popes during the nineteenth and twentieth centuries.

- **Who condemned the first "liberal Catholic" wave?**

  The first wave, led by Félicité de Lamennais (1782–1854) was condemned by Gregory XVI in the Encyclical *Mirari Vos* in 1832. Lamennais left the Church and was abandoned by his disciples.

- **Who condemned the second "liberal Catholic" wave?**

  The second "liberal Catholic" wave, led by Msgr. Felix Dupanloup (1802–1878, Bishop of Orleans) and Count Charles de Montalembert (1810-70), was condemned in 1864 by Pope Pius IX's Encyclical *Quanta Cura* and the catalogue of errors (the Syllabus) that accompanied it.

- **Who condemned the third "liberal Catholic" wave?**

  The third "liberal Catholic" wave developed in the circles that had resisted the second wave. At the end of the pontificate of Leo XIII (especially after he called upon the French monarchists to rally to the Republic in 1892), under the pressure of the contemporary world and without being aware of it, a significant part of young French Catholics gradually adopted the ideas against which their parents had fought. The "democrat priests," then the *Sillon* of Marc Sangnier (1873-1950) were at the head of this movement, which was halted by St. Pius X's Letter on the Sillon, *Our Apostolic Mandate* (August 25, 1910).

- **Was there a fourth "liberal Catholic" wave?**

  Jacques Maritain (1882-1973) was the principal leader of the fourth "liberal Catholic" wave in France beginning in the 1930's.

- **But wasn't Jacques Maritain a great Thomist philosopher?**

  Just as at the beginning of the Church's history certain men betrayed the true faith after having been its champions (Tertullian, for example), likewise Maritain, a champion of Thomism, progressively evolved towards liberalism. He went so far that, towards the end of his life, he had come to doubt the eternity of the pains of hell.[34]

- **Was this fourth "liberal Catholic" wave condemned?**

  In 1953, Cardinal Ottaviani, the Pro-Secretary of the Holy Office, refuted some of Maritain's liberal theses in a solemn speech at the Lateran; in 1958, the Holy Office prepared a document condemning certain propositions of Maritain or of the American Jesuit John Courtney Murray, but Pius XII's death prevented its publication. Ultimately, Maritain and Murray triumphed at Vatican II.

---

[34] Jacques and Raïssa Maritain, *Oeuvres complètes* (Paris: Ed. Saint-Paul) XIII, 440-478.

- **Does the religious liberty proclaimed by Vatican II incur these condemnations of "liberal Catholicism"?**

    The religious liberty taught by Vatican II incurs several of these condemnations. In *Quanta Cura*, for example, Blessed Pius IX condemned "that erroneous opinion, most fatal in its effects on the Catholic Church and the salvation of souls, called by Our Predecessor, Gregory XVI, an insanity (*deliramentum*); namely, that 'liberty of conscience and worship is each man's personal right, which ought to be legally proclaimed and asserted in every rightly constituted society....'"[35] He equally condemned the following error as contrary to Holy Scripture, the Church, and the holy Fathers: "That is the best condition of civil society, in which no duty is recognized, as attached to the civil power, of restraining by enacted penalties, offenders against the Catholic religion, except so far as public peace may require."[36]

- **Can you cite another pope?**

    Leo XIII, in *Libertas Praestantissimum*, sounded a warning not only against the irreligious State, but also against a State that would "treat the various religions (as they call them) alike, and bestow upon them promiscuously equal rights and privileges," "a line of action which would end in godlessness." Such a State would sin against justice and reason.[37]

- **Do the popes of the twentieth century teach the same doctrine?**

    Pope Pius XII taught on October 6, 1946:

    > The Catholic Church, as we have already said, is a perfect society and has as its foundation the truth of Faith infallibly revealed by God. For this reason, that which is opposed to the truth is, necessarily, an error, and the same rights, which are objectively recognized for truth, cannot be afforded to error. In this manner, liberty of thought and liberty of conscience have their essential limits in the truthfulness of God in revelation.[38]

- **But doesn't *Dignitatis Humanae* refer to papal pronouncements?**

    Dignitatis Humanae cites Pope Leo XIII's Encyclical *Libertas* in support of religious freedom. Here is the relevant paragraph (§30):

---

[35] Pius IX, Encyclical *Quanta Cura* (December 8, 1864), §3 (online at www.papalencyclicals.net).
[36] *Ibid.*
[37] Leo XIII, *Libertas* (June 20, 1888), §21.
[38] Pius XII, *Ecco che gia un anno*, October 6, 1946 [English version online at www.geocities.com/Athens/ Rhodes/3543/liberty.htm.]

Another liberty is widely advocated, namely, *liberty of conscience.* If by this is meant that everyone may, as he chooses, worship God or not, it is sufficiently refuted by the arguments already adduced. But it may also be taken to mean that every man in the State may follow the will of God and, from a consciousness of duty and free from every obstacle, obey His commands. This, indeed, is true liberty, a liberty worthy of the sons of God, which nobly maintains the dignity of man and is stronger than all violence or wrong–a liberty which the Church has always desired and held most dear.

- **What is the import of this passage of Leo XIII?**

After condemning "liberty of conscience" as it is commonly understood in the modern world, Leo XIII says that this expression can, however, be rightly understood. Speaking of "a liberty worthy of sons of God," he unequivocally means the freedom to be able to practice the true religion (the right of which he speaks has as its object the will of God and the accomplishment of His precepts). It is dishonest to pretend to apply this passage to false religions.

- **Do the authors of *Dignitatis Humanae* admit that their document contradicts the teachings of previous popes?**

Several of the authors of *Dignitatis Humanae* were obliged to admit that the text posed some difficulties. The chief inspirer of the text, Fr. John Courtney Murray, acknowledged this in his commentary: "Almost exactly a century later, the Declaration on Religious Freedom seems to affirm as Catholic teaching that which Gregory XVI and Pius IX held as 'insanity,' a mad idea."[39] Fr. Yves Congar admitted: "It cannot be denied that the Declaration on Religious Liberty does say materially something else than the Syllabus of 1864; it even says just about the opposite of Propositions 15 and 77 to 79 of this document."[40] Elsewhere he said: "I collaborated on the final paragraphs–which left me less satisfied. It involved demonstrating that the theme of religious liberty was already contained in Scripture. Now, it isn't there."[41]

---

[39] Fr. John Courtney Murray, S.J., "Towards an Understanding of the Development of the Church's Doctrine on Religious Freedom," *Vatican II: Religious Liberty* [French], Unam Sanctam 60 (Paris: Cerf, 1967), p. 111.

[40] Fr. Yves Congar, O.P., *The Crisis in the Church and Msgr. Lefebvre* [French] (Paris: Cerf, 1977), p. 51. In 1984, Fr. Congar reaffirmed: "The Declaration on Religious Freedom says the contrary of several propositions of the Syllabus of 1864" (*Ecumenical Essays: The Men, the Movement, the Problems* [French] [Paris: Centurion, 1984], p. 85).

[41] Fr. Yves Congar, O.P., interviewed by Eric Vatre in *The Father's Right Hand: A Look at Catholic Tradition Today* [French] (Paris: Trédaniel, 1994), p. 118.

- **How could Vatican II have reached the point of promulgating a declaration so radically in contradiction with the Church's practice and teaching?**

The Preparatory Theological Commission constituted by Pope John XXIII to prepare the Council had drafted an entirely traditional document, summarizing the Church's doctrine in this matter.[42] But the Secretariat for Promoting Christian Unity, presided by Cardinal Bea, had prepared an alternative schema drafted with a view to pleasing the Protestants and Freemasons. During the preparatory sessions held on June 19-20, 1962, "the texts of the Commission and the Secretariat were presented together before the Central Commission, provoking the most dramatic confrontation that body ever experienced."[43] Cardinals Ottaviani and Bea vehemently clashed. On the eve of the Council, two contrary doctrines were proposed. One referred to the unbroken tradition of the Church, the other invoked the expectations of the modern world.

- **Was the Secretariat for Christian Unity able to impose this innovative text easily?**

The Secretariat for Unity was able to impose its text only after four years of lobbying the Council Fathers. The innovators hoped to bring it to a vote in 1964 as a sort of repentance for Pius IX's Syllabus, whose centenary was being observed that year, but they did not succeed. Finally, the Declaration on Religious Freedom was voted and promulgated at the end of the Council's last session in 1965. To reduce the opposition, they had moderated the tone and added numerous apparently traditional passages. But the fundamental orientation of the document remained liberal, and the definition given to "religious freedom" contradicted the constant teaching and practice of the Church.

39) How does Vatican II try to justify religious freedom?

The Declaration on Religious Liberty bases it on the dignity of the human person: "The council further declares that the right to religious freedom has its foundation in the very dignity of the human person, as this dignity is known through the revealed Word of God and by reason itself."[44]

---

[42] The document was entitled *De Relationibus inter Ecclesiam et Statum, necnon de Tolerantia Religiosa* [On the Relations between the Church and the State, and Religious Tolerance].
[43] Giuseppe Alberigo, *Histoire du Concile Vatican II, 1959-1965* (Paris: Cerf, 1997), I, 334.
[44] Vatican II, Declaration *Dignitatis Humanae*, December 7, 1965, 2.

- **Why do the authors of this document want to found the right to religious liberty on the dignity of the human person?**

In order to bypass the Church's previous condemnations (notably against the idea that error has rights), a new foundation for religious liberty had to be found, so they tried to consider things from the viewpoint of persons: to be able to adhere freely to religious truth, they must be exempt from constraint in matters religious.

- **What should we think of this argumentation?**

It is an attempt at diversion by means of a threefold sophism.

- **Where's the diversion?**

A theoretical distinction about the foundation of religious liberty cannot change the fact that religious liberty itself is directly contrary to the constant teaching and practice of the Church. It is a fact that the Church has always striven to reduce (and if possible to ban) the practice and propagation of false religions. Regardless of the cleverness deployed to provide religious freedom with new foundations not yet explicitly condemned, a false right will always remain a false right (and the new foundations, sophisms).

- **What is the first sophism?**

Under the pretext that man must adhere to religious truth freely, Vatican II would exempt him from any constraint in this matter. *Dignitatis Humanae* thus asserts:

> ...The truth cannot impose itself except by virtue of its own truth, as it makes its entrance into the mind at once quietly and with power....
>
> It is in accordance with their dignity as persons–that is, beings endowed with reason and free will and therefore privileged to bear personal responsibility–that all men should be at once impelled by nature and also bound by a moral obligation to seek the truth, especially religious truth. They are also bound to adhere to the truth, once it is known, and to order their whole lives in accord with the demands of truth. However, men *cannot discharge* these obligations in a manner in keeping with their own nature *unless they enjoy immunity from external coercion*....
>
> Truth, however, is to be sought after in a manner proper to the dignity of the human person and his social nature. The inquiry is to be free, carried on with the aid of teaching or instruction, communication and dialogue, in the course of which men explain to one another the truth they have discovered, or think they have discovered, in order thus to assist one another in the quest for truth. (§§1-3)

● It is true after all that coercion is opposed to freedom; where then is the sophism?

An expert at the Council, Fr. Berto,[45] neatly exposed the sophism:

> Not everyone is an adult, and many adults by age are not so by intellect.
>
> The schema ignores the timid; it ignores the slaves of sin; it ignores the pressure of the passions; it ignores the spreading of errors by perverse men, and imagines an angelic man....Where in the world, or on what planet, does this schema put us? From a child's tenderest age and attainment of the use of reason there are "moral problems" to resolve, and far from having a right to be left to itself to resolve them, the child has a right not to be left to itself, but rather to be helped by the counsels, commands, injunctions, and paddle of its parents and educators to resolve its "moral problems" with rectitude. *The child has a right to have its freedom limited*; it has the right to have those in charge order it to do what is inherently right. And the parents and educators who abdicate from ordering, prescribing, ordaining, and spanking, fail in a very serious duty and heavily burden their consciences before God.
>
> The same ought to be said analogously of most men, who are not able to overcome even vincible errors unless the errors are kept far from them by those who have received the duty, and they can as it were breathe the truth. Just as sick people are sent to a sanitarium so that they can breathe the fresh air of the mountains or sea shore to rebuild their strength and they can escape the noxious air of the city, likewise the human race, sick from original sin and manifold actual sins, has a right, not to an unlimited "religious freedom," but on the contrary to such restraint on "religious freedom" that by using their liberty men embrace the truth. This does not mean that people are forced to embrace the faith against their will, but rather that the stupid and the weak are placed in a situation in which they can more easily discern and choose the truth. Unlimited "religious freedom," besides being inherently bad, opens the door to error to the great detriment of the rights of the weak and the ignorant.[46]
>
> [Moreover,] [s]ince in this world error has such power, all those endowed with authority of whatever degree–parents over their children, the State over its citizens, the Church over the baptized–have a very serious duty, whether natural or supernatural, to protect those in their charge from error. *Some say that truth can defeat error all by itself without the help of any authority.* This will be true the day when men are no longer men, but supermen or superangels! I have sufficiently shown above that error finds its accomplices within us and among us.[47]

---

[45] Fr. Victor-Alain Berto (1900-68) was a Dominican tertiary and Archbishop Lefebvre's theologian during the Council.

[46] Fr. Victor-Alain Berto, essay on religious liberty written in 1964 for the *Coetus Internationalis Patrum* and published in the anthology *La Sainte Eglise Romaine* (Paris: Cedre, 1976), pp. 405-6 (emphasis added).

[47] *Ibid.*, p. 396.

- ### What is the second sophism?

Under the pretext of not hindering the free search for truth (*DH* 2), Vatican II promotes the free propagation of error (*DH* 4).

- ### What's the answer?

This error is self-refuting. Recall that Pius IX, quoting St. Augustine, affirmed that the unrestricted freedom to publicly manifest opinions of all stripes is a "liberty of perdition" (*libertas perditionis*).[48] He also quotes St. Leo the Great: "If human arguments are always allowed free room for discussion, there will never be wanting men who will dare to resist truth, and to trust in the flowing speech of human wisdom; whereas we know, from the very teaching of our Lord Jesus Christ, how carefully Christian faith and wisdom should avoid this most injurious babbling."[49]

- ### What is the third sophism?

The third sophism hinges on the "dignity of the human person":

> The council further declares that the right to religious freedom has its foundation in the very dignity of the human person....
>
> ...Therefore the right to religious freedom has its foundation not in the subjective disposition of the person, but in his very nature. In consequence, the right to this immunity continues to exist even in those who do not live up to their obligation of seeking the truth and adhering to it and the exercise of this right is not to be impeded, provided that just public order be observed. (*DH* 2)

- ### Where is the sophism?

There is a confusion between *radical* [or *ontological*] dignity and *operative* or *terminal* dignity.

- ### What is man's radical dignity?

The radical dignity of man is tied to his human nature. It derives from man's having a spiritual soul and consequently being endowed with reason and free will. It also derives from the fact that he is called by God to a supernatural end: the beatific vision.

- ### Why is it called radical dignity?

This dignity is called *radical* from the Latin root of the word, *radix-root*, because it is the root of the voluntary acts by which man can increase, diminish, or lose his dignity.

---

[48] Pope Pius IX, Encyclical *Quanta Cura* (December 8, 1864), §3.
[49] *Ibid.*

• What is operative dignity?

Insofar as a man adheres to the good and the true, he achieves his perfection; he acquires a dignity that is called operative or terminal.

• All men, then, do not possess the same dignity?

It is obvious that a murderer does not have the same dignity as a saint, and that a man loses his dignity by adhering to error or evil. In this life, he cannot lose his radical dignity completely (even the worst criminal can convert and amend his life); but in hell, the damned (who are no longer even capable of moral good) have totally lost their dignity.

• Where can this teaching on man's dignity be found?

The Roman liturgy reminds us that our human dignity is wounded by sin and can only be restored by the practice of temperance.[50]

• Have the Doctors of the Church addressed this question?

St. Thomas Aquinas, in the *Summa Theologica*, explains: **1)** that by sinning, man departs from the order of right reason and thereby falls away from his human dignity; and that **2)** he thus loses his right to a certain liberty.[51]

• Have the popes confirmed this teaching?

Pope Leo XIII teaches in the Encyclical *Immortale Dei*:

> If the mind assents to false opinions, and the will chooses and follows after what is wrong, neither can attain its native fullness, but both must fall from their native dignity into an abyss of corruption. Whatever, therefore, is opposed to virtue and truth may not rightly be brought temptingly before the eye of man, much less sanctioned by the favor and protection of the law. (§32)

• In light of this, what should we make of the text of Vatican II?

During that Council, Fr. Berto explained:

> If the dignity of the human person is considered only in its root [the simple fact of man's being endowed with reason and free will] then these considerations will be entirely inadequate and insufficient. An adequate

---

[50] Collect for the Thursday in Passion Week: "Grant, we beseech Thee, almighty God, that the dignity of human nature, impaired by intemperance, may be restored by the practice of salutary self-denial."

[51] "By sinning man departs from the order of reason, and consequently falls away from the dignity of his manhood, in so far as he is naturally free, and exists for himself, and he falls into the slavish state of the beasts..." (II-II, Q. 64, Art. 2, ad 3). This is how St. Thomas justifies the death penalty for certain criminals.

consideration of human dignity requires that a man's acts be taken into account....A dunce and a scholar do not have the same dignity. The dignity of someone who follows error is certainly not equal to that of someone who adheres to truth; nor is it equal between one who desires the good and one who desires evil.

The drafters, who have erected their schema on an inadequate notion of the dignity of the human person, have for this reason alone presented a deformed work of an extraordinary unreality; in effect, whether one will or no, between human persons adequately considered there are vast differences in dignity. And this is even truer in the context of the schema on religious freedom; for, obviously, religious freedom is proper to a person, not in virtue of his radical or ontological dignity, but in accordance with his operative dignity. Thus freedom cannot be the same for a child and for an adult, for an idiot and for a wise man, for a dunce and for a scholar, for someone possessed by the devil and for someone inspired by the Holy Ghost, *etc.*

Now this dignity, which we call *operative*, does not belong to the physical order, but, obviously, to the order of intellect and will. The failure in the schema to take into account the deliberative aspect, namely knowledge and virtue, constitutes a very grave error....[52]

In this regard, Archbishop Lefebvre wrote: "[T]o the extent that a man adheres to error or attaches himself to evil, he loses his final dignity or does not attain it; and nothing more can be founded on it!"[53]

40) Isn't religious freedom a result of man's freedom?

Freedom is not an absolute value. It was given to man so that he might freely choose the good. That he might choose evil is only a consequence, and at the same time an abuse, of this freedom. More precisely: freedom was not given to man so that he might choose between good and evil, but so that he could freely direct himself towards the good.

• Why did God give man freedom?

Freedom of the will is a consequence of reason; it is necessary for man to be able to love God (which creatures without reason cannot do). It thus confers on men a great dignity that places them well above creatures without reason.

---

[52] Berto, "Essay on Religious Liberty" (1964), pp. 387-88. Archbishop Lefebvre developed the same idea in the dubia he presented to the Congregation for the Doctrine of the Faith in October, 1985 (*Religious Liberty Questioned* [Angelus Press, 2002], pp. 19-22, 31-36, 99-100).

[53] Archbishop Marcel Lefebvre, *They Have Uncrowned Him* (Angelus Press, 1988), pp. 192-93. This work is undoubtedly the best and most thorough study of religious liberty.

● Doesn't freedom imply the power to do evil?

In the actual state of things, for man freedom implies the ability to do evil, but not the right (a murderer does not have a right to kill his neighbor). A man who chooses evil abuses his freedom.

● For man, what is the rule of good and evil? Is it his conscience?

It is true that man must act according to his conscience, but he first has the duty to enlighten it, because the conscience is not the ultimate criterion of good and evil: it is only an intermediary transmitting an obligation that does not depend on it.

● Can a man incur guilt by following his conscience?

Yes, a man can be guilty though he follow his conscience–guilty, not because he follows his conscience, but because he previously warped it (for example, a doctor who persuaded himself that abortion is not a crime), or because he was negligent in forming it correctly in the first place (for example, an unbeliever who was never concerned about religious truth).

● Cannot a man have a warped conscience without it being his fault?

Yes, a man can have an erroneous conscience about something or other (believe that a bad action is good) without it being his fault. In such a case one speaks of an invincibly erroneous conscience (or of a person in a state of invincible ignorance). In this case, ignorance prevents the man from being guilty, but the action remains bad in itself.

● Must the State respect such a person's conscience?

Let's suppose that a murderer is subjectively innocent because his false religion inculcated in him the conviction that murder is licit in certain conditions. Yet this subjective conviction does not give him an objective right: the policeman who stops him from carrying out his act does not commit an injustice. Someone who would affirm that murder is certainly bad, but that the murderer has, because of his human dignity, a right not to be prevented from killing would be called crazy.

● Who maintains such a thing?

This is just about what *Dignitatis Humanae* claims. This document indeed teaches that all men have the duty to seek the truth and to receive it, but it adds that if someone, knowingly or unknowingly, adheres to error, he has a right not to be prevented from acting in accordance with the error, in the name of his human dignity.

- **Doesn't someone who is mistaken in good faith deserve a certain indulgence?**

Someone who is mistaken in good faith no doubt deserves to be treated with charity and prudence, but he does not thereby acquire a right to disseminate his error. A food distributor would never have a right to distribute products dangerous to health under the pretext that he is acting in good faith. Likewise, religious error being deadly to souls, it is normal for the State to prevent its propagation.

- **Is the diffusion of heresy a great evil?**

The Church rightly considers the diffusion of heresy as murder committed against souls.

41) Did the new liturgy keep the Feast of Christ the King?

The new doctrine introduced by Vatican II is translated into the liturgy: in the new missal (1969) the Feast of Christ the King was moved from the last Sunday of October to the last Sunday of the liturgical year in order to signify that the reign of Christ the King will not come until the end of time and that it cannot (or must not) be accomplished at present. They removed from the hymn for the Vespers of this feast the three stanzas which speak of Christ's reign over society:

Scelesta turba clamitat	Though evil crowds cry once again
Regnare Christum nolumus	With frenzied will, "Christ shall not reign,"
Te nos ovantes omnium	Yet our exulting voices sing,
Regem supremum dicimus.	And hail Thee, universal King.
Te nationum præsides	The rulers of the nations all
Honore tollant publico	Shall at Thy feet adoring fall,
Colant magistri, judices	All judges magnify Thy name,
Leges et artes exprimant.	All laws and arts show forth Thy fame.
Submissa regum fulgeant	Let kingly crowns more glorious shine
Tibi dicata insignia	When consecrated, Lord, as Thine:
Mitique sceptro patriam	Place Thou our land and homes today
Domosque subde civium.	Beneath Thy mild and gracious sway.

• Why did the Church's authorities denature the Feast of Christ the King in this way?

Lex orandi, lex credendi, the saying goes. The formulas of prayer are also the expression of the faith. Now, religious freedom is in total opposition to the principles formerly professed by the Church. That is why the promoters of religious liberty cannot invoke in their favor either Sacred Scripture or the Tradition of the Church. It was always the enemies of the Church (heretics, rationalists, the "Enlightenment" philosophers, Freemasons, *etc.*) who clamored for religious liberty.[54]

• Is Vatican II explicitly opposed to the social reign of Christ?

Dignitatis Humanae completely ignores Christ the King; given the subject being spoken of, it is a very serious omission. The text does not forbid States to profess Catholicism (that would be too contrary to Tradition), but it gives no encouragement whatsoever. It merely tolerates the public profession of the Catholic religion on the same basis as that of false religions.[55] In practice, since 1965, the Vatican has worked at the suppression of Catholic States.[56]

• What was the Church's conduct in this regard before Vatican II?

As soon as the Church obtained her freedom [Edict of Milan, A.D. 313], she exhorted the kings and princes, especially if they were Christians, to protect and defend the true religion. In mission lands, she principally strove to win over the princes to the Catholic Faith in order to facilitate the establishment of a society permeated with the Christian spirit.

---

[54] The high Freemasonic dignitary Yves Marsaudon, 33rd degree, minister of the Supreme Council of France of the Ancient and Accepted Scottish Rite, in his book *Ecumenism Seen by a Freemason of Tradition* [French] (Paris: Vitiano, 1964), p. 121, speaks of religious liberty as "the revolution desired by John XXIII." He insisted: "One can truly speak of a revolution" that "originating in our Masonic lodges, wonderfully extended to the dome of St. Peter's."

[55] Vatican II is content to say: "If, in view of peculiar circumstances obtaining among peoples, special civil recognition is given to one religious community in the constitutional order of society, it is at the same time imperative that the right of all citizens and religious communities to religious freedom should be recognized and made effective in practice" (*DH* 6).

[56] Moreover, Vatican II intends to forbid any discrimination based on religion, going so far as to put it on the same level as discrimination because of race, color, or class: "The Church reproves, as foreign to the mind of Christ, any discrimination against men or harassment of them because of their race, color, condition of life, or religion" (*Nostra Aetate*, §5. See also *Dignitatis Humanae*, §7).

42) What are the consequences of religious liberty?

The first consequence of the religious liberty preached by Vatican II was that the States that were still officially Catholic had to change their constitutions. Thus religious freedom led to the laicization of the State and an ever-widening dechristianization of society. Since the same rights are given to erroneous beliefs, the true faith is disappearing more and more. Man, who because of his fallen nature generally tends to follow the path of least resistance, needs the help of Catholic institutions. In a society marked by the Catholic Faith, more men will save their souls than in a society where religion is a private affair and the true Church must exist side by side with innumerable sects possessing the same rights.

- **Which countries had to change their constitutions following Vatican II?**

A characteristic example is that of Colombia. The population of this country was 98 percent Catholic, and the Catholic religion was the only one officially recognized by the Constitution. The president, reluctantly, had to yield to the pressure exerted by the Vatican in the name of the Council, and to change the Constitution, which was done on July 12, 1973. About the same time, the Protestant sects, financially supported by the United States, set out to conquer Latin America. Today, the country is overrun by the sects. Some towns have more Protestant temples than Catholic churches.[57]

- **Has the Council's religious freedom been imposed on other countries?**

Two Swiss cantons, the Tessin and the Valais, under pressure from the Apostolic Nuncio, also had to change their constitutions.[58] In Italy, a new concordat was signed on February 11, 1984: the false religions obtained equal treatment with the Church, *etc.*[59] It is Rome that has demanded these changes!

- **Can you give a final example?**

The case of Spain is particularly interesting because the concordat signed on August 27, 1953, between Spain and the Holy See was

---

[57] Archbishop Marcel Lefebvre, *L'Eglise infiltrée par le modernisme* (Broût-Vernet: Fideliter, 1993), pp. 111-13.
[58] See *DC*, No. 1653 (May 5, 1974).
[59] See *DC*, No. 1872 (April 15, 1984); Romano Amerio, *Iota Unum* (Sarto House, 1996), pp. 167-72.

considered by Pius XII as a model of its kind. The first article began like this: "The Catholic, Apostolic, and Roman religion continues to be the religion of the Spanish nation." The concordat ratified the *Fuero de los Espagnoles* [the Spanish Charter] of July 13, 1945, whose Article 6 was particularly clear:

> The profession and practice of the Catholic religion, which is that of the Spanish State, will enjoy official protection. No one shall be disturbed for his religious beliefs or the *private* exercise of his religion. There is no authorization for *external* ceremonies or manifestations other than those of the Catholic religion.[60]

• What happened after 1965?

The Declaration *Dignitatis Humanae* openly contradicted this Article 6. Under Vatican pressure, in 1967 Spain granted liberty to other religions, explicitly citing Vatican II:

> After this declaration of the Council, the necessity arose of modifying Article 6 of the Spaniards' Charter in virtue of the aforementioned principle of the Spanish State.
> This is why the organic law of the State dated 10 January 1967 has modified the aforementioned Article 6 as follows: "The profession and practice of the Catholic religion, which is that of the Spanish State, enjoys official protection. The State guarantees the protection of religious liberty, which shall be guaranteed by an effective juridical provision which will safeguard morals and public order."

It must be noted that this modification had been approved by the Holy See before publication.[61]

• What does the example of Spain show?

Spain's example shows the flagrant contradiction between the traditional doctrine and that of Vatican II, since what was praised before 1965 became worthy of condemnation immediately afterwards.

• What does the application of the Vatican II document on religious freedom prove?

The years following Vatican II have shown the truth of Leo XIII's statement that religious liberty necessarily leads to immorality. In formerly Catholic countries, it is not only faith that has disappeared, but also Christian morality. Marriages fail, families break up, criminality rises, and one can scarcely find anyone willing to exercise authority. Anyone taking a candid look at things today has to recognize that our

---

[60] See *DC*, No. 948 (September 30, 1945), p. 691 [our emphasis].
[61] See Michael Davies, "*Dignitatis Humanae* and Spain," *The Second Vatican Council and Religious Liberty* (Neumann Press, 1992), pp. 275-82.

society is descending into chaos. The situation will never really change until society once again recognizes Christ as its King and refuses to give free rein to error. For, as Cardinal Pie stated, "When He does not reign by the benefits attached to His presence, He reigns by the calamities inseparable from His absence."[62]

---

[62] Cardinal Pie, Discourse at Chartres, April 11, 1858, *Oeuvres Épiscopales*, I, 84.

VI

ECUMENISM

43) What is meant by ecumenism?

The word *ecumenism* designates the movement that arose in the nineteenth century among non-Catholics, the goal of which was to foster the reconciliation and collaboration of the various Christian confessions. This movement led to the foundation of the World Council of Churches in 1948.[1] The same ambition subsequently led to a movement of mutual understanding with non-Christian religions. This is what is called interreligious dialogue.

● Where does the term ecumenism come from?

"Ecumenical" means "universal." Fr. Charles Boyer, S.J., explains: "The renewed use of the word *ecumenism* is due to the fact that the Protestants, desiring to designate a universality and finding the word *catholic* already employed by the Roman Church, chose its equivalent: *ecumenical*."[2]

---

[1] This Council defines itself as "a community of Churches that recognizes Christ as God and Savior." The religious denominations which belong to it remain independent. The Council has no authority over them; they can accept or reject its decision as they wish. It is no longer necessary for each of its members to recognize the other communities as Churches in the strict sense. The Catholic Church is not a Member of the WCC, even if it has moved closer to it.

[2] *Dictionnaire de Théologie Catholique*, s.v. "Christian Ecumenism" [French]. In its primary meaning, the word *ecumenical* ("universal") was used to designate the *general* councils of the Church, distinguishing them from *particular* councils (see Question 19 of this catechism). Today the word has acquired a new meaning.

- **Why did the Protestants feel the need to work towards the unity of Christians?**

Having rejected the Church's teaching authority, or magisterium, which alone can guarantee unity in the true faith, the Protestants very rapidly split into countless sects and confessions. To preserve some credibility and retain their members drawn by Catholic unity (the threefold unity of faith, worship, and government), they needed to find a way to unite in a different manner: the ecumenical movement was born.

- **What was the Church's attitude towards the ecumenical movement?**

In the beginning, the Catholic Church clearly kept its distance. It was only during Vatican II that ecumenism officially entered the Church.

- **Did Vatican II treat of ecumenism and interreligious dialogue?**

Vatican II consecrated a special decree to ecumenism, called *Unitatis Redintegratio*. It also promulgated the Declaration *Nostra Aetate*, which treats of the relations of the Church with the non-Christian religions.

- **Where can one find the veritable Catholic position on ecumenism?**

The veritable Catholic position on ecumenism is expressed in the Encyclical *Mortalium Animos* (1928). In it, its author, Pope Pius XI, describes the efforts of the "ecumenists" in a way that remains pertinent:

> Assured that there exist few men who are entirely devoid of the religious sense, they seem to ground on this belief a hope that all nations, while differing indeed in religious matters, may yet without great difficulty be brought to fraternal agreement on certain points of doctrine which will form a common basis of the spiritual life. With this object, congresses, meetings, and addresses are arranged, attended by a large concourse of hearers, where all without distinction, unbelievers of every kind as well as Christians, even those who unhappily have rejected Christ and denied His divine nature or mission, are invited to join in the discussion.[3]

- **How did Pius XI judge these ecumenical activities?**

He continues:

---

[3] Pius XI, Encyclical *Mortalium Animos* (January 6, 1928), §2 [English version: Angelus Press, 1998].

Now, such efforts can meet with no kind of approval among Catholics. They presuppose the erroneous view that all religions are more or less good and praiseworthy, inasmuch as all give expression, under various forms, to that innate sense which leads men to God and to the obedient acknowledgment of His rule. Those who hold such a view are not only in error; they distort the true idea of religion, and thus reject it, falling gradually into naturalism and atheism....[4]

- **How does the Pope conclude?**

He concludes: "To favor this opinion, therefore, and to encourage such undertakings is tantamount to abandoning the religion revealed by God."[5]

44) What judgment should we make of ecumenism in keeping with the Catholic Faith?

Since the Catholic Church is the only Church founded by Christ and the sole possessor of the fullness of truth, the unity of Christians can only be re-established by the conversion and return to its bosom of all the separated brethren and communities. Such is the teaching of Pope Pius XI in *Mortalium Animos*: "There is but one way in which the unity of Christians may be fostered, and that is by furthering the return to the one true Church of Christ of those who are separated from it; for far from that one true Church they have in the past fallen away."[6] This judgment is simply the logical consequence of the Church's claim to alone possess the truth, for there can only be true religious unity in the true faith.

- **Before Vatican II, was the Church disinterested in the separated communities?**

The Church has always striven to bring the members of separated Christian communities to the unity of the Mystical Body. More often its efforts were brought to bear upon individuals, but sometimes, too, upon entire separated communities. During the Councils of Lyons (1245 and 1274) and of Florence (1439), for instance, the hierarchy was intent upon restoring the union of the Eastern schismatics separated from the Church since 1054. In 1869, while convoking the first Vatican Council, Pope Pius IX invited the separated Christians to put an end

---

[4] *Ibid.*
[5] *Ibid.*
[6] *Ibid.*, §15.

to the schism and to return to the bosom of the Church;[7] Leo XIII addressed a similar appeal to all the Christian confessions in 1894.[8]

- **How did these initiatives differ from today's ecumenism?**

These initiatives differed from today's ecumenism because they were accompanied by the firm conviction that it is not up to the Church to change, but to those who are separated from it. The Church was always ready to facilitate their return, but never at the expense of the Faith.

45) What is the new conception of ecumenism?

At Vatican II, the Church adopted a new attitude corresponding to a new doctrine. The Catholic Church is no longer presented as the unique religious society leading to salvation; the other Christian confessions, and even the non-Christian religions, are considered as other expressions (undoubtedly less perfect, but nevertheless valid) of the divine religion, paths really leading to God and eternal salvation. It is no longer question of the conversion of non-Catholics to the Catholic Church, but of dialogue and religious pluralism.

- **Can you give an example of this new attitude?**

The Decree on Ecumenism uses the word "Church" (in the plural) to designate the other Christian communities, whereas previously this had always been avoided. When "Churches" were spoken of, local Churches were meant, like the Church (that is to say, the diocese) of Lyons or Milan.

- **Wasn't the word "Church" used to designate the Eastern schismatics?**

The word "Church" was sometimes used broadly to designate the schismatic confessions that have conserved the apostolic succession and all the sacraments, but it was firm teaching that there is only one Church in the strict sense, because our Lord has only one Spouse. The heretical dissidents received the name of *confessions* or *communities*, but they were not ascribed the title of *Church*. Today, however, this has become completely common.

---

[7] Pius IX, Letter *Iam Vos Omnes* (September 13, 1868).
[8] Leo XIII, Letter *Præclara Gratulationis* (June 20, 1894).

- **What is the theological foundation of this new attitude?**

    The theological foundation of this new attitude has already been indicated in Question 29: it is the *"subsistit in"* of *Lumen Gentium*.[9] Instead of saying that the Church of Christ *is* the Catholic Church, the document of Vatican II says that the Church of Christ "subsists in" [*subsistit in*] the Catholic Church.[10]

- **Why did Vatican II introduce the expression "*subsistit in*"?**

    By the expression *"subsistit in,"* Vatican II posits a distinction between the Church of Christ and the Catholic Church (whereas for traditional theology, these two terms are synonymous: The Church of Christ, that is to say the supernatural society founded by our Lord Jesus Christ for the salvation of mankind, *is* the Catholic Church.)

- **What exactly does the expression "*subsistit in*" mean for Vatican II?**

    Vatican II indeed is willing to admit that the Church of Christ has its perfect realization (its "subsistence") in the Catholic Church,[11] but it conveys the idea that it is not *identical* to the Catholic Church: the Church of Christ would extend beyond it, imperfectly, thanks to "elements of the Church" present in other Christian confessions.

- **Is this really the correct interpretation of the "*subsistit in*"?**

    This interpretation was officially confirmed by the Congregation for the Doctrine of the Faith in the Declaration *Dominus Jesus* of August 6, 2000:

    > With the expression *subsistit in*, the Second Vatican Council sought to harmonize two doctrinal statements: on the one hand, that the Church of Christ, despite the divisions which exist among Christians, continues to exist fully only in the Catholic Church, and on the other hand, that "outside of her structure, many elements can be found of sanctification and truth,"[12] that is, in those Churches and ecclesial communities which are not yet in full communion with the Catholic Church.

---

[9] It should be remembered that the father of the expression *"subsistit in"* is a Protestant: Pastor Wilhelm Schmidt.

[10] Vatican II, Constitution *Lumen Gentium* on the Church, I, 8. The same expression is employed in the Declaration on Religious Freedom, *Dignitatis Humanae* §1: "We believe that this one true religion subsists in the Catholic and Apostolic Church."

[11] Note 56 of the Declaration *Dominus Jesus* (August 6, 2000) specifies that the Church of Christ only has this concrete realization (has its "subsistence") in the Catholic Church.

[12] Vatican II, Dogmatic Constitution *Lumen Gentium*, §8; see John Paul II, Encyclical *Ut Unum Sint*, §13. See also *Lumen Gentium*, §15 and the decree on Ecumenism, *Unitatis Redintegratio*, §3.

● What is noteworthy in this text?

First of all, it is worth pointing out that this passage designates heretical and schismatic communities as "ecclesial communities which are not yet in *full* communion with the Catholic Church." This implies that they are nonetheless in partial or imperfect communion.

● Is the expression "full communion" novel?

The distinction between full and imperfect communion is a major innovation of Vatican II.[13]

● What is the Church's traditional teaching on this subject?

The Church's teaching is very simple: to be saved it is necessary to belong to the Church either *in re* (*in reality*, that is, by fulfilling the three classic conditions: baptism, Catholic faith, submission to the hierarchy), or at least *in voto* (by a desire, explicit or implicit).[14] Consequently, those who do not have the Catholic faith or who are not submissive to the hierarchy, and who, moreover, have not even an implicit desire to change their state, do not belong to the Church at all. They cannot secure their salvation with these dispositions.

● What is Vatican II's innovation?

The Council tried to find intermediate states between belonging to the Church and not belonging. The non-Catholic Christians would be in "imperfect communion" with the Church (*UR* 3; *LG* 15) and all men, even non-Christians, would be "related in various ways to the people of God" (*LG* 16). This implies that they could be confident of their salvation without having the desire (at least implicit) of changing their state and becoming a member of the Church.

● How can heretical or schismatic communities be, according to Vatican II, in "imperfect communion" with the Church?

To affirm that the Christians and communities separated from the Church are in "imperfect communion" with it, the Council invokes, like Cardinal Ratzinger [in *Dominus Jesus*], the "elements of sanctifica-

---

[13] This innovation figures in the document *Unitatis Redintegratio* [*UR*] §3; see also *Lumen Gentium* §14, which speaks of "full incorporation."

[14] Those who are not incorporated in the Church *in re* (in reality) can, in certain circumstances, be so *in voto* (by desire: this is what is sometimes called belonging to the *soul* of the Church). This desire can either be *explicit* (for example, in a catechumen preparing for baptism) or *implicit* (for example, in a person brought up in heresy but who only adheres to this heresy from a non-culpable ignorance: he does not possess the means to discern that the Catholic Church is the only true religion, but is fundamentally disposed to accept it).

tion" they contain, and by which they would be in communion with the unique Church of Christ.

- **Isn't it true that the schismatic communities, or even the heretical communities, conserve some elements of sanctification?**

It is true that the Protestants conserve Sacred Scripture (more or less altered), and that the Eastern schismatics conserve the sacraments. But traditional theology did not designate these realities stolen from the Catholic Church as "elements of sanctification" or "elements of the Church," but rather as "vestiges" of the true religion.

- **Is the replacement of the term "vestiges" by the term "elements of the Church" important?**

This change of vocabulary is not innocent, for the word *vestiges* expressed an important truth: the elements stolen from the Catholic Church by the separated communities by that very fact cease to be a living reality. They become "ruins."

- **Yet the sacrament of baptism administered in a community separated from the Church can be valid. Isn't the term "element of sanctification" more appropriate than "ruin"?**

Here we must carefully distinguish between a valid sacrament and a fruitful sacrament. A sacrament can be valid without being fruitful, that is, without giving grace, if it encounters in the soul an impediment to this grace.

- **Can you clarify this by giving an example of the distinction between a valid sacrament and a fruitful sacrament?**

The sacrament of marriage would be received validly but not fruitfully by a person in the state of mortal sin. He would be really married but would not receive the graces usually given by this sacrament (and, moreover, would commit a sacrilege).

- **How does this distinction between valid sacrament and fruitful sacrament concern the heretical or schismatic communities?**

The distinction between a valid sacrament and a fruitful sacrament is important because adherence to schism or heresy is *per se* an impediment to grace. It implies that a sacred reality, even holy in itself, cannot be an "element of holiness" inasmuch as it is in a community separated from the Church. The community is, in and of itself, an impediment to the sanctifying efficacy of the element it has taken.

- ### Yet are there not cases in which the sacraments dispensed outside the Church can be fruitful (that is to say, give grace)?

The sacraments given outside the Church can only be fruitful in cases where the person who receives them does not adhere formally to the heresy or schism. (This is the case, for example, of children below the age of reason, or of people who are in what is called a state of "invincible ignorance.") In this case, even if the sacrament is received materially from a community separated from the Church, the person only receives it fruitfully because by his intention (*in voto*) he escapes from this community.

- ### Is this a certain and traditional teaching in the Church?

St. Augustine explains that all the goods which are in the Church can be found, in a certain measure, outside the Church, except the grace by which these goods are salutary:

> God in His unity can be honored outside the Church; the faith which is one can be encountered outside her; baptism, which is unique, can be validly administered outside her bosom. And yet, just as there is only one God, one faith, one baptism, there is only one incorruptible Church: not only in which the true God is honored but alone in which He is honored with piety; not only in which the one true faith is conserved, but alone in which it is conserved with charity; not only in which true baptism exists, but alone in which it exists for salvation.[15]

- ### Can you cite another Father of the Church on this subject?

St. Bede the Venerable, in his *Commentary on the First Epistle of St. Peter*, expresses this truth in a striking manner. Speaking of the analogy made by St. Peter between the Flood and baptism (I Pet. 3:21), he explains that for those who are baptized outside the Church, the water of baptism is not an instrument of salvation, but rather of damnation: "The fact that the floodwater does not save, but kills those situated outside the ark prefigures without the least doubt that every heretic, though he possess the sacrament of baptism, is not plunged into hell by other waters than by the very waters that lift the ark to heaven."[16]

- ### Isn't it an exaggeration to say that baptism received outside the Church would be a cause of damnation?

Active participation in a religious ceremony of a heretical or schismatic community is of itself, by its very nature, an act of assent to the faith of this community. Thus even baptism becomes, in these

---

[15] *Ad Cresc.*, Bk. I, ch. 29.
[16] *PL*, 93, 60.

circumstances, sinful and an occasion of scandal. That is why St. Bede the Venerable says that the very water of baptism is in this case a cause of damnation.

- **Is the Second Vatican Council opposed to this teaching?**

Yes, Vatican II is opposed to this teaching by affirming that the heretical or schismatic communities are in imperfect communion with the Church, and by implying that there is a certain (imperfect) presence of the Church of Christ in the Christian communities separated from the Catholic Church.

- **Has this idea of an (imperfect) presence of the Church of Christ in the communities separated from the Church of Christ been enounced explicitly?**

John Paul II affirmed in his Encyclical *Ut Unum Sint* (§11):

Indeed, the elements of sanctification and truth present in the other Christian Communities, in a degree which varies from one to the other, constitute the objective basis of the communion, albeit imperfect, which exists between them and the Catholic Church. *To the extent that these elements are found in other Christian Communities, the one Church of Christ is effectively present in them.*

- **But is this idea to be found in the documents of Vatican II?**

We read in the Decree *Unitatis Redintegratio* (§15), regarding the schismatic Eastern Churches: "Hence, through the celebration of the Holy Eucharist in each of these churches, the Church of God [!] is built up and grows in stature and through concelebration, their communion with one another is made manifest." A community which is separated from the true Church is considered as belonging to "the Church of God."

- **What does Vatican II think of the non-Christian religions?**

Even towards the non-Christian religions, the Council makes an effort to have the most positive view possible. The conciliar Declaration *Nostra Aetate* sings the praises of Hinduism, Buddhism, Islam, and Judaism.

- **How can this change of attitude towards the non-Christian religions be characterized?**

Whereas formerly the Church worked to evangelize the adepts of pagan religions, the post-conciliar Church engages in "dialogue" with them.

- **Is this change of attitude publicly recognized?**

    The document *Dialogue and Mission* of the Pontifical Council for Interreligious Dialogue explicitly states in its opening lines: "The Second Vatican Council marked a new stage in the relations of the Catholic Church with the believers of other religions....This new attitude took the name of dialogue."[17]

- **What does the word dialogue mean in the Council's language?**

    The document *Dialogue and Mission* explains in depth the meaning of the word *dialogue*: "It signifies not only the fact of engaging in conversation, but also the ensemble of positive, constructive interreligious relations among individuals and communities of diverse beliefs for the sake of getting to know one another and for mutual enrichment."[18] The same document gives this definition of dialogue in its §13: "Dialogue [is] the meeting of Christians with the believers of other religious traditions so that they can work together in search of the truth [!] and collaborate in works of common interest."[19]

- **What ought we to conclude from these affirmations?**

    If the Catholics work with the non-Christians in search of the truth and it is question of reciprocal enrichment, clearly the Church has abandoned any claim to alone possess the truth!

- **Have the partisans of conciliar ecumenism explicitly renounced the goal of converting the non-Catholics?**

    Very many partisans of the Council's brand of ecumenism have renounced any intention of seeking the conversion of non-Catholics. We read, for example, in the Ecumenical Catechism prefaced by the Most Reverend Degenhardt, Archbishop of Paderborn, and highly praised by several bishops: "The goal is not the return, but rather the communion of the Sister-Churches; unity in reconciled diversity; the unity of Churches. The Churches remain, but become one single Church."[20]

---

[17] *DC*, No. 1880 (September 2, 1984), p. 844. This document was approved by Pope John Paul II on June 10, 1984.
[18] *Ibid.*
[19] *Ibid.*, p. 845.
[20] Heinz Schütte, *Glaube im ökumenischen Verständnis: Ökumenischer Katechismus* (Paderborn, 1994), p. 33.

46) Are the non-Catholic Christian confessions really partial embodiments of the Church of Christ?

The Christian confessions separated from the Catholic Church are dissidents and do not belong to it. Even if they keep some Christian truths, and even a valid baptism, they remain separated from the Mystical Body of Christ. Consequently, no one can be saved who, having recognized that the Catholic Church is the one true Church of Christ, fails to enter it and stays in a heretical or schismatic community.

● How does one belong to the true Church of Christ?

In *Mystici Corporis*, Pope Pius XII teaches that three elements are necessary for belonging to the true Church of Christ–baptism, true faith, and submission to the legitimate authority: "Actually only those are to be included as members of the Church who have been baptized and profess the true faith, and who have not been so unfortunate as to separate themselves from the unity of the Body, or been excluded by legitimate authority for grave faults committed" (§22).

● Then, even though they keep the seven sacraments and agree with the Catholic Church on most points of faith, the schismatic Churches do not belong to the true Church of Christ?

The schismatic Eastern Churches, even if they keep the sacraments and are in agreement with the Catholic Church about most points of faith, are not the true Church of Christ, for they refuse to recognize the primacy and the infallibility of the Successor of Peter, and Christ said that whoever refuses to hear the Church is to be considered as a heathen and a publican (Mt. 18:17).

● What should be said of the heretical communities?

If the schismatic communities do not belong to the one Church of Christ, this is all the more true of the heretical communities (Protestants, for example), who depart from the true faith on numerous points.

● Has this truth been called into question within the Church?

Unfortunately, this truth has frequently been called into question. On May 6, 1983, a joint Lutheran-Roman Catholic commission met at Kloster Kirchberg in Wurtemberg, issued a statement concerning the heresiarch Luther:

> Together, we begin to recognize him as a witness to the Gospel, as a master in the faith, as a herald of a spiritual renewal....The taking into

account of the historically conditioned nature of our modes of expression and thought has equally contributed to a broader acknowledgment in Catholic circles of Luther's thought as a legitimate form of Christian theology....[21]

47) Are non-Catholic Christian confessions and the non-Christian religions means of salvation?

The non-Catholic Christian confessions and the non-Christian religions are not means of salvation, but rather, perdition. Certainly, the adepts of the false religions can be saved *in* them, if, living heedful of their consciences and striving to fulfill the will of God insofar as they know it, they receive from God the theological virtues; but God only knows when this happens. We can only say that one may be able to be saved *in* the false religions—or, rather, despite them—but never *by means of* them.

- **The non-Catholic Christian communities (the Protestants, for instance) provide their members a certain number of goods useful for salvation (baptism, Holy Scripture, etc.); in this are they not means of salvation?**

Everything that can be found of truth and goodness in Protestantism or in the schismatic Churches belongs by right to the Church. Even the conciliar Decree on Ecumenism, *Unitatis Redintegratio*, was made to include a statement to that effect in its §3, at the express demand of Pope Paul VI.

- **How was this addition, imposed by the Pope, received?**

One readily gathers that the liberal theologians were dissatisfied. Rahner and Vorgrimler had these comments:

> The statement that these goods belong by right (*jure*) to the Church of Christ is one of the nineteen modifications made by the Pope that were added in November 1964 to a text that had already been voted, and that, because of their narrowness, left a rather more unfavorable impression than is warranted by the teaching contained in the document (here we are alluding only to the changes that especially offended the non-Catholics).[22]

---

[21] *DC*, No. 1855 (July 3, 1983), pp. 694-95.
[22] Karl Rahner and H. Vorgrimler, *Kleines Konzilskompendium* (Fribourg: Herder, 1986), p. 220.

- **So then Vatican II does reiterate Catholic doctrine on this point?**

The very same §3 of the Decree *Unitatis Redintegratio* unfortunately contains a "monstrosity," a good example of the Council's contradictions: "For the Spirit of Christ has not refrained from using them [the separated Churches and Communities] as means of salvation."

- **Concretely, is it not through their heretical or schismatic communities that the Christians separated from the Church receive certain means of salvation (even if these means belong, *per se*, to the Catholic Church)?**

The sacred realities kept unduly by the heretical or schismatic societies can only give grace and salvation insofar as those who receive them *refuse* (albeit implicitly) formal adherence to the heresy or schism; in other words: only insofar as they escape from these societies by the inmost intention of their wills. Far from being "means of salvation," these societies, in and of themselves, render sterile everything they have taken from the Catholic Church, even the sacraments (which are nonetheless, *per se*, the means of salvation par excellence).

- **The communities separated from the Church and the non-Christian religions, then, cannot be ordinary means of salvation?**

Not only are the false religions not *ordinary* means of salvation, they are not even *extraordinary* means; they are only obstacles to salvation.[23] If some of their members are in the state of grace, it is uniquely because they are in a state of ignorance and thus not guilty of their separation from the body of the Church. According to traditional teaching, they can belong to *the soul* of the Church. But they belong individually, and not in and by their communities. The false religions, far from leading people to the Catholic Church, turn them away from it. They are not willed by God.

---

[23] Cardinal Joseph Ratzinger, in *The Ratzinger Report*, an interview on the state of the Church with Vittorio Messori [English version: Ignatius Press, 1985], contests the idea that the non-Christian religions can be *ordinary* means of salvation, but he admits that they can be *extraordinary* means.

- **What should we think of the reasoning of those who affirm that the separated communities are means of salvation because of the elements of sanctification to be found in them?**

  This reasoning is a sophism because it is based on something that happens *per accidens* (incidentally), by reason of the personal dispositions of this or that member of the community, from which it draws a conclusion about the value of the society as a whole (*per se*). With that kind of reasoning, it could be argued that Judas is a saint and that he did an eminently meritorious act by delivering up Christ, since he thus allowed the redemption of the human race to occur!

- **What should we think of Vatican II's positive assessments of Hinduism, Buddhism, Islam, and Judaism to be found in *Nostra Aetate*, the Declaration on the Non-Christian Religions?**

  The conciliar declaration *Nostra Aetate* is deliberately partial. Its official reporter declared publicly that it was drafted in keeping with a decision not to tell the whole truth about these religions, but only what could make them appear to be compatible with Christianity.[24] This deliberate misrepresentation of those religions is quite simply an act of treason against our Lord Jesus Christ.

- **Isn't the Declaration *Nostra Aetate* redeemed by the statement that the Church "proclaims, and ever must proclaim, Christ 'the way, the truth, and the life' (Jn. 14:6), in whom men may find the fullness of religious life, in whom God has reconciled all things to Himself" (§2)?**

  Our Lord Jesus Christ not only affords us "the fullness" of religious life; He is the *only* mediator between God and men (I Tim. 2:5), the *only* ambassador received by God, and who intercedes unceasingly for us (Heb. 7:25). "Who is a liar, but he who denieth that Jesus is the Christ? This is Antichrist, who denieth the Father, and the Son. Whosoever denieth the Son, the same hath not the Father" (I Jn. 2:22-23). "For there is no other name under heaven given to men, whereby we must be saved" (Acts 4:12). Every religion that refuses this mediation is intrinsically evil. It is contradictory to pretend to announce Christ while vaunting of (even partially) the religions that reject Him.

---

[24] *Acta Synodalia Sacrosancti Concilii Oecumenici Vaticani II*, vol. IV, periodus quarta, pars IV (Typis polyglottis Vaticanis, 1977), p. 698 (response to the second modus) and p. 706 (response to modus 57).

● Despite all of that, surely these religions contain some good elements?

Even in the material order, the judgment of whether a cake is good or bad depends not only on its ingredients, but on the cake as a whole. Good ingredients, excellent in themselves, mixed in the wrong proportions can spoil it; the introduction of one rancid ingredient can make it inedible, and the addition of a few drops of poison would have a greater effect upon the final result than a lot of good butter, flour, and chocolate. In the spiritual order, this reality applies all the more. A religion is not merely a material agglomeration of "elements"; it forms a whole (just as a scientific or philosophical system or a demonstration, *etc.*). This whole is good or bad, true or false, as a whole. And if it is bad as a whole, then the good elements matter little.

● Despite that, can one not underscore the parcels of truth these religions contain?

Every erroneous system contains parcels of truth; an obvious folly would have no adherents. But these parcels of truth are captured by the false system that makes use of them (and that utilizes their verisimilitude and attractiveness to its advantage). Moreover, these elements of truth are themselves falsified because they are linked to errors that distort them.

● Can you give an example of this?

Islam presents itself as a monotheistic religion. This just and reasonable tenet (stolen from the true religion) lends it much of its force. But this monotheism is fiercely anti-Trinitarian. While true in itself, it is falsified by the erroneous system in which it is enmeshed.

● Can it not be argued, however, that there are degrees of error, and that a religion that, while being false, recognizes the existence of one God and imposes on its adherents a certain moral code is better than doctrinaire atheism and absolute amorality?

There are degrees of error, but, paradoxically, it could be argued that a system that incorporates many truths is more dangerous than one containing fewer. A chair with just three legs is more dangerous than a two-legged chair no one would think of sitting on. A very good counterfeit bill is more dangerous than a less skillfully executed fake.

- **Can you give an example?**

It has been said quite justly that "Islam is the religion that, having known Christ, refused to acknowledge His divinity. If it is true that the worst form of falsehood is that which least contradicts the truth, then the falsehood that consists in saying all the good possible about Christ except that He is God is the most redoubtable."[25] In fact, missionaries have always had much more trouble converting Muslims than Animists.

- **What should we make of the argument that God is at work in the non-Christian religions because good can be found there, and good can only come from God?**

This reasoning is a sophism that relies upon a failure to distinguish between the natural order and the supernatural order, for it is obvious that when we speak of the action of God in a religion, we understand an action that leads to salvation. God saves by supernatural grace, while the good referred to in the other religions (at least the non-Christian religions) is only a natural good. In these occurrences, God acts as the Creator who gives being to all things, and not as the Savior. The Second Vatican Council's desire to disregard the distinction between the natural and the supernatural orders yields its worst fruits in the domain of ecumenism. People start thinking that any religion is able to procure the greatest gifts of the good Lord. This is an enormous deception.

- **By stimulating man's religious sentiment, are not all these religions nonetheless doing good?**

What is the good of urging someone down the wrong path? Far from leading to God and life eternal, the non-Christian religions turn people away.

- **Does Hinduism turn people away from eternal salvation?**

By preaching reincarnation, Hinduism removes the seriousness of our earthly existence. It is no longer the decisive test upon which our eternity depends, but rather a simple stage since the soul must be reincarnated–in a rat, a dog, or some other thing–as often as necessary to expiate its faults. For the same reason, Hinduism is devoid of mercy (even if today it tries to imitate the beneficent works of Christianity). It coldly passes by the poor and suffering, deeming that they justly bear the weight of their past sins.

---

[25] Joseph Hours, "The Christian Conscience before Islam" [French], *Itinéraires*, 60, 121.

• Does Buddhism turn people away from eternal salvation?

Buddhism is a religion without God. Man believes that he can save himself, and this salvation consists in entering nothingness, Nirvana. Buddhism does not look forward to an eternal life in union with God, but only at the end of suffering in the dissolution of existence itself.

• Does Islam turn people away from eternal salvation?

Islam rejects as blasphemy the Holy Trinity and, consequently, the divinity of Christ. It encourages cruelty (praising the murder of a Christian as a good work) and sensuality (encouraging polygamy and promising men a paradise of sensual delights). To give some examples, let us quote from a few passages of the Koran:

> The Christians say, "The Messiah is the Son of God." That is the utterance of their mouths, conforming with the unbelievers before them. God assail them! How they are perverted![26]

> When you meet the unbelievers, smite their necks, then, when you have made wide slaughter among them, tie fast the bonds; then set them free, either by grace or ransom, till the war lays down its loads.[27]

As for Paradise, besides the "wide-eyed houris as the likeness of hidden pearls" (Sura LVI, 22, *etc.*) there are also immortal youths to be found there.[28]

• Can it be said truly that Judaism turns people away from eternal salvation?

Present-day Jews also refuse our Lord Jesus Christ. Before the coming of Christ, Judaism was the true religion, but it no longer is since it failed to recognize its vocation and refused the Savior. The true Jews converted to Christ, for, at His coming, the religion of the Old Testament lost its object. Thus it is contrary to the faith to assert, as did Cardinal Walter Kasper (President of the Pontifical Commission for Religious Relations with the Jews), that the Jews need not convert to Christianity to be saved.

• Did Cardinal Kasper really say that?

In a speech given on November 6, 2002, at the Center for Christian-Jewish Learning of the University of Boston, Cardinal Kasper began by affirming that Jesus Christ is the Savior of all men. Then he continued:

---

[26] *The Koran Interpreted*, a translation by A. J. Arberry (version online at arthursclassicnovels.com), Sura IX, 30.
[27] *Ibid.*, Sura XLVII, 4.
[28] Suras LXXVI, 19; LII, 24; LVI, 17. See J. Bertuel, *L'Islam, ses véritables origines* (Paris: NEL, n.d.), p. 187.

"This does not mean that Jews in order to be saved have to become Christians; if they follow their own conscience and believe in God's promises as they understand them in their religious tradition, they are in the line with God's plan, which for us comes to its historical completion in Jesus Christ."[29]

- **What is Catholic belief on this subject?**

St. Paul speaks explicitly of the Jews' unbelief (Rom. 11:20) and of their blindness (Rom. 11:25; II Cor. 3:15; *etc.*); he asserts that, in this state, they "please not God," but rather are the object of His wrath (I Thess. 2:14-16). The gentle St. John speaks of "them that say they are Jews and are not, but are the synagogue of Satan" (Apoc. 2:9). St. Peter says to their face on the day of Pentecost: "Therefore let all the house of Israel know most certainly that God hath made both Lord and Christ, this same Jesus, whom you have crucified....Do penance: and be baptized every one of you in the name of Jesus Christ, for the remission of your sins" (Acts 2:36-38). St. Thomas explains that the practice of the Jewish religion is today a sin, for it manifests a refusal of the Messias, who has already come.[30]

- **How has the traditional doctrine of the Church on Judaism been attacked?**

The traditional doctrine of the Church on Judaism has been attacked by the Declaration *Nostra Aetate* (of Vatican II), which opened the door to the innovators;[31] and also by the modification of the Good Friday prayer for the Jews.

- **What is the Good Friday prayer for the Jews?**

The traditional wording of the prayer (which already occurs in seventh-century sacramentaries) is as follows:

---

[29] The audio of the speech is online at http://forum-network.org/lecture/crucial-endeavor-catholic-jewish-relations (beginning at 43:40 into the speech).

[30] St. Thomas (*ST,* I-II, Q. 103, Art. 4) reiterates the teaching of the Fathers of the Church: the Jewish religion, which expired on Good Friday (that is to say, it lost its religious value when our Lord inaugurated the new Covenant by His sacrifice, and when the veil of the Temple was torn), is, moreover, lethal (that is to say, matter of mortal sin) at least since the destruction of the Temple of Jerusalem in the year 70. (Deprived of the Temple, priests, and sacrifices, the Jews had at that time every means of recognizing the lapse of their religion and the veracity of Christ, who had foretold this destruction.)

[31] Once the door was opened, the attack against the Church's traditional doctrine on Judaism advanced in stages, of which four can be distinguished: (1) from 1965 to 1975, the policy and practice [*engrenage*] of dialogue; (2) from 1975 to 1985, of self-censorship; (3) from 1985 to 2000, of apology (which culminated in the ceremony of apologies of March 12, 2000, at Rome); and (4) since the year 2000, of collaboration. These four stages have been analyzed in detail by Michel Laurigan in his work *Chronologie d'un engrenage* (Editions du Sel, 2008).–*Ed.*

Let us pray also for the perfidious Jews [*perfidis* = unfaithful to their covenant with God], that the Lord our God may take the veil from their hearts and that they also may acknowledge our Lord Jesus Christ. Let us pray: Almighty and everlasting God, You do not refuse Your mercy even to the unfaithfulness of the Jews [*perfidiam judaicam*]; hear the prayers which we offer for the blindness of that people so that they may acknowledge the light of Your truth, which is Christ, and be delivered from their darkness.

• What is noteworthy in this prayer?

The words "*perfidis*" and "*perfidiam*" clearly show that belonging to the Jewish religion today does not constitute faithfulness but, on the contrary, unfaithfulness to the covenant with God (since this was oriented towards Christ). One should also note the triple mention of the blindness of the Jews ("the veil [over] their hearts," "the blindness of that people," "their darkness").

• Weren't the expressions of this prayer too harsh, and might they not incite anti-Semitism?

The Apostles, who were Jews, were the first to speak of the blindness of their people (Rom. 11:25) and of the "veil" preventing them from understanding the true sense of the Bible (II Cor. 3:15). Nineteen centuries later, the image of a "veil" naturally came to the mind of the young Jew Alphonse Ratisbonne to describe his miraculous conversion (on January 20, 1842): "All I can say is, that the moment when the Blessed Virgin made a sign with her hand, the veil fell from my eyes; not one veil only, but all the veils which were wrapped around me disappeared, just as snow melts beneath the rays of the sun. I came forth from a tomb, from an abyss of darkness...."[32]

• How was the Good Friday prayer changed?

John XXIII censored the words "*perfidis*" and "*perfidiam*" in 1959. Paul VI in turn modified the prayer in 1965 (by suppressing the three mentions of the Jews' blindness[33]). Then in 1969 he replaced it by a brand new prayer that says the contrary of the ancient one (it asks of God that the Jews "may continue to grow in the love of his name and in faithfulness to his covenant"). As the 1962 missal was unaffected by Paul VI's decisions, Benedict XVI changed its wording in February 2008.

---

[32] *The Conversion of Marie-Alphonse Ratisbonne: Original Narrative of Baron Théodore de Bussière*, edited by the Rev. W. Lockhart, of the Order of Charity (New York: T. W. Strong Catholic Publishing House, n.d.). Online at www.todayscatholicworld.com/conv-ratisbonne.pdf.

[33] The petition "that He take the veil from their hearts" was replaced by "that our Lord and God let his face shine upon them" (Decree of the Sacred Congregation of Rites, March 7, 1965, *AAS*, 57, 412-13; in English: Bouscaren & O'Connor, *Canon Law Digest*, 6, 108-109).

- **What is the new prayer of 2008?**

   Benedict XVI's prayer is:

   Let us also pray for the Jews: that our God and Lord may illuminate their hearts, that they acknowledge that Jesus Christ is the Savior of all men. Let us pray. Let us kneel. Arise. Almighty and eternal God, who want that all men be saved and come to the recognition of the truth, propitiously grant that even as the fullness of the peoples enters Your Church, all Israel may be saved. Through Christ our Lord. Amen.

- **This prayer, then, asks of God the conversion of the Jews?**

   Yes, the 2008 prayer asks for the conversion of the Jews (unlike the prayer of the Missal of Paul VI). On the other hand, like the 1965 prayer, it suppresses the three mentions of their blindness.

- **Is it so important to mention the blindness of the Jews?**

   The question still is to know whether modern Judaism should be considered in the same way as the Judaism of the Old Testament (that is, as a religion pleasing to God, albeit imperfect), or, on the contrary, as a religion that has become false because of its refusal of the Messias. The traditional prayer answered this question clearly by speaking of the "*perfidis*" Jews (unfaithful to their covenant with God). Once this word had been suppressed, the threefold reminder of the Jews' blindness continued to evince that they are still in error. But by the suppression of this triple mention, the way is opened to the idea that the Jewish religion is still pleasing to God (albeit deprived of the full light). One thus foments an error that is very common today.

- **Should the modern Jewish religion, like Islam or Buddhism, be considered a false religion?**

   Yes, the modern Jewish religion, because of its refusal of Christ and its obstinacy in practices that only had meaning before the coming of the Messias, is today a false religion. Moreover, very many of its beliefs and practices are far removed from the Old Testament. Modern Judaism is based more on the Talmud than the Bible.

- **Finally, what can be said with regard to these non-Christian religions?**

   We ought to repeat tirelessly St. Peter's words: "For there is no other name under heaven given to men, whereby we must be saved" (Acts 4:12).

- **May one hope, in spite of everything, for the salvation of non-Christians?**

The Church has always admitted that non-Christians can have implicit baptism of desire (if they are in a state of error without personal fault and accept the grace of God), but she has not been optimistic about the number of those saved in this way. Blessed Pope Pius IX denounced as an error this proposition: "We must have at least good hope concerning the eternal salvation of all those who in no wise are in the true Church of Christ."[34]

48) Do the non-Christian religions honor the true God?

The non-Christian religions do not honor the true God. The true God, in effect, is the Triune God who was revealed in the Old Testament and especially in the New Testament by His Son Jesus Christ. "Whosoever denieth the Son, the same hath not the Father" (I Jn. 2:23). "No man cometh to the Father, but by Me" (Jn. 14:6).

- **Might it not be said that the Jews and the Muslims have a correct but incomplete idea of God, and that consequently they honor the true God?**

This was the case for the Jews of the Old Testament. To them, the Blessed Trinity had not yet been revealed. They did not believe this dogma explicitly, but neither did they reject it. Today, the Mohammedans and the Jews expressly deny the Holy Trinity revealed by our Lord Jesus Christ. They pray to a God who would be but a solitary person. But such a God does not exist.

- **Yet the Jews and the Muslims mean to honor the one God that exists, the One who created heaven and earth, the One who revealed Himself to Abraham, Isaac, and Jacob; so doing, are they not addressing the true God?**

The non-Christians are able to have a certain natural knowledge of God as the author of nature, and even as the author of certain revelations (to Abraham, Isaac, and Jacob, *etc.*) to which they adhere by a purely human faith. But this purely natural knowledge leaves them as strangers to God. Only supernatural faith enables its possessor to glimpse into the divine intimacy and enter into familiar relations with Him.

---

[34] Syllabus of Errors, Proposition 17 (DS 2917, Dz. 1717).

- **But in the eleventh century, didn't Pope Gregory VII write to a Muslim king that Christians and Muslims have the same God?**

Indeed, in a letter to King Anzir,[35] Pope St. Gregory VII did write: "We and you, who, while in a different manner, believe and profess one God; who daily praise and venerate Him as the Creator and ruler of the world...."[36]

- **What exactly does this passage mean?**

This sentence of Pope St. Gregory VII means this: Christians and Muslims believe, profess, praise, and venerate the one God, but in the case of the Christians, this faith and love are supernatural virtues that make them adhere to God, whereas for the Muslims, it involves a virtue of natural religion that leaves them far from the true God.[37] Thus it can be said in a certain sense that only the Christians possess or attain the true God, and that only they honor Him truly because they are in an intimate relation with Him.

- **Doesn't a person who prays to God in virtue of a merely natural knowledge of Him accomplish a good action?**

Such a prayer would be a good action in and of itself (though devoid of supernatural value) if it were not mingled with errors or superstitious rites that, far from honoring God, insult Him. The Muslim who, several times a day, affirms that God neither begets nor is begotten, blasphemes the God he pretends to honor. Ultimately, he may be excused for this blasphemy because of his invincible ignorance, just as someone who engages in false worship, but, in fact, it is not an act of religion that is being performed, but of superstition (and even idolatry).

- **Have these fundamental truths been challenged since Vatican II?**

During the retreat that Cardinal Wojtyla, the future John Paul II, preached at the Vatican in 1976 for Pope Paul VI, he developed an

---

[35] This Berber prince (En Nacir Ibn Alennas) reigned over the former Roman province of Mauritania...from 1062–88. Gregory VII could consider him as being influenced by the Christianity of his ancestors, and perhaps even secretly Christian since the prince had sent presents to the Pope, had asked him to consecrate a bishop, and had released Christian prisoners, as he explained at the beginning of the letter. Pope Gregory VII's letter might have been written to sound out the king's thinking, which would explain his unusual turn of phrase (it is the only letter of this kind prior to Vatican II).

[36] "*Nos et vos...qui unum Deum, licet diverso modo, credimur et confitemur, qui eum creatorem huius mundi quotidie laudamus et veneramur....*"

[37] Except for those that may have received baptism of desire, in which case they would no longer be acting as Muslims but as Christians.

absolutely modernist conception of faith and, subsequently, the thesis according to which all men, regardless of the religion to which they belong, pray to the true God.

- **Can you quote these modernist statements of Cardinal Wojtyla?**

    Cardinal Wojtyla declared: "The *itinerarium mentis in Deum* emerges from the depths of created things and from a man's inmost being. The modern mentality as it makes its way finds its support in human experience, and in affirmation of the transcendence of the human person."[38]

- **What makes these statements modernist?**

    These statements are modernist because faith is not understood as man's response to divine revelation, but as a search for God issuing from the depths of man's soul.[39]

- **What did Cardinal Wojtyla say about prayer in the false religions?**

    A little further on, the Cardinal states:

    ...This God is professed in his silence by the Trappist or the Camaldolite. It is to him that the desert Bedouin turns at his hour for prayer. And perhaps the Buddhist too, wrapt in contemplation as he purifies his thought, preparing the way to Nirvana. God in his absolute transcendence, God who transcends absolutely the whole of creation, all that is visible and comprehensible.[40]

- **What can be said about these statements?**

    This way of thinking is completely foreign to Holy Scripture. The Old Testament is full of the wrath of God against the false religions; the Chosen People is often punished for worshipping false gods.

- **Is the same vision of things to be found in the New Testament?**

    St. Paul writes in a trenchant phrase: "The things which the heathens sacrifice, they sacrifice to devils, and not to God" (I Cor. 10:20).

---

[38] Karol Wojtyla, *Sign of Contradiction* (New York: The Seabury Press, 1979), pp. 15-16.
[39] See Question 11.
[40] Wojtyla, *Sign of Contradiction*, pp. 16,

- **A non-Christian cannot honor the true God, then?**

God is surely attentive to the good dispositions that Jews, Muslims, or pagans have when they set about to pray. It is even possible that, pushed by grace, some of them really honor God in their hearts, but that happens *despite* the false ideas their religion gives them. The false religion itself is not addressed to God, but to an illusion; of itself, it does not lead its adherents to God, but turns them away from Him.

49) What should we think of the "anonymous Christians" theory?

For Karl Rahner, the non-Christian religions are an anonymous Christianity. They are ways of salvation "by which men approach God and His Christ."[41] Of course, they do not profess belief in Christ as the Christians do, but they seek Him. This opinion is totally false. Rather, the non-Christian religions *prevent* men from believing in Christ and being baptized. When Islam proclaims that it is a blasphemy to say that God has a Son, it keeps its adepts from embracing the true faith.

- **But did not the Fathers of the Church acknowledge that the pagan religions contained "seeds of the Word"?**

John Paul II claimed as much, in line with Vatican II.[42] But the Fathers of the Church saw no such thing. The passages of St. Justin and Clement of Alexandria cited in this context are in fact not speaking about the pagan religions, but of the philosophers and poets. And St. Justin even specifies that this "seed" spread throughout the human race is that of (natural) reason, which he carefully distinguishes from supernatural grace.

- **So, then, are there no "anonymous Christians"?**

If it were absolutely necessary, one might call "anonymous Christians" those who, despite the false doctrines of their religion, are interiorly disposed by a special grace of God to receive all that God has revealed. But it would be better to employ the traditional expression describing this case, "baptism of implicit desire."

---

[41] Karl Rahner, *Schriften zur Theologie* (Einsiedeln, 1978), III, 350.

[42] John Paul II wrote in his first encyclical, *Redemptor Hominis* (March 4, 1979): "The Fathers of the Church rightly saw in the various religions as it were so many reflections of the one truth, 'seeds of the Word'" (§11). In a footnote he cites St. Justin and St. Clement of Alexandria, but especially the documents of Vatican II that launched this idea: *Ad Gentes* 11 and *Lumen Gentium* 17.

50) Are all men automatically saved by Christ?

Christ died for all men in the sense that all have the possibility of gaining salvation. No one is excluded. But to be saved in fact, a man must accept the grace Christ merited for him and offers him. If he refuses, he remains in the state of perdition and will be damned eternally (unless he converts before his death).

• Where is the error of universal salvation to be found?

The error of universal salvation, that is, the thesis according to which all men have received from Christ not just the possibility of being saved but salvation in fact, seems to have been taught by Cardinal Wojtyla in the 1976 Lenten retreat he preached to Pope Paul VI and his household. Here is what he says:

> Thus the birth of the Church, at the time of the messianic and redemptive death of Christ, coincided with the birth of "the new man"–whether or not man was aware of such a rebirth and whether or not he accepted it. At that moment man's existence acquired a new dimension, very simply expressed by St. Paul as "in Christ."[43]

He adds: "All men, from the beginning of the world until its end, have been redeemed by Christ and his cross."[44]

• What do these words of Cardinal Wojtyla imply?

If every man, "whether or not man was aware of it and whether or not he accepted it," possesses being in Christ and is justified, then it follows that, according to the Cardinal, all are saved and none are damned.

• Did John Paul II continue to favor this error after his election to the papacy?

Once pope, John Paul II wrote in his first encyclical, *Redemptor Hominis*:

> We are dealing with "each" man, for each one is included in the mystery of the Redemption, and with each one Christ has united himself for ever through this mystery...man in all the fullness of the mystery in which he has become a sharer in Jesus Christ, the mystery in which each one of the four thousand million human beings living on our planet has become a sharer from the moment he is conceived beneath the heart of his mother.[45]

---

[43] Karol Wojtyla, *Sign of Contradiction* (New York: The Seabury Press, 1979), p. 91.
[44] *Ibid.*, p. 87.
[45] *Redemptor Hominis*, III, 13.

If every man is united with Christ from the first instant of his conception, what need can there still be of baptism and membership in the Church?

● Are we really to understand that John Paul II intended to preach universal salvation?

We need only consider the fact that this pope wanted to elevate to the cardinalate Hans Urs von Balthasar, a theologian who held the opinion that hell is empty.

● How do we know that hell is not empty?

Sacred Scripture speaks of hell in very many passages. In the parable of the last judgment, Christ made it clear that men will go into hell: "Then he shall say to them also that shall be on his left hand: Depart from me, you cursed, into everlasting fire which was prepared for the devil and his angels" (Mt. 25:41).

● Will very many men go to hell?

It seems that indeed very many will go to hell: "Wide is the gate, and broad is the way that leadeth to destruction, and many there are who go in thereat" (Mt. 7:13).

The Church has always been convinced that many men are lost. This conviction was a stimulus to her missionary activity, and many Catholics accepted untold hardships to go and preach the Gospel and thus save the greatest possible number of souls.

● Yet did not John Paul II often speak of evangelization? Of what use are the Church and evangelization if all men are saved?

If all men are already saved, the mission consists of telling men: I bring you good tidings; unbeknownst to you, you have already been saved by the Christ!

● Are there any signs that John Paul II understood evangelization in this way?

In fact, it is in this way that Cardinal Wojtyla explained the text of *Gaudium et Spes* 22, which affirms: "Christ, the final Adam, ...fully reveals man to man himself." This would mean that Christ manifests to man what has already happened to him, namely, that he possesses "being in Christ": "This revelation...consists in a fact–the fact that by his incarnation the Son of God united himself with every man."[46]

---

[46] Wojtyla, *Sign of Contradiction*, p. 102.

- **What can be said about this interpretation?**

The Church has never understood her mission in this way. Being a missionary has always meant bringing salvation to men through the preaching of the gospel and the administering of the sacraments. It has never meant announcing to them that they have possessed salvation all along. "He who believes and is baptized will be saved; he who refuses belief will be condemned" (Mk. 16:16).

51) How should the prayer meeting of religions at Assisi be judged?

The prayer meeting of religions held at Assisi on October 27, 1986, was an unprecedented scandal inducing souls into error.[47] It was also a sin against the First Commandment of God: "I am the Lord thy God; thou shalt not have strange gods before me." Never had the Church been so humiliated as when the Pope put himself on the same level as the heads of all the religions and sects. So doing, he gave the impression that the Catholic Church is but one religious community amongst many others that must work together to establish peace on earth–as if there could be another peace than in the conversion of men to Christ and His Church! "You must not consent to be yoke-fellows with unbelievers. What is there in common between light and darkness? What harmony between Christ and Belial? How can a believer throw in his lot with an infidel? How can the temple of God have any commerce with idols?" (II Cor. 6:14-16).[48]

- **How did the Pope put himself on the same level as the heads of all the false religions and sects?**

During his welcome address, which took place in Notre Dame Basilica, the Pope was seated on the same kind of chair as the heads of the other religions. Everything that might have given the impression of the Pope's precedence was avoided; all had to appear to be equals.

- **Didn't the Pope make a profession of his faith in Jesus Christ at Assisi?**

The Pope gave witness to his *personal* faith in Jesus Christ; but, despite the command given by Christ in sending His Apostles on their mission, he did not ask the representatives of these religions to convert to Christ. To the contrary, he invited them to pray to their false gods:

---

[47] The same kind of interreligious ceremony was repeated at Assisi in January 1993, at Rome in 1999, then again at Assisi, in the Pope's presence, in January 2002.
[48] Knox version.

We shall go from here to our separate places of prayer. Each religion will have the time and opportunity to express itself in its own traditional rite. Then from these separate places of prayer, we will walk in silence towards the lower Square of Saint Francis. Once gathered in the Square, again each religion will be able to present its own prayer, one after the other.

Having thus prayed separately, we shall meditate in silence on our own responsibility to work for peace. We shall then declare symbolically our commitment to peace. At the end of the Day, I shall try to express what this unique celebration will have said to my heart, as a believer in Jesus Christ and the first servant of the Catholic Church.[49]

● Afterwards, weren't efforts made to convert to Christ the representatives of the different religions?

Not only was nothing done at Assisi for the conversion of non-Christians, but Cardinal Etchegaray even declared on the square of St. Francis's Basilica that it was very important that the members of the different religions remain faithful to their false faith:

> We come from numerous religious traditions across the world; we are meeting together in total fidelity to our own religious traditions, quite conscious of the identity of the involvement of everyone in his own faith. We are gathered here without any trace of syncretism. This is what makes for the richness and value of this prayer meeting.[50]

● Did non-Christian religious worship take place during the World Day of Prayer at Assisi?

Not only did non-Christian worship take place publicly, but places of Catholic worship were placed at the disposition of the false religions. When one considers that a Catholic church is a sacred place consecrated uniquely to the worship of the most Blessed Trinity, one cannot but think of the "abomination of desolation" announced by Christ (Mt. 24:15).

● But didn't the Vatican nonetheless scrupulously avoid common prayer of Christians with non-Christians, and specify that it was not a matter of praying together, but of being together to pray?[51]

This formula seems more like a temporary concession made to the opponents of the meeting at Assisi than the expression of the Pope's thought. As early as 1979, in his inaugural encyclical *Redemptor Hominis*, John Paul II announced his intention of establishing "prayer

---

[49] John Paul II, Allocution of October 27, 1986, in the Basilica St. Mary of the Angels.
[50] Cardinal Etchegaray, *DC*, No. 1929 (December 7, 1986), p. 1074.
[51] The expression is John Paul II's (*DC*, No. 1929, p. 1071).

in common" with the members of other religions.⁵² In any case, the simple fact of publicly promoting the practice of false religions, with the implication that they are pleasing to God, is already an enormous scandal even if one does not participate in it directly. God has often shown that He holds false religions in abomination, and especially idolatry, the *summum* of all superstitions.

- **Can it not be said that John Paul II encouraged these prayers and worship as expressions of natural religion, and not as false religions?**

The gathering at Assisi was not a matter of individual prayer, of man in his personal relationship with God, but rather of the prayer of the divers religions as such, with their own rites addressed to their particular divinities. These cults, being the public expression of false beliefs, are, in and of themselves, insults proffered to God. Moreover, Sacred Scripture, in both the Old and the New Testaments, teaches that the only prayer pleasing to God is the prayer of the one He has established as the sole mediator between Himself and men, our Lord Jesus Christ, and that this prayer is only to be found in the true religion.

- **Didn't John Paul II attempt to justify his initiative at Assisi?**

John Paul II tried several times to justify the meeting at Assisi, particularly in the speech he addressed to the cardinals on December 22, 1986.

- **What is most striking in the speech of December 22?**

What is most striking about this speech is that the Pope cites the Second Vatican Council thirty-five times, without mentioning any other magisterial document. He notably asserts that "the appropriate key to understanding so great an event is found in the teaching of the Second Vatican Council."⁵³ He elaborates: "The event of Assisi can thus be considered as a visible illustration, an object lesson, a catechesis understandable by all, of the presuppositions and signification of our commitment to the ecumenism and interreligious dialogue recommended and promoted by the Second Vatican Council."⁵⁴

---

⁵² John Paul II, *Redemptor Hominis*, §6.
⁵³ John Paul II, "The State of the World and the Spirit of Assisi," Discourse to the Cardinals and the Curia, December 22, 1986; *DC,* No. 1933 (February 1, 1987), p. 133.
⁵⁴ *Ibid.,* p. 134.

- **In this speech, how does John Paul II justify theologically the interreligious gathering at Assisi?**

Besides the thirty-five references to Vatican II, John Paul II justifies the interreligious prayer meeting of Assisi by asserting: "All authentic prayer is inspired by the Holy Ghost, who is mysteriously present in the heart of every man."

- **What can be said about this statement?**

This statement contains two affirmations, the first of which is ambiguous ("All authentic prayer is inspired by the Holy Ghost"), and the second is clearly false ("The Holy Ghost is mysteriously present in the heart of every man").

- **Why is it ambiguous to assert that every authentic prayer is inspired by the Holy Ghost?**

The sentence is ambiguous because its truth or falsehood depends on the meaning given to the word "authentic." If by "authentic prayer" is meant a prayer in which a person really elevates his heart and mind to the one true God, then the sentence is undoubtedly true. But if it means "any sincere prayer," it is seriously erroneous (the prayer of the Buddhist before an idol of Buddha, like that of the animist sorcerer or the terrorist Muslim, can be sincere, but that certainly does not mean that it is inspired by the Holy Ghost).

- **Why is it false to say that the Holy Ghost is mysteriously present in the heart of every man?**

In the language of Catholic theology, as in Sacred Scripture, the expression "presence of the Holy Ghost" or "indwelling of the Holy Ghost" designates the *supernatural* presence of God by sanctifying grace. Now, even if the word "mysteriously" may lead some to think otherwise, it is certain that the Holy Spirit is not thus present in the heart of every man.

- **What does Church tradition have to say about this?**

During a baptism, the priest commands the devil: "Depart from him, unclean spirit, and give place to the Holy Ghost, the Consoler."[55] This surely indicates that the Holy Ghost was not indwelling in that soul.

---

[55] *Exi ab eo, immunde spiritus, et da locum Spiritui Sancto Paraclito.*

● What may we conclude on this subject?

Clearly, a false proposition underlies the justification of the prayer meeting of religions at Assisi.

● If John Paul II showed great respect for the false religions at Assisi, did these religions show a like respect for Catholicism?

The Muslims shamelessly took advantage of the meeting at Assisi to profess their faith in Allah as the only correct way. This is the prayer they offered for peace:

> It is Thou whom we adore, it is Thou whom we implore. Lead us on the straight path, the path of those upon whom Thou dost bestow blessings and not of those who anger Thee or go astray.

Sura II:36 of the Koran followed:

> Say: We believe in Allah and (in) that which had been revealed to us, and (in) that which was revealed to Abraham and Ishmael and Isaac and Jacob and the tribes, and (in) that which was given to Moses and Jesus, and (in) that which was given to the prophets from their Lord. We do not make any distinction between any of them, and to Him do we submit.

The Muslims' prayer for peace concluded with Sura 112, recited in Arabic by all the Muslims present:

> In the name of Allah, the Beneficent, the Merciful. Say: He, Allah, is One. Allah is He on Whom all depend. He begets not, nor is He begotten. And none is like Him.[56]

● What is remarkable about the Muslim prayers?

The assertions that God does not beget nor is He begotten and that they make no distinction amongst the prophets expressly take aim against the Catholic Faith, which professes that Jesus Christ is not a prophet like the others, but the true Son of God, begotten by the Father before all ages.

● How did the Assisi meeting conclude?

When all the delegations had completed their separate worship service for peace, they returned in silence like pilgrims to the Basilica of St. Francis, where each made a prayer for peace. In the speech closing the day, the Pope alluded to this procession:

> While we have walked in silence, we have reflected on the path our human family treads: either in hostility, if we fail to accept one another in love; or as a common journey to our lofty destiny, if we realize that other

---

[56] *DC,* No. 1929 (December 7, 1986), pp. 1076-77.

people are our brothers and sisters. The very fact that we have come to Assisi from various quarters of the world is in itself a sign of this common path which humanity is called to tread. Either we learn to walk together in peace and harmony, or we drift apart and ruin ourselves and others. We hope that this pilgrimage to Assisi has taught us anew to be aware of the common origin and common destiny of humanity. Let us see in it an anticipation of what God would like the developing history of humanity to be: a fraternal journey in which we accompany one another towards the transcendent goal which he sets for us.[57]

● What can be said about this speech?

We shall leave the commentary to a high dignitary of Freemasonry–Armando Corona, Grand Master of the Grand Lodge of the Vernal Equinox (Italy):

> Our interconfessionalism earned us the excommunication declared by Clement XI in 1738. But the Church was surely in error, if it is true that on October 27, 1986, the current pontiff at Assisi gathered men from every religious confession to pray together for peace. What else were our brethren seeking when they gathered in our temples if not brotherly love, tolerance, solidarity, the defense of the dignity of the human person; considering themselves equals, above political creeds, religious creeds, and skin color?[58]

The ecumenism of Assisi meshes with the Masonic plan: the establishment of a great temple of universal brotherhood above religions and creeds, the "unity in diversity" so dear to the New Age movement and globalism.

52) What are the results of ecumenism?

The results of ecumenism are religious indifferentism and the ruin of the missions. Today the opinion is widespread among Catholics that one can save one's soul equally well in any religion. Missionary work no longer makes sense, and it often happens that churchmen refuse to receive members of other religions into the Catholic Church in spite of their petitions. Missionary activity becomes an aid to socioeconomic development. This is in flagrant opposition to the Lord's command: "Going therefore, teach all nations; baptizing them in the name of the Father, and of the Son, and of the Holy Ghost. Teaching them to observe all things whatsoever I have commanded you" (Mt. 28:19).

---

[57] Pope John Paul II, Address to the Representatives of the Christian Churches and Ecclesial Communities and of the World Religions at the St. Francis of Assisi Basilica, October 27, 1986.
[58] Remarks published in *Hiram*, the bulletin of the Grand Orient of Italy, April 1987.

- **Can you cite an example of an actual refusal to convert non-Catholics?**

One unimaginable example of this ecumenism is the Balamand Declaration, signed June 23, 1993, at the conclusion of a meeting between the Roman Catholic Church and the Orthodox Church.[59]

- **In what context was this meeting at Balamand, Lebanon, held?**

It is necessary to understand that since the Greek Schism, several parts of the Eastern Church were reunited to Rome. While keeping their Eastern Rite, they recognize the papal primacy, as did the entire Eastern Church before the schism. These Eastern Catholic Churches experienced a great expansion after the political changes that took place in the Soviet Union (many Orthodox were only in the schism as a result of external pressure and desired to be reunited with the See of Peter). One can comprehend the anger of the Orthodox authorities, who threatened to break off ecumenical relations. The Balamand conference was an attempt to salvage ecumenism.

- **What does the Balamand Declaration say?**

In paragraph 8 of the Declaration, the Eastern Catholic Churches are called "a source of conflicts and of suffering." It states that in order to justify its "proselytism"–that is to say, its efforts to bring the schismatics back to Catholic unity–"the Catholic Church developed the theological vision according to which she presented herself as the only one to whom salvation was entrusted" (§10). In other words, the constant teaching of the Church, according to which all Christians must be united to the pope, the Supreme Pastor, is reduced to a simple theological opinion developed to justify selfish interests.

- **How does the Balamand agreement conceive of the relations between the Catholic Church and the schismatics?**

The Oriental schismatic Churches are henceforth considered as Sister Churches:

> It is in this perspective that the Catholic Churches and the Orthodox Churches recognize each other as Sister Churches, responsible together for maintaining the Church of God in fidelity to the divine purpose, most especially in what concerns unity. According to the words of Pope John Paul II, the ecumenical endeavour of the Sister Churches of East and West, grounded in dialogue and prayer, is the search for perfect and total communion which is neither absorption nor fusion but a meeting in truth and love (cf. *Slavorum Apostoli*, 27). (§14)

---

[59] The text was made public on July 15, 1993, by the Pontifical Council for Promoting Christian Unity.

- **What are the consequences of the practical rules agreed to in the Balamand Declaration?**

The Catholic Church expressly renounces trying to convert Eastern schismatics (§12). She even agrees to renounce creating Catholic organizations against the will of the Orthodox where none presently exist (§29). The Declaration concludes:

> By excluding for the future all proselytism and all desire for expansion by Catholics at the expense of the Orthodox Church, the commission hopes that it has overcome the obstacles which impelled certain autocephalous Churches to suspend their participation in the theological dialogue and that the Orthodox Church will be able to find itself altogether again for continuing the theological work already so happily begun. (§35)

- **How might one summarize the Balamand accords?**

In short, the Eastern Catholic Churches are considered to be an obstacle to ecumenism. Since, unfortunately, they exist, at the very least they must be forbidden to develop. This policy constitutes a betrayal of all the Christians who for centuries endured great sufferings and even martyrdom to remain faithful to the See of Peter. The churchmen sacrifice their own brothers in the faith solely to keep ecumenical dialogue with the Orthodox from stagnating.

- **What realistic assessment of ecumenical dialogue in general can we make?**

After all is said and done, ecumenical dialogue always turns to the detriment of the Catholic Church. It is always the Church that retreats and yields, while the other confessions and religions rejoice over the Church's concessions without taking a single step towards truth.

53) Isn't ecumenism required for the sake of fraternal charity?

Ecumenism as preached by Vatican II is not an exigency of fraternal charity, but rather a crime committed against it. True charity requires that one both desire and do good to one's neighbor. In matters religious, this means leading one's neighbor to the truth. It was an act of true charity when the missionaries of old left their countries, families, and friends to go and preach Christ in foreign lands amidst unspeakable dangers and toil. Many laid down their lives, carried off by sickness or violence. Ecumenism, on the contrary, leaves men in their false religions and even confirms them in their errors. It abandons them to error and to the immense danger of losing their souls. While ecumenism may be more comfortable for its proponents than the missionary apostolate, it is not a sign of charity, but rather of laziness, indifference, and human respect. The ecumenical theologians act like doctors who encourage the self-delusion of a gravely ill patient instead of alerting him to the gravity of his condition and treating him.

VII

THE NEW MASS

54) What is the holy Mass?

The holy Mass is the renewal and the representation of the sacrifice of the Cross. By the intermediary of the priest, Christ offers to His Father in an unbloody manner His Body and Blood, which He offered on the Cross. Thus the Mass is a true sacrifice by which the merits of the sacrifice of the Cross are applied to us.

- **Where is the Church's teaching on the holy sacrifice of the Mass to be found?**

The Council of Trent teaches:

> He, therefore, our God and Lord...at the Last Supper, on the night He was betrayed, so that He might leave to His beloved spouse the Church a visible sacrifice (as the nature of man demands), whereby that bloody sacrifice once to be completed on the Cross might be represented, and the memory of it remain even to the end of the world and its saving grace be applied to the remission of those sins which we daily commit...offered to God the Father His own Body and Blood....[1]

- **Is it certain that the Mass is a true sacrifice strictly speaking?**

The Council of Trent is explicit: "Canon 1. If anyone says that in the Mass a true and real sacrifice is not offered to God...let him be anathema."[2] The same Council declares that by the words "Do this in

---

[1] Council of Trent, Session XXII, Ch. 1 (Dz. 938).
[2] *Ibid.* (Dz. 948).

commemoration of me," Christ constituted the apostles priests of the New Testament and gave them power to celebrate this sacrifice.[3]

● What precisely is the relation between the sacrifice of the Mass and that of the Cross?

The sacrifice of the Mass has the same victim, the same priest, and the same intentions as that of the Cross; it is the same sacrifice but offered in a different manner.[4]

● What victim is offered in the sacrifice of the Mass?

Our Lord Jesus Christ is the victim of the sacrifice of the Mass as He is of the sacrifice of the Cross; it is He who is essentially offered at Mass, and not the bread and wine, which cease to exist during the consecration.

● Might it be said that our Lord is present in the holy Eucharist as victim?

Yes, it is as *victim* that our Lord Jesus Christ is present in the holy Eucharist.

● How can our Lord, whose body is henceforth glorious, be present in a state of victimhood?

Our Lord is in a state of victimhood in the holy Eucharist because in it His Body and Blood are *sacramentally* separated in order to represent the *physical* separation effected by the Passion.

● Yet isn't our Lord entirely present—Body, Blood, Soul, and Divinity—under the appearances of both the bread and the wine?

Since our Lord Jesus Christ is now living (risen and glorious), the presence of His Body or His Blood necessitates the presence of His whole person (body, blood, soul, and divinity); His Body and Blood can no longer be separated physically. And yet, *per se, merely by the power of the consecratory words,* it is the Body that is made present under the appearances of the bread, and the Blood under the appearances of wine; the Body and Blood of Christ are in a certain way *separated* by the sacrament (because of the double consecration).

---

[3] *Ibid.* (Dz. 938).
[4] *Ibid.* (Dz. 940).

- **Does this sacramental separation of the Body and Blood of our Lord Jesus Christ constitute immolation?**

The *sacramental* separation of the Body and Blood of our Lord constitutes an immolation in that it represents the *physical* separation that took place during His Passion, and, by the Savior's will, applies its fruits.

- **In the Mass, then, there really is an immolation?**

In the Mass there is an immolation, a *sacramental* immolation. The Council of Trent affirms that in the Mass, Christ "is contained and immolated in an unbloody manner."[5]

- **Who is the priest of the sacrifice of the Mass?**

The veritable priest of the sacrifice of the Mass is our Lord Jesus Christ, as He was on the Cross. The only difference is that Christ offered Himself on the Cross, whereas in the Mass He makes use of a human priest, who acts as Christ's instrument.

- **What are the intentions of the sacrifice of the Mass?**

Like the sacrifice of the Cross, the sacrifice of the Mass is offered by our Lord Jesus Christ for four great intentions: to adore God, to thank Him for His favors, to make reparation for the offenses committed against Him (in this sense, the sacrifice is called *propitiatory* or *satisfactory*), and to obtain graces for men.

- **In what way is the sacrifice of the Mass offered differently from that of the Cross?**

On the Cross, Christ was sacrificed in a bloody manner, while in the Mass He is sacrificed in an unbloody manner.

- **Is this the doctrine of the Fathers of the Church?**

St. Augustine teaches that "Christ was sacrificed once in Himself, and yet He is sacrificed daily in the sacrament"[6]; and St. Ambrose teaches that "just as what is offered everywhere is one body, and not many bodies, so also is it but one sacrifice."[7]

---

[5] *Ibid.* (Dz. 940). See also Dz. 938.
[6] St. Augustine, quoted by St. Thomas in the *ST*, III, Q. 83, Art. 1.
[7] Statement attributed to St. Ambrose, cited by St. Thomas, *ibid.*, ad 1: "*Sicut enim quod ubique offertur unum est corpus et non multa, ita et unum sacrificium.*"

55) Who has denied that the Mass is a sacrifice?

For more than a thousand years, no one dared to deny that the Mass is a sacrifice. Catholics enjoyed peaceful possession of this truth. It was not until the twelfth century that some sects began to attack it. But it was especially Martin Luther and Protestantism that induced numerous Christians to reject this dogma.

- **How did God reveal to us that the Mass is a sacrifice?**

The fact that the Mass is a sacrifice emerges clearly from Sacred Scripture. In the Old Testament, God, through the prophet Malachias, announced a future sacrifice in these terms: "From the rising of the sun even to the going down my name is great among the Gentiles, and in every place there is sacrifice, and there is offered to my name a clean oblation: for my name is great among the Gentiles, saith the Lord of hosts" (Mal. 1:11).

- **What is noteworthy in this prophesy of Malachias?**

The Jews had the right to offer sacrifice in only one place: the Temple at Jerusalem. Yet the prophet foretells a clean oblation that will be celebrated in every place. From the beginning, Christians recognized in this statement the sacrifice of the Mass.

- **Are there any other prophecies of the sacrifice of the Mass in the Old Testament?**

In the Old Testament, Christ's priesthood is figured by Melchisedech's (St. Paul says that Jesus Christ is "a high priest according to the order of Melchisedech"[8]). Melchisedech is only mentioned in the Bible for having offered a sacrifice of bread and wine (Gen. 14:18). This was a figure of the sacrifice of the Mass, instituted by Christ and offered under the species of bread and wine.

- **Do the Gospels speak of the Mass as a sacrifice?**

During the institution of the Mass on Holy Thursday, Christ used words expressive of a sacrifice: "This is my body, which shall be delivered for you" (I Cor. 11:24); "this is my blood of the new testament, which shall be shed for many unto remission of sins" (Mt. 26:28).

---

[8] Hebrews 6:20.

● Are there other passages of Sacred Scripture that can be cited?

In the first Epistle to the Corinthians, St. Paul opposes "the table of devils" and "the table of the Lord" (10:18-21). As the expression "the table of devils" designates the sacrifices pagans offer to idols, the expression "the table of the Lord" thus designates the Christian sacrifice. Similarly, the Epistle to the Hebrews affirms: "We have an altar, whereof they have no power to eat who serve the tabernacle [Jewish worship]" (Heb. 13:10). Now, by definition an altar is made for the offering of sacrifice.

● What do the early Fathers of the Church say about the Mass?

The most ancient ecclesiastical writings speak of the Eucharist as a sacrifice. One might cite, among others, the Didache (ca. A.D. 100), Pope St. Clement (d. 101), and St. Cyprian of Carthage (d. 258). I What does the *Didache* teach?

The *Didache*, one of the first Christian writings, declares: "But every Lord's day do ye gather yourselves together, and break bread, and give thanksgiving after having confessed your transgressions, that your sacrifice may be pure."[9]

● What does Pope St. Clement teach?

St. Clement of Rome (pope 92-101) wrote: "The Lord prescribed that sacrifices and liturgical actions be accomplished at specific seasons and times."[10]

● How does St. Cyprian speak about the sacrifice of the Mass?

St. Cyprian of Carthage (d. 258) devotes his Letter 63 to the sacrifice of the Mass. In it he states that Christ offered His Body and Blood in sacrifice to the Father (n. 4), that He commanded that this sacrifice be celebrated in memory of Him (n. 14), and that the priest acts as Christ's representative.

● Can you cite another Father of the Church on the sacrifice of the Mass?

St. Gregory Nazianzen (d. 390) exhorts a priest thus: "But, most reverend friend, cease not both to pray and to plead for me when you draw down the Word by your word, when with a bloodless cutting

---

[9] The *Didache*, Chapter 14 [English version: available online at www.newadvent.org/fathers].
[10] St. Clement of Rome, First Letter to the Corinthians, Chapter 14.

you sever the Body and Blood of the Lord, using your voice for the glaive."[11]

• What do we observe in this passage of St. Gregory Nazianzen?

St. Gregory very clearly mentions the unbloody sacrifice of Christ effected by the separation of His Body and Blood by means of the double consecration.

• What can we conclude from all these passages from Sacred Scripture and the Fathers?

The passages cited and many others plainly show that one cannot deny that the Mass is essentially a sacrifice without betraying Christ's teaching.

• Is this truth about the sacrifice of the Mass very important?

All the truths revealed by our Lord Jesus Christ are important, and none of them can be neglected with impunity. But the sacrifice of the Mass is truly at the heart of the whole Christian life. An error on this point would have disastrous consequences.

• How is the sacrifice of the Mass at the heart of Christian life?

The Jewish religion of the old Testament was already centered on the sacrifices offered in the Temple. It would be surprising if these numerous sacrifices had no counterpart in the new Testament. In fact, our Lord essentially came on earth to offer Himself in sacrifice to His Father. In the name of all mankind, He offered this perfect sacrifice of adoration, thanksgiving, reparation for sin, and petition. The essential of our Christian life must be to unite ourselves, day after day, to this sacrifice. It is precisely by the Mass that we do this.

• Thus Christianity without the Mass is inconceivable?

Even in the natural order, sacrifice is an essential element of the worship due to God. All the ancient religions have their sacrifices (one of the proofs of the caducity of the Jewish religion is the very fact that since the year 70, date of the destruction of the Temple, its sacrificial rites can no longer be performed). In the modern era, the Protestants tried to invent a Christianity without the Mass; the result was a complete denaturing of Christian faith and morals, which led rather rapidly to contemporary humanism. When man ceases offering sacrifices to God, he quickly tends to take himself for God.

---

[11] Letter 171, to Amphilochium [English version: available online at www.newadvent.org/fathers].

- **Isn't it especially the real presence of our Lord in the Blessed Sacrament that is denied by the Protestants?**

Luther did not deny some kind of real presence of Christ in the sacrament of the Eucharist, even if he understood it in an heretical way. However, he rejected the teaching on the sacrifice of the Mass and proffered scurrilous insults against it.

- **What did Luther say about the holy sacrifice of the Mass?**

Luther announced clearly that he wanted to destroy the Mass in order to strike at the heart of the Church. For example, he said:

> Once the Mass has been overthrown, I say we'll have overthrown the whole of Popedom. It is indeed upon the Mass as on a rock that the whole Papal system is built, with its monasteries, its bishoprics, its collegiate churches, its altars, its ministries, its doctrine, *i.e.,* with all its guts. All these cannot fail to crumble once their sacrilegious and abominable Mass falls.[12]

- **But doesn't Luther admit that the Mass can, in a sense, be called a sacrifice?**

Luther admits and sometimes employs the term *sacrifice* to designate the Mass, but only in a broad sense ("a sacred thing"). He obstinately refuses to believe that the Mass is literally a sacrifice: "The principal element of their worship, the Mass, exceeds every impiety and abomination; they make of it a sacrifice and a good work."[13]

- **What is the Mass, then, for Luther?**

For Luther, the Mass is simply a *memorial* of the Passion. His goal is to instruct the faithful, to remind them of the sacrifice of Calvary in order to prompt an interior act of faith. If he speaks of sacrifice, it is solely in the sense of a sacrifice of praise or thanksgiving without redemptive value.

- **What does Luther absolutely refuse in the Catholic doctrine of the Mass?**

Luther absolutely refuses the doctrine that the Mass has a *propitiatory* or *satisfactory* value, that is, that it really and effectively applies to our souls the fruits of the sacrifice of the Cross, thereby acquitting the debt we have incurred towards God because of our sins.

---

[12] Luther, *Contra Henricum regem Angliæ* (1522), *Werke*, X, 220. [English version: Michael Davies, *Cranmer's Godly Order* (Ft. Collins, Colorado: Roman Catholic Books, 1995), p. 55-56.]

[13] Luther, *De votis monasticis judicium* (1521), *Werke*, VIII, 651.

- **What exactly do the words *propitiatory* and *satisfactory* mean?**

The sacrifice of the Mass is said to be *propitiatory* because it renders God *propitious*, favorably inclined, towards us by destroying the reasons for the wrath He may bear towards us because of our sins. It is called *satisfactory* because it *satisfies* divine justice, that is, it does enough (*satis facere* = to do enough) to appease it.

- **What does Luther have to say on this subject?**

Luther teaches:

> The Mass is not a sacrifice or the action of a sacrificer. Let us regard it as a sacrament or a testament. Let us call it benediction, Eucharist, or remembrance of the Lord.[14]
>
> The blessed Sacrament was not instituted to be made into an expiatory sacrifice...but to serve to awaken faith in us and to console consciences; ...the Mass is not a sacrifice offered for others, whether living or dead, for the remission of their sins, but...a communion in which priest and faithful receive the sacrament, each for himself.[15]
>
> It is a blatant and blasphemous error to offer or to apply the Mass for sins, in satisfaction for them, or on behalf of the deceased....[16]

- **What were the liturgical consequences of Luther's errors on the Mass?**

For Luther, the "liturgy of the Word" must hold the first place and communion, second. By progressively modifying the traditional rites and ceremonies of the Mass, Luther intended to induce the faithful gradually to change their faith. He advised his co-revolutionaries not to go too fast: "To reach the goal safely and successfully, certain ceremonies of the ancient Mass must be kept for the sake of the weak, who might be scandalized by too sudden a change."[17]

- **Did the Protestants deliberately introduce their new belief in a calculated way, by changing the liturgy little by little?**

The Anglicans in particular adopted this cunning strategy,[18] but Luther had articulated it very clearly: "The priest can very well

---

[14] Luther, Sermon for the First Sunday of Advent, *Werke*, XI, 774.
[15] The Confession of Augsburg, Art. 24, "Of the Mass."
[16] Luther, *De Captivitate Babylonica* (1520), *Werke*, VI, 521.
[17] *Ibid.*, XII, 212.
[18] See *Cranmer's Godly Order* by Michael Davies. The first Anglican Book of Prayer (1549) suppressed the Offertory, altered the Canon, and adopted the Lutheran version of the Institution narrative: no mention is made of the propitiatory sacrifice, but it is not explicitly

manage so that the man of the people is still unaware of the change that has taken place, and can assist at Mass without finding anything to scandalize him."[19]

• What changes did Luther introduce into the liturgy?

Luther attacked the Offertory, which he eliminated, and the Canon, which he modified considerably. He kept the general outline of the Mass, but skillfully erased the essential. At Christmas 1521, the Lutheran worship service comprised the Confiteor, Introit, Kyrie, Gloria, Epistle, Gospel, sermon, no Offertory, the Sanctus, narration of the institution of the Supper recited aloud in the popular language, Communion under both kinds (in the hand and from the chalice) with no preliminary confession, the Agnus Dei, and Benedicamus Domino. Latin would only disappear little by little.

• What can be said of the hatred with which Luther pursued the Catholic Mass?

Luther was right about one thing: the whole Christian life rests upon the sacrifice of Calvary renewed in an unbloody manner on the altar. Denaturing the Mass is one of the most effective ways of destroying the Church. Several Catholic authors have remarked that this would be the work of Antichrist.

• Can you quote some of these authors?

St. Alphonsus Liguori alerts us: "The Mass is the best and most beautiful thing in the Church....That is why the devil has always sought to deprive the world of the Mass through the actions of heretics, making them precursors of Antichrist."[20]

Dom Guéranger gives the same warning: "Were the Mass to be done away with, we should quickly fall again into the state of depravity in which pagan nations are sunk: and this is to be the work of Antichrist. He will take every possible means to prevent the celebration of the Holy Sacrifice of the Mass, so that this great counterpoise being taken away, God would necessarily put an end to all things, having now no object left in their further subsistence."[21]

---

denied. This was but the first stage: once it was widely adopted, a second Prayer Book was published (1552), which more closely resembled the Calvinist Supper.

[19] Luther, quoted by Jacques Maritain in *Three Reformers* (New York: Charles Scribner's Sons, 1934), p. 181-2.

[20] *Oeuvres du B. Alphonse de Liguori* (Avignon: Seguin, 1827), p. 182.

[21] Dom Prosper Guéranger, O.S.B., *Explanation of the Holy Mass* (1885; reprint: Loreto Publications, n.d.), p. 109.

- **Does Sacred Scripture foretell that the Antichrist will attack the Holy Sacrifice of the Mass?**

    Concerning Antichrist, the Prophet Daniel says: "And strength was given him against the continual sacrifice, because of sins" (Dan. 8:12).

56) Does the Church's teaching about the holy sacrifice of the Mass lessen the importance of the sacrifice of the Cross?

The sacrifice of the Mass in no way lessens the importance of the sacrifice of the Cross because it depends on it totally and draws from it all its efficacy. Its whole worth consists in making it present through its commemoration and in applying to men the graces Christ merited for them on the Cross.

- **Who has accused the sacrifice of the Mass of lessening the importance of the sacrifice of the Cross?**

    The Protestants have accused the sacrifice of the Mass of being an outrage against the sacrifice of the Cross. According to them, the Catholics think that the sacrifice of the Cross did not suffice for the salvation of mankind and that another perpetual sacrifice is needed.

- **How should the Protestants' accusations be answered?**

    The Protestants completely misunderstand the Church's teaching. On the cross, Christ merited all the graces necessary for the salvation of all men of all time.[22] The sacrifice of the Mass is not *another* sacrifice than that of the Cross, but *the same* sacrifice made present to all Christians. Its purpose is not to gain new graces, but to apply to men the graces already merited on the Cross.

- **Why is the sacrifice of the Mass needful for applying to us the graces merited on the Cross?**

    According to Christ's will, the fruits of the redemption are not dispensed automatically, but are linked to the sacraments: "He that believeth and is baptized shall be saved" (Mk. 16:16); "Except you eat the flesh of the Son of man and drink his blood, you shall not have life in you" (Jn. 6:54).

---

[22] "But Christ...neither by the blood of goats, or of calves, but by his own blood, entered once into the holies, having obtained eternal redemption" (Heb. 9:12).

- **But why is a sacrifice required for dispensing the fruits of the redemption?**

The Christian life is a participation in the life of Christ. But He became incarnate in order to be able to offer in His own person, and in our name, a perfect sacrifice to His Father. The essential act of our Christian life must be to unite ourselves to Christ's sacrifice, according to St. Paul's word: "[I] fill up those things that are wanting of the sufferings of Christ, in my flesh, for his body, which is the church" (Col. 1:24). In the Mass, the Church, the priest, and the faithful continually unite their life to Christ's sacrifice; they give themselves, and they receive graces for giving themselves ever more.

57) Is the Holy Mass also a meal or supper?

In its very essence, the Mass is neither a meal nor a meal including a sacrifice, but simply a sacrifice. Holy Communion, which strictly speaking could be called a meal, is a fruit of this sacrifice but does not belong to its essence.

- **What does the Church's magisterium say about this subject?**

The Council of Trent clearly affirms that the Mass is a sacrifice. It never says that it is also a meal. The thesis according to which the Holy Mass, in its essential nature, would be both a sacrifice and a meal was explicitly condemned by Pope Pius XII:

> They, therefore, err from the path of truth who do not want to have Masses celebrated unless the faithful communicate; and those are still more in error who, in holding that it is altogether necessary for the faithful to receive holy communion as well as the priest, put forward the captious argument that here there is question not of a sacrifice merely, but of a sacrifice and a supper of brotherly union, and consider the general communion of all present as the culminating point of the whole celebration.
>
> Now it cannot be over-emphasized that the Eucharistic sacrifice of its very nature is the unbloody immolation of the divine Victim, which is made manifest in a mystical manner by the separation of the sacred species and by their oblation to the eternal Father. Holy Communion pertains to the integrity of the Mass and to the partaking of the august sacrament; but while it is obligatory for the priest who says the Mass, it is only something earnestly recommended to the faithful.[23]

---

[23] Pius XII, Encyclical *Mediator Dei*, November 20, 1947, §§114-115.

- **Is there a way to tell on a practical level that the Mass is not essentially a supper?**

The Church has imposed the obligation to attend the holy sacrifice of the Mass every Sunday, but has never required the faithful to receive Holy Communion weekly. If the Holy Mass were essentially a supper, the faithful present would all have to communicate since one who attends a meal without eating anything has not taken part!

- **So it is possible to really participate in the holy sacrifice of the Mass without receiving Holy Communion?**

Yes, the faithful can really participate in the holy sacrifice of the Mass without communicating (even though, obviously, communicating increases one's participation). The Council of Trent declared: "If anyone says that Masses in which the priest alone communicates sacramentally, are illicit and are therefore to be abrogated: let him be anathema."[24]

- **Are there other proofs that the Mass is not essentially a supper?**

The rite of Mass itself shows that the Mass is not essentially a meal. How strange a meal it would be in which after such lengthy rites and ceremonies so miniscule a morsel were served! If the Mass were a meal, those who would like to organize the Mass with the form of a genuine supper would be right.

58) Who teaches that the Mass is both a sacrifice and a supper?

Nowadays the theory that the Mass is a supper during which a sacrifice takes place is widely held by many "Catholic" theologians. According to them, the Mass is firstly a meal, but also comprises a sacrifice because Christ gives Himself to us as food. It is Christ's self-donation in the supper that would impart to the Mass its sacrificial character. But this notion has nothing to do with Catholic theology, for it completely skews the reality. Sacrifice consists in an offering made to God, not to men. On the cross, Christ offered Himself to His Father and not to us. If this new theory were true, the sacrifice of the Mass would be offered to us and not to God.

---

[24] Dz. 955.

- **Where are these new theories on the nature of the Mass to be found?**

This theory is propounded, for example, in the Common Declaration of the Lutheran-Roman Catholic Joint Commission that worked from 1976 to 1982.

- **Who were the Catholic participants in the commission?**

Among the Catholic members of this commission were future Cardinals Karl Lehmann and Walter Kasper, and Cardinals Hermann Volk and Joseph Ratzinger.

- **What did the Lutheran-Roman Catholic Declaration say?**

The Lutheran-Roman Catholic Declaration states:

> The visible sign of Jesus Christ's offering in the celebration of the Eucharist and of our incorporation in this sacrifice is...the Supper. This means that, in the realization of this Supper, the sacrifice that Jesus Christ makes of Himself is made present and effected. That is why the traditional distinction, which only became habitual after the Council of Trent, according to which in the Eucharist are distinguished the sacrament and the sacrifice, cannot be retained by theology because it falsifies the fundamental structure. It is in the fact of His offering Himself as food that the sacrifice of Jesus finds its expression in the liturgy.[25]

- **What may be said of this teaching?**

This theory really constitutes a new teaching that implies the rejection of the traditional theology. Therefore it must be firmly refused.

59) Was the Tridentine Mass abolished?

Since the introduction of the New Mass (Paul VI's Mass, in 1969), Rome endeavored to make people believe that the traditional Mass was abolished and its celebration prohibited. But in his Motu Proprio *Summorum Pontificum* (July 7, 2007), Pope Benedict XVI publicly recognized that it had never been abrogated. All those who were accused of disobedience for nearly forty years because of their fidelity to this Mass indeed suffered persecution for justice' sake.

- **Could the traditional Mass have been abolished?**

Celebration of the traditional Mass could not easily be prohibited, for the Church has always respected rites of immemorial custom instead of forbidding them. Moreover, in promulgating the Tridentine

---

[25] Lehmann Schlink, *Das Opfer Jesu Christi und seine Gegenwart in der Kirche* (Herder, 1983), p. 223.

Missal (by the Bull *Quo Primum* of July 14, 1570), St. Pius V granted a perpetual privilege by which no priest could ever be prevented from being faithful to this rite for the celebration of the Mass.

- **Were not the stipulations of St. Pius V's Bull *Quo Primum* abrogated by Paul VI's Apostolic Constitution *Missale Romanum* (April 3, 1969) promulgating the New Mass?**

It is difficult to determine the exact juridical scope of Paul VI's Constitution *Missale Romanum* because of the ambiguities it contains. What is sure is that it did not attempt to abolish the privilege accorded by St. Pius V. The defenders of the traditional Mass saw this right away and said so, but the bishops, and even Pope Paul VI, tried to make the faithful believe that the new Mass was obligatory.

- **So it took nearly forty years for Rome to notice that the traditional Mass had not been abolished?**

The Roman authorities were well aware, at least since 1986, that the traditional Mass had not been abolished. But it was necessary to wait twenty more years for the fact to become official. According to Cardinal Stickler's account:

> In 1986, Pope John Paul II asked a commission of nine cardinals two questions. First: Did Pope Paul VI or any other competent authority legally forbid the widespread celebration of the Tridentine Mass in the present day?
>
> The Cardinal explained, "I can answer because I was one of the Cardinals."
>
> He continued: "The answer given by the nine Cardinals in 1986 was 'No, the Mass of St. Pius V (Tridentine Mass) has never been suppressed.'"
>
> In answer to the second question, Can any bishop forbid any priest in good standing from celebrating the Tridentine Mass?, Cardinal Stickler replied, "The nine Cardinals unanimously agreed that no bishop may forbid a Catholic priest from saying the Tridentine Mass....There is no official interdiction, and I believe that the Pope will never issue one... precisely because of the words of Pius V, who said that this Mass would be valid in perpetuity."[26]

60) Is the new rite of Mass an adequate expression of Catholic teaching on the holy sacrifice of the Mass?

In the judgment of Cardinals Ottaviani and Bacci, the new rite of Mass promulgated in 1969 "represents, both as a whole and in

---

[26] Cardinal Alphonse Stickler, *Latin Mass Magazine*, May 1995.

its details, a striking departure from the Catholic theology of the Mass."[27] All the changes tend to silence any mention of propitiatory sacrifice in favor of the Protestant Supper.

● How, concretely, does the New Mass resemble the Protestant Supper?

The most serious changes were those touching the Offertory and Canon. It could be said that the demands of Luther, who called for abolishing the Offertory and the Canon, are substantially satisfied in the New Order.

● What did Luther say about the Offertory?

Luther affirmed: "That abomination called the Offertory, and from this point almost everything stinks of oblation."[28]

● Why did Luther so hate the Offertory of the Mass?

The ancient Offertory clearly expresses that the Mass is a sacrifice offered in propitiation for sins. The priest prays:

> Receive, O holy Father, almighty, eternal God, this spotless host which I, thine unworthy servant, offer unto Thee, my living and true God, for my own countless sins, offenses, and negligences, and for all here present; as also for all faithful Christians, living or dead; that it may avail for my own and for their salvation unto life eternal. Amen.

● What has become of this Offertory in the new rite?

In the new rite, the Offertory was suppressed and replaced by a preparation of the gifts, the text of which was taken from a Jewish table blessing:

> Blessed are you, Lord, God of all creation. Through your goodness we have this bread to offer, which earth has given and human hands have made. It will become for us the bread of life.

● What might be noticed in this new prayer?

Besides its markedly naturalist tone (there is no allusion to supernatural truths revealed by God), this prayer completely voids the notions of sacrifice and propitiation. It is the equivalent of a simple prayer before a meal.

---

[27] Cardinals Ottaviani and Bacci, letter to Pope Paul VI dated September 29, 1969, accompanying the *Short Critical Study of the New Order of Mass* written by a group of theologians. [In English, it is known as *The Ottaviani Intervention*, tr. Fr. Anthony Cekada (Rockford, Ill.: TAN Books & Publishers, 1992).]

[28] Luther, in *Formula Missæ et Communionis* (1523), XII, 211.

● But isn't the most important thing that the Canon of the Mass—the very ancient and venerable Roman Canon—was preserved?

It cannot really be said that the Roman Canon was retained in the new liturgy. Firstly, it lost its character of *canon*, that is to say, a fixed, obligatory rule: now it is but one option among others (it became "Eucharistic Prayer I," to which, in fact, one of the other three "Eucharistic prayers" introduced in 1969 is often preferred, or else one of the many others authorized by the Holy See). Secondly, even "Eucharistic Prayer I" distorts the Roman Canon.

● Isn't "Eucharistic Prayer I" the same as the Roman Canon?

At first glance "Eucharistic Prayer I" of the new liturgy may seem to be the ancient Roman Canon, but in fact several modifications have been introduced. Noteworthy among these are the following: **1)** recitation in a loud voice (which leads to a desacralization of the Canon); **2)** the alteration of the formula of consecration (made to resemble the Lutheran rite); **3)** the banalization of the formula of consecration (henceforth recited in a narrative tone rather than in the customary low voice); **4)** the suppression of the priest's genuflection between the consecration and the elevation (which favors the heresy that teaches that the faith of the assembly, and not the words of consecration, are the cause of the Real Presence); **5)** the elimination of numerous signs of the cross; **6)** the addition of an ambiguous acclamation after the consecration.

● Are these new ways of doing things really bad?

Taken separately, these practices are not necessarily bad *in themselves* (one or the other of them can even be found in an Eastern rite). But taken together and compared with what was previously done, they all tend toward a weakening of the faith.

● Are the three other "Eucharistic prayers" also contestable?

The three new "Eucharistic prayers" add several grave deficiencies to the defects of the first, which Fr. Roger Calmel summarized thus:

> They begin by putting the larger part of the *Preces Eucharisticae* after the consecration, with just a short invocation to the Holy Ghost bracketed between the *Sanctus* and the narrative of the institution. By all means they want to rush the priest into the consecration without leaving him suitable time to become focused on what he is going to do, without allowing him to prepare himself for the infinite mystery he is to accomplish....Lastly, if, despite everything, certain ideas from the Roman Canon on the nature of the Mass and its effects have been retained, they have been systematically weakened by well-calculated omissions: the Lord God to whom the

sacrifice is offered is no longer invoked under the titles of His omnipotence or His infinite mercy; there is not a word of our condition of servants and sinners, constrained by these two titles to offer the holy sacrifice; nothing on the Church as Catholic and apostolic....[29]

• Aren't these criticisms a bit severe?

These criticisms are *true*. And many more omissions common to the three new "Eucharistic prayers" could still be catalogued: the *propitiatory* end of the sacrifice of the Mass is never explicitly affirmed (even if the words *sacrifice* and *victim* figure in Prayers III and IV); all the types and figures of the sacrifice of Christ (Abel, Abraham, Melchisedech) have disappeared; the Virgin Mary is never called *ever* virgin; the merits of the saints are ignored (the saints themselves being reduced to anonymity: even St. Peter is not named); hell is never mentioned, *etc*.

• Isn't "Eucharistic Prayer II" very old?

"Eucharistic Prayer II" does deserve a special mention for, as has been written, "a priest who no longer believed in either Transubstantiation or the sacrificial character of the Mass could recite it with perfect tranquility of conscience," and "a Protestant minister...could use it in his own celebrations just as well."[30] Not once does the notion of sacrifice occur, yet it is the most often used because it passes for ancient and venerable, and especially because it is the shortest of the four (it has been nicknamed the "mini-canon").

• Isn't this Eucharistic Prayer II the Canon of St. Hippolytus (third century)?

Some claim that this prayer is the ancient canon of Hippolytus, but: **1)** at best, it would only be a truncated version of that canon (the passage affirming that Christ voluntarily gave Himself up to suffering in order to "destroy death, to break the bonds of the devil, to trample hell underfoot, and to enlighten the just" has, for example, been suppressed[31]); and **2)** it is forgotten that Hippolytus was the second antipope, and that it is not at all certain that his liturgy was ever celebrated in the Catholic Church.

---

[29] Fr. Roger-Thomas Calmel, O.P. "Apology for the Roman Canon" [French] *Itinéraires*, No. 157, Nov. 1971, p. 38. In the rest of the article, Fr. Calmel fully develops the facts enumerated here.
[30] Ottaviani and Bacci, *The Ottaviani Intervention*, Chapter VI.
[31] See Hippolytus of Rome, *La Tradition apostolique, texte Latin*, edited by Dom Botte, O.S.B., Sources Chrétiens (Paris: Cerf, 1946), p. 32.

● But isn't this Hippolytus a saint?

Father Roguet, who cannot be suspected of hostility towards the new liturgy, explains:

> Hippolytus does not give his text as a canon, that is to say a fixed, obligatory rule, but rather as a model for improvisation; his text, then, was probably never pronounced as written. Lastly, he was a very reactionary character, so opposed to the Roman hierarchy as to play the antipope (which he redeemed by martyrdom) and it is highly likely that he presented his anaphora in opposition to the Eucharistic prayer then in use by Rome.[32]

● What are the consequences of the deficiencies of these new Eucharistic prayers?

Fr. Calmel remarked:

> As a result of these alterations and manipulations, the inexhaustible but well-defined riches of the consecratory rite are no longer suitably set forth. The interior dispositions required for receiving the supernatural fruits of the holy sacrifice are no longer fostered as they ought to be. The unavoidable consequences seem to be that priests and the laity cease to perceive the significance of the Mass, and the Catholic Mass more closely resembles the Protestant Supper.[33]

● Are all the deficiencies of the New Mass fortuitous, or do they correspond to some overarching idea?

The new liturgy is the bearer of its own spirit, which is a new spirit. Its principal author, Fr. Annibale Bugnini, could declare: "The image of the liturgy given by the Council is completely different from what it was before."[34]

● How might we summarize the spirit that inspired the redaction of the New Mass?

The spirit that inspired the redaction of the new rite of Mass is clearly visible in the General Introduction to the new Missal. It is especially manifest in its Article 7, which states:

> The Lord's Supper or Mass is the sacred assembly or meeting of the People of God, met together with a priest presiding, to celebrate the Memorial of the Lord. For this reason the promise of Christ is particularly true of a local congregation of the Church: "Where two or three are gathered in my name, there I am in their midst" (Mt. 18:20).

---

[32] Amon-Marie Roguet, O.P., *Pourquoi le canon de la messe en français?* (Paris: Cerf, 1967), p. 23.
[33] Calmel, "Apology for the Roman Canon," *Itinéraires*, p. 38.
[34] Annibale Bugnini, *DC*, No. 1491, Jan. 4, 1967, col. 824.

- **What stands out in Article 7?**

The description Article 7 gives of the Mass has nothing specifically Catholic and could just as easily apply to the Protestant Supper. If Article 7 is taken as a definition, it must even be considered heretical.

- **How does Article 7 contradict Church teaching?**

Article 7 contradicts Church teaching on the three essential points that distinguish the Catholic Mass from the Protestant Supper:

1) The Mass is essentially a (propitiatory) sacrifice, not an assembly of the faithful met together to celebrate a "memorial."

2) The priest is essentially a (free and voluntary) instrument by which Christ renews His sacrifice, and not a mere president of an assembly.

3) Our Lord is present in the Eucharist with His body and blood, and not only in a spiritual manner (as when two or three persons are gathered in His name).

- **Yet is it not true that the Mass is an assembly of the faithful?**

The presence of the faithful is not necessary for the celebration of holy Mass (even if it is desirable). The third Eucharistic prayer favors error on this point by affirming: "From age to age you gather a people to yourself, so that...a perfect offering may be made to the glory of your name."

- **Is this bad presentation of the Mass proper to Article 7, or is it to be found throughout the General Introduction of the new missal?**

This bad presentation of the Mass is to be found throughout the General Introduction of the 1969 missal, of which Article 7 is the perfect summary:

1) The word *sacrifice* appears a few times in the 341 articles of this Introduction with a vague meaning, but *propitiatory* sacrifice is never spoken of (the Mass is presented, rather, as a banquet, a feast, *etc.*).

2) The fact that the priest–and he alone–is the instrument by which our Lord renews His sacrifice during the consecration is never mentioned either.[35]

---

[35] Pius XII taught very clearly: "The unbloody immolation at the words of consecration, when Christ is made present upon the altar in the state of a victim, is performed by the priest and by him alone, as the representative of Christ and not as the representative of the faithful" (*Mediator Dei*, §92). The General Introduction, however, asserts that in the Mass the priest speaks sometimes in the name of the people and sometimes in his own name (Art. 13), but

3) The expression "real presence" is equally absent. The "presence" of Christ in the Eucharist is mentioned, but in the same way as one speaks of His "presence" in sacred Scripture. And the term *transubstantiation*, which is the only word that unequivocally expresses the Catholic faith, is also omitted.[36]

- **Surely the mere fact that the word transubstantiation does not appear in the General Introduction to the 1969 missal is not enough to support the conclusion that its authors do not believe it.**

It is not a matter of judging the personal faith of the new missal's authors, but of knowing whether, objectively, the Catholic Faith is expressed in it. In 1794, Pius VI condemned a proposition of the Jansenist Synod of Pistoia, which did express the Catholic doctrine on the Eucharist correctly, *for the sole reason* that if failed to employ the word *transubstantiation.* This single omission was reason enough for Pius VI to declare that the proposition was favorable to heretics.[37] Now, the General Introduction of the 1969 missal is much less clear on this subject than the Synod of Pistoia; and at the same time, the new missal suppresses many marks of respect towards the Blessed Sacrament. It is obviously dangerous to the faith.

- **Wasn't the General Introduction of the new missal subsequently corrected?**

The General Introduction of the Missal, and especially its Article 7, raised such an outcry that it was modified as early as 1970. The words *transubstantiation* and *propitiatory* were notably added (once, so that it could no longer be said that they were absent) in the "typical" (that is to say, official) edition of the new Missal, promulgated March 26, 1970, by the Roman Congregation on Divine Worship. But *the new rite itself,* of which Article 7 perfectly expressed the spirit, *was not changed!* It continues to impart to the faithful who participate in it the same idea of the Mass: an assembly of the People of God celebrating a memorial under the presidency of the priest. This is nearly the Protestant conception.

---

fails to say that at the essential moment, at the consecration, he is the representative of Christ alone.

[36] If absolutely necessary, some Protestants will accept the term "real presence," but not "transubstantiation," which very precisely designates the change of the entire substance of the bread into the substance of the glorious body of our Lord, the outward appearances alone remaining.

[37] Dz. 1529.

61) Was the protestantization of the new rite of Mass intentional

The French Academy member Jean Guitton, a great friend and confidant of Paul VI, declared that the Pope had intended to remove from the Mass anything that might trouble the Protestants. In fact, Paul VI asked six Protestant pastors to collaborate in the drafting of the New Mass. A famous photograph shows him in the company of these Protestant ministers. One of them, Max Thurian, a member of the Protestant monastic community of Taizé, later explained: "There is nothing in this renewed Mass that can really bother evangelical Protestants."[38] Later, in 1988, he was ordained priest without previously having abjured Protestantism.

- **When did Jean Guitton reveal this intention of Paul VI?**

During a radio program devoted to Paul VI (December 19, 1993, on Radio Courtoisie), Jean Guitton described in the following terms the intention Paul VI had in devising the new rite:

> First of all, Paul VI's Mass is presented as a banquet, and emphasizes much more the participatory aspect of a banquet and much less the notion of sacrifice, of a ritual sacrifice before God with the priest showing only his back. So, I do not think I'm mistaken in saying that the intention of Paul VI and the new liturgy that bears his name is to ask of the faithful a greater participation at Mass; it is to make more room for Sacred Scripture and less room for everything...some would say for magic, others for transubstantiation, which is of Catholic faith. In other words, Paul VI evinced an ecumenical intention to efface, or at least to correct, or at least to relax what is too Catholic, in the traditional sense, in the Mass, and to converge the Mass, I repeat, with the Calvinist Supper.

- **Are there other testimonies about the ecumenical orientation of the new liturgy?**

The principal author of the liturgical reform, Fr. Annibale Bugnini (1912-82) never made a secret of his ecumenical intentions. He made a rather significant admission of as much in 1965, in a striking sentence worth reading twice: "The Church was guided by the love of souls and the desire to do everything in order to smooth the way to union, to remove every stone which could represent even the shadow of a risk of a stumbling block or some displeasure for our separated brethren."[39]

Let's reread it: remove every stone (1) that might represent (conditional tense) (2) even the *shadow* (3) of a *risk* (4) of *displeasure*.

---

[38] Quoted in *La Croix*, May 30, 1969.
[39] *L'Osservatore Romano*, March 17, 1965.

- **How did the Protestants understand Paul VI's New Mass?**

Many Protestants, who obviously refused the traditional Mass, stated that they saw no difficulty henceforth in using the new rite to celebrate their Protestant Supper. In addition to Max Thurian (*La Croix,* May 30, 1969), one can quote G. Siegvalt (*Le Monde,* November 22, 1969); Roger Mehl (*Le Monde,* September 10, 1970); Ottfried Jordahn (conference of June 15, 1975, at Maria Laach); and lastly, the official declaration of the Supreme Consistory of the Church of the Augsburg Confession of Alsace and Lorraine on December 8, 1973.

- **Were the Protestants the only non-Catholics to influence the preparation of the new liturgy?**

Besides the influence of Protestants, the liturgical reform of 1969 was influenced by Freemasonry.

- **How did Freemasonry exert its influence on the liturgical reform of 1969?**

Freemasonry influenced the liturgical reform indirectly at first, thanks to the opening to the world preached by Vatican II at the very moment that civil society began to be dominated by Masonic slogans: progress, the cult of man, freedom, secularization, tolerance, equality, *etc.* Everything that manifested divine transcendence, the sense of the sacred, respect for authority, contempt for the world, the acknowledgment of our status as sinners, the importance of the spiritual combat, the need for sacrifice and reparation, or simply the clear acknowledgment of a *supe*rnatural order, seemed ill-adapted to "modern man," and was eliminated or watered down.

- **Can you give some examples of these changes?**

The new liturgy modified or expurgated texts speaking too clearly of *hell* or the *devil* (the *Dies Irae* in the Mass for the Dead; the Collects of the 17th Sunday after Pentecost and the feasts of St. Nicholas, St. Camillus de Lellis, *etc.*); of *original sin* (Collect of Christ the King); of *penance* (Collects of St. Raymond of Peñafort, St. John-Marie Vianney, the Curé of Ars; of the Thursday after Ash Wednesday); the *contempt of the things of the earth* (Collect of St. Francis of Assisi, the Postcommunion of the second Sunday of Advent, the Secret of the third Sunday after Easter); the need to make satisfaction for sins (Collect of the Sacred Heart); the *enemies* of the Church (Communion of the Feast of the Exaltation of the Holy Cross, and the Collects of St. Pius V, St. John Capistrano, *etc.*); the *dangers of error* (the Good Friday prayer for the conversion of heretics and schismatics, and the Collects of St. Peter Canisius, St. Robert Bellarmine, and St. Augustine of Canterbury);

the miracles of saints (Collects of St. Nicholas, St. Francis Xavier, St. Raymond of Peñafort, St. John of God, St. Frances Roman, *etc.*).[40]

- **Were these suppressions really the expression of a new spirit?**

That same year of 1969, Paul VI declared: "After the Council a wave of peace and optimism has swelled in the Church, a stimulating and positive Christianity, the friend of life, of worldly values....[result of] an intention to render Christianity acceptable and lovable, indulgent and open, rid of every trace of medieval rigorism or pessimistic outlook on men and morals."[41]

- **Was there any *direct* influence by Freemasonry on the liturgical reform of 1969?**

In 1975, the great architect of the New Mass, Annibale Bugnini, was denounced as a Freemason to Paul VI; the cleric who accused him furnished proofs and threatened to make the matter public. Paul VI took it very seriously and, to avoid scandal, immediately dismissed Msgr. Bugnini from his functions as secretary of the Congregation for Divine Worship before appointing him apostolic pro-nuncio to Iran (January 1976).[42] In 1976 and 1978, Annibale Bugnini's name appeared on lists of Freemasonic prelates published by the Italian press.[43]

62) Is the promulgation of a rite covered by the Church's infallibility?

Sometimes it is asserted that the promulgation of a new rite or the publication of an universal law (for example, a liturgical law) would automatically come under the Church's infallibility, such that there could be nothing in it false or detrimental to the Church. But this is not true. The same rule applies to the liturgy as applies to papal teaching. Just as not every word of the pope is infallible, but rather he is only infallible under certain conditions, so also not every liturgical rule is infallible per se. It will only be infallible in the event that

---

[40] Here we are summarizing the study of Dom Edouard Guillou, O.S.B., "Les oraisons de la nouvelle messe et l'esprit de la réforme liturgique," *Fideliter,* No. 86, March-April 1992, 58ff. It provides the complete text of these prayers and some complementary examples.

[41] Pope Paul VI, *DC,* No. 1538 (October 20, 1969), col. 1372.

[42] See, among others, Archbishop Bugnini's memoirs (*The Reform of the Liturgy, 1948-1975* [1983; The Liturgical Press, 1990], pp. 91-95) and the study by Michael Davies, *Liturgical Revolution,* Vol. III: *Pope Paul's New Mass* (1980; Angelus Press, 2009), pp. 533-37.

[43] Lists published in *Panorama,* No. 538 (August 10, 1976) and in Mino Pecorelli's *Osservatore Politico* (September 12, 1978). Note that the journalist Mino Pecorelli was himself a Freemason. He was shot to death a few months later (March 20, 1979). Cf. Professor Carlo-Alberto Agnoli's study, *La Maçonnerie à la conquête de l'Église* (Versailles: Publications du Courrier de Rome, 2001).

the ecclesiastical authority promulgates it with the full weight of his authority and invokes his infallibility.

- **Has it ever happened in the past that the Holy See published liturgical books that might favor error?**

Yes, it has happened (though exceptionally) that the Holy See published liturgical books favoring error.

- **Can you give an example?**

For a long time the Roman Pontifical contained a rubric recommending that, during an ordination to the priesthood, the bishop assure that the ordinand touch the chalice and the paten, since it was by his so doing that the sacerdotal character was conferred. This rubric was suppressed after the declaration of Pope Pius XII (*Sacramentum Ordinis*, 1947) clarifying that only the imposition of hands constitutes the essential matter of priestly ordination.

- **Can you provide another example?**

The Roman Pontifical of the thirteenth century contained an even more surprising error: it affirmed that the consecration of wine into the blood of Christ could be effected even without the words of consecration by mere contact of the wine with a consecrated host.

- **How can the presence of such errors in liturgical books approved by the Holy See be explained?**

These errors are possible because in approving these rubrics, the Holy See did not intend to give them the value of dogmatic definitions. That was clear to all. (Theologians were discussing the question of the matter of the sacrament of holy orders until the time of Pius XII; they did not consider the rubrics as sufficient to decide the question.)

- **What can we conclude from these examples?**

These examples clearly show that the Holy See does not always engage its infallibility in liturgical matters; in order to ascertain to what extent infallibility is engaged, one must carefully consider the nature, the essential content, the circumstances, and the degree of authority of official decisions.

- **Isn't it surprising that the Church does not always engage its infallibility in the liturgy?**

Even the Ecumenical Councils and pontifical documents are far from engaging infallibility in each of their parts, even when they have as a direct and primary end to teach doctrine. It is therefore logical that liturgical rites, which only teach indirectly, do not always engage it either.

● If the liturgy does not always engage infallibility, may one then freely criticize the Church's established liturgy?

Even though it does not always engage infallibility (and thus it can exceptionally contain errors), the liturgy established by the Church must be venerated and respected. It would be rash, scandalous, and offensive to pious ears to pretend to submit it in principle to one's particular judgment.[44]

● Must the discipline and liturgy established by the Holy See always be accepted, even when they do not engage infallibility?

As a general rule, yes, the discipline and liturgy established by the Holy See must always be accepted integrally (just as one must adhere to the whole of its teaching without limiting oneself to believing infallible dogmas). In case of an exceptional crisis, however, should one possess evidence that a non-infallible decision endangers one's faith, one may, and even *must,* resist it.

● It is then possible that a pope might require the promulgation of a liturgy dangerous to the faith?

The present situation unfortunately shows that, in a time of exceptional crisis, a pope might promulgate a liturgy which, without being properly heretical, is dangerous to the faith. Such a catastrophe is facilitated by the liberal mentality of the post-conciliar popes, who visibly shrink from exercising their infallibility. However, it is impossible for such a liturgy to be peacefully accepted by the whole Church (which would mean that the gates of hell had prevailed[45]). In fact, the detrimental character of the new liturgy was solemnly denounced at

---

[44] In the Bull *Auctorem Fidei*, Pope Pius VI condemned the Jansenist Synod of Pistoia (1786), which had declared that, in the discipline established and approved by the Church, it is necessary to distinguish "what is necessary or useful...from that which is useless or too burdensome..., but more so, from that which is even dangerous and harmful and leading to superstition and materialism." Pius VI declared this proposition "false, rash, scandalous..." (DS 2678, Dz. 1578).

[45] Pius VI, in the Constitution *Auctorem Fidei* (August 28, 1794), condemned the Jansenists, who spoke "as if the Church which is ruled by the Spirit of God could have established discipline which is not only useless and burdensome, but which is even dangerous and harmful..." (Dz. 1578). This text, which has neither the authority nor the precision of a dogmatic definition, shows very well that the ecclesiastical authorities enjoy a certain infallibility in disciplinary and liturgical matters, but does not indicate the conditions of its exercise nor its exact limits. While waiting for the Church to decide the matter, theologians are reduced to hypotheses on the matter.

Rome itself by cardinals (among whom, Cardinal Ottaviani, who had been the pro-prefect of the Holy Office, hence second in command in the Vatican, under three popes in succession); throughout the world, bishops, priests, and faithful publicly refused to celebrate it or associate with it.

- **Can one be sure that Paul VI's new liturgy does not engage papal infallibility?**

As regards the New Mass, Pope Paul VI himself declared that its rites can receive differing theological evaluations:

> ...no particular rite or rubric amounts in itself to a dogmatic definition. Such things are all subject to a theological evaluation, differing according to their context in the liturgy. They are all gestures and words related to a religious activity that is lived and living by reason of an inexpressible mystery, a divine presence, and that is carried out in diverse ways. Such religious activity is of a kind that only a theological critique can analyze and articulate in doctrinal formulas that satisfy logic.[46]

- **What should we conclude?**

The assertion that the New Mass is an object of the Church's infallibility cannot be sustained.

63) What should we think of celebrating Mass facing the people?

The purpose of celebrating Mass facing the people is to present it as a meal (the altar for such Masses generally takes the form of a table); the priest is in this case the one who is at the head of the table, and naturally he turns towards the people. But since the Mass is not essentially a meal, this practice should be rejected.

Moreover, celebration facing the people gives the impression of a purely worldly ceremony in which man is at the center. Prayer becomes more difficult, for this human face to face is not oriented towards the Lord (*ad Dominum*).

- **Is not the Mass facing the people a return to the usages of the early Church?**

It is in reality very doubtful that the Mass was said facing the people during Christian antiquity. But even were that the case, a return to

---

[46] Paul VI, Address to a general audience on the new Order of Mass about to be introduced, November 19, 1969: *AAS* 61 (1969), 777-780; English version: *Documents on the Liturgy, 1963-1979: Conciliar, Papal, and Curial Texts* (Collegeville, Minn.: The Liturgical Press, 1982), p. 539.

liturgical forms abandoned long ago would not be a good thing. Such an attitude goes against true tradition (which is attached to what has been *transmitted* [in Latin, *tradere*], and not to what has been discarded). It constitutes what Pius XII in his Encyclical *Mediator Dei* denounced as *archaeologism*, an "exaggerated and senseless antiquarianism."

● Did Pius XII elaborate on his condemnation of "archaeologism"?

Pius XII explained:

> The liturgy of early ages is worthy of veneration; but an ancient custom is not to be considered better, either in itself or in relation to later times and circumstances, just because it has the flavour of antiquity....The desire to restore everything indiscriminately to its ancient condition is neither wise nor praiseworthy. It would be wrong, for example, to want the altar restored to its ancient form of a table; to want black eliminated from liturgical colours, and pictures and statues eliminated from our churches; to require crucifixes that do not represent the bitter sufferings of the divine Redeemer.... (§66)
>
> ...Just as obviously unwise and mistaken is the zeal of one who in matters liturgical would go back to the rites and usage of antiquity, discarding the new patterns introduced by disposition of divine Providence to meet the changes of circumstances and situation. (§63)

It should also be added that the liturgical practices of antiquity are only imperfectly known. Those who pretend to be reverting to them run the risk of falling into many errors.

● Doesn't the orientation of the Roman basilicas prove beyond the shadow of a doubt that in the early Christian era Mass was celebrated facing the people?

On the contrary, it is quite likely that celebration facing the people never existed in antiquity. It is true that some basilicas give the impression that the priest celebrated Mass turned towards the people. In fact, he was turning towards the east and not the people. If the basilica were situated facing west, the priest would turn towards the east during the Canon because the rising sun was seen as a symbol of the risen Christ. The priest indeed had the people before him, but they also turned eastwards and so had the priest *behind* them. All prayed together *towards the Lord* (*ad Dominum*).

● Can it be said, then, that in Christian antiquity there was no celebration of Mass facing the people?

What is certain is that **1)** this was not the general rule, and **2)** if it ever happened, it was not done *with the intention* of putting the priest and the faithful face to face. The idea that the celebrant must face the people is of Lutheran origin; it does not appear earlier.

64) Is the New Mass valid?

The validity of the Mass depends on the validity of the consecration (transubstantiation of the bread into the Body of Christ and the wine into His Blood).

The New Mass is valid if it is celebrated by a *validly ordained* priest who uses the *required* matter (wheaten bread and wine) while pronouncing the required *words* (those of the consecration) and having the required *intention*. The priest must indeed desire to do what Christ and the Church do during the celebration of Mass (he must be a conscious instrument at their service). Were he to deliberately oppose the Church's intention (by refusing, for example, to celebrate a sacrifice or by not intending to commemorate the Last Supper), the Mass would be invalid.

Now, by the very fact that the new rite can easily be understood in a Protestant sense, it can also easily be used by priests who would no longer have the required intention for celebrating Mass. Such an eventuality is not in the least unlikely considering the totally false image of the Church, the priesthood, and the Mass that has been communicated to very many future priests in the new seminaries. Moreover, the use of any bread besides unleavened bread, or of any wine made of something else than the fruit of the vine, or the omission of the consecratory words would also render the Mass invalid.

- **Might not the fact that the words of the consecration were modified in the new missal cast some doubt upon the validity of the New Mass?**

This modification of the consecratory formula, which converges it with Lutheran worship, is regrettable, but is not sufficient to cast a doubt on the validity of the New Mass (the essential meaning of the words of consecration is conserved). On the other hand, some translations are problematic.

- **Might some translations of the words of consecration raise doubts about the validity of the New Mass?**

The problem arises from the fact that in several countries the words for consecrating the wine have been badly translated. The Latin text reads: "My Blood, which shall be shed for you and *for many* [*pro multis*]." The French adopted an ambiguous translation: "For you and for the multitude." But for the translation in many languages, notably English, a patently false translation was adopted: "My Blood, which shall be shed for you *and for all*." But this translation alters the meaning of the text. The words "for all" do not occur in the narratives of the institution of the holy Eucharist in Sacred Scripture, nor in the consecratory words of any traditional liturgy.

● But is it not true that Jesus Christ shed His blood for all men?

It is indeed true that Christ shed His blood for all and that for this reason it is possible for all to be saved (salvation is offered to all). But the Mass is about the new covenant ("For this is the chalice of My Blood, of the new and eternal testament"), and not all men belong to this covenant, but only many, namely, those who receive salvation. At Mass, what is involved is not the offer of salvation, but the actual gaining possession of it.

● Does this mistranslation have consequences?

Obviously, this mistranslation is linked to the modern theory of universal salvation (no one is damned). This bad translation, which is a factual error, thus favors a veritable heresy!

● Does this mistranslation render the Mass invalid?

It is not certain that this mistranslation renders the consecration invalid (particularly as the priest could understand the "for all" in a way that does not go against the faith, namely, that salvation is *offered* to all). But it renders this validity at least doubtful (especially if the priest understands the formula in the heretical sense: all men are saved).

● Doesn't this objection exaggerate the importance of a slight error in translation?

The translation is not the result of a slight error, but of a deliberate alteration to which the innovators themselves attach great importance. In Hungary, for example, there were still missals a few years ago with the translation "for many." After the fall of the Iron Curtain, new missals were published with the formula "for all." If the innovators go to so much trouble for a single word, it is because they think it is important.

● Are there other signs of the importance the innovators attach to the replacement of the phrase "for many" by "for all"?

One indication of the importance the innovators attach to this erroneous formulation is that, having tried to impose it by means of a bad translation, they stooped to falsifying the Latin itself. The Latin text of the New Mass still had the formula "*pro multis*" (for many). But this formula was replaced by "*pro omnibus*" (for all) in the *Latin* text of John Paul II's Encyclical *Ecclesia de Eucharistia* (April 17, 2003, §2), as it was disseminated by the Holy See's news services (and by the Vatican's Web site).

- **Surely such a falsification provoked an outcry?**

This falsification provoked such an outcry that, finally, the official version (the one published in the *Acta Apostolicæ Sedis*) was corrected and contains the phrase "*pro multis*."[47] But the episode remains significant. The partisans of universal salvation intend to bend the liturgy to their heresy. They already partially succeeded with the New Mass of 1969 (which suppressed or attenuated the mentions of hell), and they continue their efforts.

65) Is it permissible to take part in the New Mass?

Even if the New Mass is valid, it is displeasing to God inasmuch as it is ecumenical and protestantizing; moreover, it represents a danger to our faith in the holy sacrifice of the Mass. Thus it must be rejected. Whoever has understood the problem of the New Mass must no longer attend it because he would be deliberately endangering his faith, and at the same time would be encouraging others to do likewise by seeming to assent to the reforms.

- **How can a valid Mass be displeasing to God?**

Even the sacrilegious Mass an apostate priest might celebrate to mock Christ would be valid yet clearly offensive to God, and it would not be permissible to take part. Likewise, the Mass of a schismatic Byzantine-Rite priest (valid and celebrated according to a venerable rite) is displeasing to God inasmuch as it is celebrated in opposition to Rome and the one Church of Christ.

- **Surely one may attend a New Mass when it is devoutly and piously celebrated by a Catholic priest with an absolutely unquestionable faith?**

The celebrant is not at issue, but the rite he uses. It is, unfortunately, a fact that the new rite has given many Catholics a false idea of the Mass, one much closer to the Protestant supper than to the holy sacrifice. The New Mass is one of the main sources of the current crisis of faith. It is thus imperative to distance oneself from it.

---

[47] *AAS*, July 7, 2003, p. 434.

66) May one attend the New Mass in some circumstances?

One should apply rules analogous to those governing attendance at non-Catholic ceremonies to attendance at the New Mass. One may attend for family or professional reasons, but without actively participating; and, of course, one does not go to Communion.

67) What should be done when it is not possible to attend a traditional Mass every Sunday?

One for whom attendance at a traditional Mass is not possible is excused from the obligation to attend Mass that Sunday. The precept of hearing Mass on Sunday only applies to attendance at a true Catholic Mass. One must, however, in this case at least try to attend a traditional Mass at regular intervals. Moreover, even if one is dispensed from attending Mass (which is a commandment of the Church), one is not dispensed from the commandment of God ("Remember thou keep holy the Lord's Day"). Thus, the Mass one could not attend must be replaced by something; for example, by reading the text of the Mass in one's missal, by uniting one's attention for the duration of a Mass with a Mass celebrated elsewhere, and by making a spiritual communion.

68) How should Holy Communion be received?

Holy Communion must be received reverently, for it contains our Lord Jesus Christ, Body, Blood, Soul, and Divinity. The best way to express this reverence is to receive Holy Communion on the tongue from the hand of the priest while kneeling.

• Did Jesus Christ Himself state that He is really present in the Eucharist?

Yes, Jesus Christ solemnly affirmed His *Real* Presence in the Eucharist: "For my flesh is meat indeed: and my blood is drink indeed. He that eateth my flesh, and drinketh my blood, abideth in me, and I in him" (Jn. 6:56-57).

• Did our Lord express this truth other times?

Our Lord clearly expressed what the holy Eucharist is during its institution when He celebrated the first Mass during the Last Supper:

Jesus took bread, and blessed, and broke: and gave to his disciples, and said: Take ye, and eat. This is my body. And taking the chalice, he gave thanks, and gave to them, saying: Drink ye all of this. For this is my blood of the new testament, which shall be shed for many unto remission of sins. (Mt. 26:26-28)

● Who denied the Real Presence of Christ in the Blessed Sacrament?

For fifteen centuries, with a few very rare exceptions (for instance, the heretic Berengarius of Tours in the eleventh century, who ultimately abjured his error), Christians unanimously believed in the Real Presence of Christ in the Blessed Sacrament. They held this sacrament in great honor, considering it the Lord's most precious gift. It was only during the sixteenth century that the leaders of the Protestant revolt succeeded in dragging the multitudes into rejecting faith in the Blessed Sacrament.

69) Is Communion in the hand a worthy way to receive Holy Communion?

As it is practiced today, Communion in the hand does not respect our Lord Jesus Christ truly present in the host. It thwarts faith in the Real Presence, and so it must be rejected. Moreover, it has never existed in this form in the Church.

● Is not the distribution of Communion in the hand a practice of the early Church?

Holy Communion was indeed distributed in the hand in certain parts of the early Church, but quite differently from the way it is today. The communicant bowed to receive it and, at least in some places, had to have his hand veiled. The priest would place the host in the *right* hand, and the faithful carried it to his mouth without picking it up with his other hand.

● Do these differences of detail really matter?

These differences reveal a different attitude from that which prevails at present. The manner, widespread today, of taking the host resembles an act of taking possession or of domination, which is out of place in the reception of the Body of Christ.

- **Does this difference in attitude between the practice of the early Church and the current practice show up in any other way?**

The difference in attitude is revealed in the very great attention formerly given to particles of the hosts. St. Cyril of Jerusalem exhorted the faithful to take care lest the least particle fall on the ground: "Take care that nothing fall on the ground. What you would let fall would be as the loss of one of your members. Tell me: if someone gave you gold powder, wouldn't you gather it so carefully that none of it would be lost to your disadvantage? Should you not then be much more attentive that not a crumb be lost, which is much more precious than gold or diamonds?"[48]

- **What does St. Cyril's exhortation show?**

Everything about it exudes reverence! Where do we hear such warnings today? With Communion in the hand, many particles fall on the ground without anyone's noticing. It is an objective lack of respect for Christ.

- **But if Communion in the hand was practiced before in the Church, how can it be rejected now?**

This argument relies on one of the major sophisms of the liturgical revolution: the sophism of *archaeologism*, already denounced and condemned by Pius XII.[49]

- **How is this argument sophistical?**

This argument presupposes that what was good in Christian antiquity is necessarily better now and must be preferred to whatever the Church instituted over the course of centuries. This is obviously false. What was in the beginning without danger thanks to the early Christians' fervor and because there had not yet been any heresy against the Real Presence could become dangerous since the Protestants' denial of transubstantiation. Moreover, love is inventive, and progressive development is the law of life in creatures. So it is normal that the Church should have developed over time the expression of its faith in and reverence towards the Blessed Sacrament. The desire to revert to the (material) practices of the early Church in reality betrays its spirit, for it means refusing the development it carried within itself and to which it imparted the impetus.

---

[48] St. Cyril of Jerusalem, Fifth Mystagogical Catechesis, 21; *PG*, XXXIII, 1126.
[49] See above Question 63.

- **Might it not be said that the refusal of Communion in the hand today is tantamount to refusing the impetus and the progressive development which is natural to the Church?**

    A change can only be qualified as "progress" in relation to a set of criteria by which to evaluate it. (The anarchic proliferation of cells in a living organism marks a progress of a sort, but that of a cancer and not that of life.) The right criteria, in this instance, are these: the manifestation of faith and reverence towards our Lord. It is obvious that Communion in the hand does not constitute progress, but rather regression. Moreover, this practice was introduced in a revolutionary and subversive manner into the Church.

- **Why do you say that Communion in the hand was introduced in the Church in a revolutionary and subversive way?**

    Communion in the hand was first practiced without any authorization in a few very progressive groups against the explicit rules of the Church. On May 29, 1969, the Instruction *Memoriale Domini* took cognizance of this disobedience and reiterated in detail the advantages of Communion on the tongue. It reported that a survey of the Latin-Rite bishops showed that a very large majority of them were opposed to the introduction of Communion in the hand.[50] It concluded that the traditional usage was to be maintained, and vigorously exhorted the bishops, priests, and faithful to carefully respect the custom.

- **How did Communion in the hand spread after having been thus condemned?**

    Communion in the hand spread because this document (drafted in Paul VI's name by Cardinal Gut and the ubiquitous Annibale Bugnini) was liberal. Having expounded all the reasons necessitating retention of the traditional usage and having stated the Pope's desire to maintain it, it closed by allowing the contrary! Just when the question seemed to be settled by all that went before, the authors added that, in those places where the habit of giving Communion in the hand had already been formed (that is to say, where they had already been disobeying the Church's rules), the episcopal conferences could authorize this new practice under certain conditions if the faithful requested it.

---

[50] Of 2,115 valid responses, 1,233 bishops [more than 58 percent] were categorically against the introduction of Communion in the hand, while only 567 [fewer than 27 percent] approved it unconditionally.

- **What was the aftermath of the Instruction *Memoriale Domini*?**

The Instruction *Memoriale Domini* actually authorized Communion in the hand even as it made a pretense of forbidding it. In Western Europe and North America, the consequences were immediate: the new practice, which the Pope had only authorized with reservations and for the sake of toleration and because of the pressing demand of the faithful, was imposed almost everywhere on the faithful who had never asked for it *in the name of obedience to the Pope.*

70) What are the consequences of Communion in the hand?

Besides occasioning sacrileges, Communion in the hand (received standing) is at least partly responsible for the loss of faith of many Catholics in Christ's Real Presence in the Blessed Sacrament. One who seriously believes he receives the Man-God in Holy Communion cannot approach this Sacrament without showing his respect. Communion in the hand thus leads first to lukewarmness and indifference, and then to loss of faith.

- **Can loss of faith in the Real Presence of our Lord correctly be attributed to Communion in the hand?**

Communion in the hand is probably not the only cause. Errors or gaps in catechesis and preaching certainly share the blame since the Real Presence has often been presented as a symbolic presence, denying the actual change of the bread into the Body of Christ. But Communion in the hand prepared the faithful to accept these false teachings, for if the host is merely a symbol of Christ, it is not surprising that people receive Communion without any special sign of reverence.

71) Is it necessary to celebrate Mass in Latin?

Just as it is fitting to change out of one's work-clothes for an important ceremony, it is likewise most fitting that the language of sacred liturgy be different from that of everyday life. The vernacular is not apt for the sacred action. In the West, Latin has been the liturgical language for centuries. But in other parts of the Church, and even in numerous non-Christian religions, there is also a sacred language.

- **Do non-Catholics also use a sacred language?**

The establishment of a fixed liturgical language while the common language evolves seems to be a constant of mankind. The schismatic

Greeks employ ancient Greek in their liturgy; the Russians use Slavonic. At the time of Christ, the Jews already utilized ancient Hebrew for the liturgy, which was no longer the common language (and neither Jesus nor the Apostles criticized this). The same thing is found in Islam (literary Arabic, the language of prayer, is no longer understood by the multitudes) and some Oriental religions. The Roman pagans also had archaic formulations in their worship that had become incomprehensible.

- **How can this universal custom of the use of a sacred language for divine worship be explained?**

Man naturally has a sense of the sacred. He understands instinctively that divine worship does not depend on him, that he must respect it and transmit it as he has received it, without allowing anything to disrupt it. The use of a fixed, sacred language in religion is in conformity with human psychology as well as the immutable nature of divine realities.

72) Don't the faithful understand the Mass better when it is celebrated in their own language?

The Mass works ineffable mysteries that no man can perfectly understand. This mysterious character finds its expression in the use of a mysterious language that is not immediately understood by all. (It is for this reason that some parts of the Mass are recited in a low voice.)

The vernacular language, on the contrary, gives the superficial impression of a comprehension which in reality does not exist. People think they understand the Mass because it is celebrated in their mother tongue. In fact, they generally understand nothing of the essence of the holy sacrifice.

- **Is the function of Latin, then, to place a barrier between the faithful and the holy mysteries?**

The purpose is not to build an opaque wall that would conceal everything, but, rather, to better appreciate the perspectives; for that, a certain distance is necessary. In order to penetrate a little into the mystery of the Mass, the first condition is to humbly acknowledge that it involves a *mystery*, something that goes beyond us.

- **If the mysterious character of Latin is so beneficial, should the faithful be dissuaded from learning it, and those who do understand it be pitied?**

The use of Latin in the liturgy keeps up the sense of mystery even for those who know this language. The mere fact that it involves a special language, distinct from one's maternal tongue and common speech (a language which, of itself, is not immediately understood by all even if in fact it is understood), is enough to create a certain distance that fosters respect. The study of Christian Latin should be heartily encouraged. The effort it requires helps to lift up its students towards the mystery, whereas the liturgy in the vernacular tends to bring it down to the human level.

- **Doesn't the use of Latin risk leaving some of the faithful in ignorance of the sacred liturgy?**

The Council of Trent imposed upon priests the duty to preach often about the Mass and to explain its rites to the faithful. In addition, the faithful have missals in which the Latin prayers are translated, so they can have access to the beautiful prayers of the liturgy without the advantages of Latin being lost. Experience also proves that in Latin countries, the understanding of liturgical Latin (if not in all its details, then at least globally) is relatively easy for anyone who is interested. The demand it makes on their attention fosters the faithful's genuine participation in the liturgy: that of the mind and will; whereas the vernacular language, to the contrary, is likely to encourage laziness.

- **Doesn't the use of a sacred language in the liturgy introduce an arbitrary break between everyday life ("profane") and the spiritual life, while the role of Christians should be, on the contrary, to consecrate everything to God (even one's everyday language)?**

In order to keep the spirit of prayer in all our activities, we must sometimes break away from these activities to devote ourselves to prayer. The same applies here: sometimes using a sacred language in order to realize more deeply the transcendence of God will be an aid, and not an impediment, to continual prayer.

73) What other reasons militate in favor of using Latin in the liturgy?

Three more reasons militate in favor of using Latin: **1)** its immutability (or, at least, its very great stability); **2)** its almost bimillennial use in the liturgy; and **3)** the fact that it symbolizes and fosters Church unity.

● In what way is the immutability of Latin an advantage?

An immutable faith requires a proportionate linguistic instrument; namely, a language that is as immutable as possible and which can serve as a reference. Latin, which is no longer a modern language, no longer (or rarely) changes. In a modern language, on the contrary, words can rapidly undergo significant changes of meaning or tone (they can acquire a pejorative or derisive connotation which they formerly lacked). The usage of such a language can thus easily lead to errors or ambiguities, while the use of Latin preserves both the dignity and orthodoxy of the liturgy.[51]

● In what way is the nearly bimillennial use of the Latin language in the liturgy an advantage?

Used in the liturgy for nearly two thousand years, the Latin language has been, as it were, hallowed. It is a comfort to be able to pray with the same words that our ancestors and all the priests and monks have prayed for centuries. We feel concretely the continuity of the Church through time, and we unite our prayer with theirs. Time and eternity converge.

● How does Latin symbolize the unity of the Church?

Latin not only manifests the Church's unity in time, but also in space.[52] Favoring union with Rome (its usage kept Poland from the Slavic schism), it also unites all Christian nations with one another. Before the Council, the Roman-Rite Mass was celebrated everywhere in the same language. On five continents, the faithful would find the Mass as celebrated in their own parish. Today, this image of unity has been shattered. There is no longer any unity in the liturgy, neither in language nor in rites. This is true to such an extent that someone attending a Mass celebrated in an unfamiliar language has a hard time even distinguishing the principle parts of the Mass.

---

[51] "The use of the Latin language, customary in a considerable portion of the Church, is...an effective antidote for any corruption of doctrinal truth" (Pope Pius XII, *Mediator Dei*, §60).– "For immutable dogmas, an immutable language is necessary, which will guarantee that the formulation of these same dogmas will not be altered....The Protestants and all the enemies of the Catholic Church have always harshly reproached its use of Latin. They feel that the immobility of this breast-plate wonderfully defends against any alteration of the ancient Christian traditions whose testimony crushes them. They would like to shatter the form in order to strike the heart. Error willingly speaks a variable, changing language" (Msgr. De Segur).

[52] "The use of the Latin language, customary in a considerable portion of the Church, is a manifest and beautiful sign of unity..." (Pope Pius XII, *Mediator Dei*, §60).

● How might one sum up the utility of Latin?

Our Church is one, holy, catholic, and apostolic. The Latin language in its way contributes to each of these characteristics.[53] By its native genius (an imperial language), its hieratic character (a "dead" language), and, especially, the consecration it received, together with Hebrew and Greek, on the *titulum* of the Cross,[54] it perfectly serves the *holiness* of the liturgy; by its universal, supranational usage (it is no longer the language of any one people), it manifests *catholicity*; by its living link with the Rome of St. Peter and with so many of the Fathers and Doctors of the Church who were both the echo of the Apostles and the artisans of liturgical Latin (they forged not only its prayers, hymns, and responses, but Christian Latin itself, which is, in many aspects, a complete renewal of classical Latin), it is the guarantee of its *apostolicity*; by its official usage, lastly, which makes it the language of reference for the magisterium, canon law, and liturgy, it contributes efficaciously to the Church's triple *unity*: unity of faith, unity of government, and unity of worship.

---

[53] "For the Church, precisely because it embraces all nations and is destined to endure until the end of time, and because it totally excludes the simple faithful from its government, of its very nature requires a language which is universal, immutable, and non-vernacular" (Pope Pius XI, Apostolic Letter *Officiorum Omnium*, August 1, 1922).

[54] "And the writing was: Jesus of Nazareth, the King of the Jews....and it was written in Hebrew, in Greek, and in Latin" (Jn. 19:19-20).

VIII

THE CATHOLIC PRIESTHOOD

74) What is the Catholic priest?

The Catholic priest is the minister on earth of the great eternal priest, Jesus Christ, the only mediator (*pontiff*: bridge-builder) between God and men. By his sacerdotal ordination, he participates in His powers. He alone is able validly to celebrate the holy sacrifice of the Mass, to forgive sins, to bless and to consecrate. The priest is therefore not first and foremost the president of an assembly; he possesses faculties the simple faithful do not. For it was to the Apostles alone and not to all the disciples that Christ said: "Do this in memory of me" (Lk. 22:19).

- **Where is a definition of priesthood to be found?**

The Epistle to the Hebrews teaches: "For every high priest taken from among men is ordained for men in the things that appertain to God, that he may offer up gifts and sacrifices for sins" (Heb. 5:1).

- **What does this definition show?**

This definition shows that the priest is taken from among men and thus set apart to be consecrated to God; he is ordained for men and thus entrusted with a public function: the relations of the faithful with God; he is consecrated as one who offers sacrifice.

- **So the priest is essentially a mediator?**

Yes, the priest is essentially a *mediator*, an intermediary, between God and the faithful. (It is absurd to claim, as Luther did, that all the faithful are priests!)

• What is the priest's most important function?

The priest is above all the man of sacrifice, as the Epistle to the Hebrews says. Now, there is only one efficacious sacrifice in the New Testament: that of our Lord Jesus Christ, which the priest as minister may offer in His name by celebrating Mass. The priest is first of all the man of the Mass.

• Where is this truth expressed?

In the Ordination rite, the bishop says to the newly ordained priest when he gives him the chalice and the paten: "Receive the power to offer to God the sacrifice and to celebrate Mass for the living and the dead" (Roman Pontifical).

• Why so much insistence on the link between priest and sacrifice?

Since Vatican II, the Catholic priesthood has suffered a veritable identity crisis. Many priests no longer know *why* they were ordained. The crisis can only be overcome by insisting on the essential: the priest is separated from other men and ordained to render to God, by the sacrifice of the Mass, the worship due Him and to communicate to the faithful, by the sacraments, the fruits of this sacrifice—notably the forgiveness of sins.

How can the priest forgive sins? The power to forgive sins was given by Christ to the Apostles and their successors after His resurrection:

> Peace be to you. As the Father hath sent me, I also send you. When he had said this, he breathed on them; and he said to them: Receive ye the Holy Ghost. Whose sins you shall forgive, they are forgiven them; and whose sins you shall retain, they are retained. (Jn. 20:21-23)

• Who is attacking the Catholic priesthood today?

The Catholic priesthood is unfortunately being attacked within the very bosom of the Church, even by priests! One priest, a Father Pesch, wrote: "Many things that appear evident to us today were unknown to the first Christian communities. There was no pope, nor bishops, nor priests, nor major or minor orders. There was no link between the validity of the Mass or absolution and certain orders."[1]

---

[1] *Zur Zeit*, journal of the German Redemptorists, July-August 1980, p. 91.

● Are these attacks against the Catholic priesthood new?

There is nothing original about these heretical affirmations, for the Protestants said the same thing in the sixteenth century. The Council of Trent solemnly condemned their errors:

> If anyone says that order or sacred ordination is not truly and properly a sacrament instituted by Christ the Lord, or that it is some human contrivance, devised by men unskilled in ecclesiastical matters, or that it is only a certain rite for selecting ministers of the word of God and of the sacraments: let him be anathema.[2]
>
> If anyone says that in the Catholic Church a hierarchy has not been instituted by divine ordinance, which consists of the bishops, priests, and ministers: let him be anathema.[3]

● Is Vatican II at all to blame for the present crisis of the priesthood?

Vatican II contributed to the crisis of the priesthood by its exaggerated insistence upon the "common priesthood of the faithful."

● Is it untrue that by their baptism all Christians participate in the priesthood of Christ?

The expression "participate in the priesthood of Christ" can designate two very different things: **1)** *Benefitting* from the effects of this priesthood; being able to enter into Christ's sacrifice in order *to be offered* with Him and *to receive* the fruits of this sacrifice. This is chiefly a passive participation that does not require priesthood (in the proper sense of the word). **2)** *Exercising* this priesthood as minister; being really able *to offer* Christ's sacrifice and *to bestow* its fruits. This is *active* participation, that of the priest in the strict sense of the word.

● Is this distinction between active participation and passive participation of Christ's priesthood traditional?

St. Thomas Aquinas explains:

> The worship of God consists either in receiving Divine gifts, or in bestowing them on others. And for both these purposes some power is needed; for to bestow something on others, active power is necessary; and in order to receive, we need a passive power....But it is the sacrament of order that pertains to the sacramental agents: for it is by this sacrament that men are deputed to confer sacraments on others: while the sacrament of Baptism pertains to the recipients, since it confers on man the power to receive

---

[2] The Council of Trent, Session XXIII, Canon 3 (Dz. 963).
[3] *Ibid.*, Canon 6 (Dz. 966).

the other sacraments of the Church; whence it is called the "door of the sacraments."[4]

● But haven't the faithful some activity to exercise?

The faithful must actively prepare to unite themselves with Christ's sacrifice by working at their own self-sacrifice: thus they have an important *activity* to exercise,[5] but it is not the same as the priest's. They remain passive in relation to the essential act of Divine worship, which is the sacrifice of Christ: their own sacrifice is *assumed* by Christ's without having any influence over Him. The ordained priest as minister, however, really and actively offers Christ's sacrifice.

● But don't the faithful also offer the Divine Victim at Mass?

Our Lord is offered in the name of His Mystical Body; by offering themselves with Him and for the same intentions, the faithful participate in the offering He makes of Himself; in this sense it may be said that they also offer the Divine Victim. But in the proper sense of the word, only the priest, as Christ's minister, offers the sacrifice; he alone is the efficient (instrumental) cause. Pope Pius XII recalled these truths in the Encyclical *Mediator Dei* in 1947.

● May it be said that the faithful exercise a certain kind of priesthood?

In the strict sense, it is false that the faithful exercise a priesthood (the word *exercise* bespeaks an action, and the faithful benefit only passively from Christ's priesthood). Nonetheless, it is sometimes permissible to speak figuratively. We say, for example, that a brave man is "a lion," or that a Christian who leads an ascetic life is "a real monk"; it is a manner of speaking that is not false provided that it is understood for what it is: simply a manner of speaking, a metaphor, an image, and not an exact definition. The same is true of what is sometimes called "the priesthood of the faithful." Since every Christian is called to worship God and to make sacrifices (which must be inserted into that of Christ), we may say that, seen from this angle, he acts *as* a priest.

---

[4] *ST*, III, Q. 63, Arts. 2 & 6 (English Dominican Fathers' version, online at newadvent.org/summa).

[5] "I beseech you therefore, brethren, by the mercy of God, that you present your bodies a living sacrifice, holy, pleasing unto God, your reasonable service" (Rom. 12:1).

- **Hasn't the "priesthood of the faithful" some foundation in Sacred Scripture?**

The "priesthood of the faithful" has as foundation in Sacred Scripture a few texts which are precisely metaphors. Thus, St. Peter compares the Christians to living stones of a temple and to a "royal priesthood": these are expressive images, but images nonetheless as the context shows.[6]

- **How did Vatican II exaggerate the "common priesthood of the faithful"?**

Vatican II placed an exaggerated emphasis upon the "common priesthood of the faithful" in the very outline of its Dogmatic Constitution on the Church, *Lumen Gentium*. Before speaking of the hierarchy and of priesthood in the proper sense, the conciliar constitution treats of "the people of God" and its universal priesthood (Chapter 2). Only afterwards (Chapter 3), speaking of particular vocations and functions within the Church, does it treat of ministerial priesthood as a special form of the universal priesthood of which the laity (Chapter 4) would also be a particular form!

- **What does the order of presentation in *Lumen Gentium* signify?**

The "order" in *Lumen Gentium* is in reality a big disorder since priesthood strictly so-called is put on the same plane as priesthood metaphorically so-called, as if they were two species of the same genus. It clearly serves to muddle everything.

- **Has Vatican II's exaggerated emphasis on the "common priesthood of the faithful" any consequences?**

Vatican II's exaggerated emphasis on "the common priesthood of the faithful" was relayed far and wide by preaching and teaching, but also by the new Mass (1969), the new Code of Canon Law (1983), and the new Catechism (1993). Hence it has had tremendous consequences.

---

[6] "Be you also as living stones built up, a spiritual house, a holy priesthood, to offer up spiritual sacrifices, acceptable to God by Jesus Christ....But you are a chosen generation, a kingly priesthood, a holy nation, a purchased people: that you may declare his virtues, who hath called you out of darkness into his marvelous light" (I Pet. 2:5, 9). Similarly, St. John twice states in the Apocalypse that Jesus Christ has made us "a kingdom and priests to God" (Apoc. 1:6 and 5:10).

- **How did the new Mass emphasize the "common priesthood of the faithful"?**

One of the guiding ideas of the new Mass was precisely to show that the liturgy is an action of the whole People of God, and not just of the clergy. The "active participation" of the faithful had to be promoted. But this expression is ambiguous, as has been seen (the faithful ought to *actively dispose themselves to be united* to Christ's sacrifice, of which only the priest is the *minister*). In fact, instead of fostering the *spiritual* and supernatural participation of the faithful, the new liturgy insists on their outward participation, and entrusts them with functions formerly reserved to sacred ministers (the readings, *etc.*). The priest is more the delegate and leader of the assembly than the minister of our Lord Jesus Christ.

- **Does the new Catechism also promote this error?**

The new Catechism of the Catholic Church (1992) adopts the ideas of Vatican II. It also states: "In the celebration of the sacraments it is thus the whole assembly that is *leitourgos*, each according to his function" (§1144). Now, the word *leitourgos* is a Greek word, and in the Byzantine liturgy, it is only used in reference to bishops, priests, and deacons, and never the assembly.

- **Does the new Code of Canon Law also exaggerate the "common priesthood of the faithful"?**

The new Code of Canon Law (1983) was presented by John Paul II as "a great effort to translate this same doctrine, that is, the conciliar ecclesiology, into canonical language," especially "the doctrine, moreover, according to which all the members of the People of God, in the way suited to each of them, participate in the threefold office of Christ: priestly, prophetic and kingly."[7]

- **In the new Code, how is this emphasis on "the common priesthood of the faithful" translated in practice?**

The outline of the new Code (as also the outline of the Constitution *Lumen Gentium*) is very instructive. The traditional Code (1917), after

---

[7] John Paul II, Apostolic Constitution *Sacrae Disciplinae Leges* (January 25, 1983), promulgating the new Code of Canon Law. The Pope adds: "It could indeed be said that from this there is derived that character of complementarity which the Code presents in relation to the teaching of the Second Vatican Council, with particular reference to the two constitutions, the Dogmatic Constitution *Lumen gentium* and the Pastoral Constitution *Gaudium et spes*. Hence it follows that what constitutes the substantial 'novelty' of the Second Vatican Council, in line with the legislative tradition of the Church, especially in regard to ecclesiology, constitutes likewise the 'novelty' of the new Code."

a first book presenting the general norms, treated of persons in its second book. It was divided into three parts: Clerics, Religious, and the Laity. The new Code also devotes its first book to general norms, but it entitles its second book "The People of God." It treats first of all of the faithful in general, then of the hierarchy, and finally of religious.

• Does this change of outline really mark a change of doctrine?

The change of order in the new Code is explained by Canon 204 (which is the first canon of Book II):

> The Christian faithful are those who, inasmuch as they have been incorporated in Christ through baptism, have been constituted as the people of God. For this reason, made sharers in their own way in Christ's priestly, prophetic, and royal function, they are called to exercise the mission which God has entrusted to the Church to fulfill in the world, in accord with the condition proper to each.

• What does the definition given in Canon 204 show?

Like the Constitution *Lumen Gentium*, the new Code begins by affirming that *all* Christians are priests, albeit in diverse ways. The ministerial priesthood (proper to priests) would only be a special modality of the universal priesthood. Likewise, *all* Christians are presented as participating in the power of government ("royal function"), and the role of the hierarchy is only presented afterwards as a "service" rendered to the community.

• Is this new way of presenting things really opposed to Tradition?

It suffices to compare it with the teaching of St. Pius X:

> It follows that the Church is essentially an *unequal* society, that is, a society comprising two categories of persons, the Pastors and the flock, those who occupy a rank in the different degrees of the hierarchy and the multitude of the faithful. So distinct are these categories that with the pastoral body only rests the necessary right and authority for promoting the end of the society and directing all its members towards that end; the one duty of the multitude is to allow themselves to be led, and, like a docile flock, to follow the Pastors.[8]

• What are the consequences of this exaggerated insistence upon "the priesthood of the faithful"?

The exaggerated insistence upon "the priesthood of the faithful" obviously promotes a penury of priests. What young man would

---

[8] St. Pius X, Encyclical *Vehementer Nos* (February 11, 1906), §8.

embrace such a demanding vocation had he not a glimpse of its greatness?

75) Can the ministers of Protestant communities be likened to priests?

The "ministers of worship" of Protestant communities are not priests, but laymen. This holds true for Anglicans, too. These ministers of worship hence do not have the power to change bread and wine into the Body and Blood of Christ, nor to forgive sins.

● **Why do you say that Protestant ministers are not priests?**

The sacerdotal powers were conferred by the Apostles to their successors and so on to the bishops and priests of today. This is what is called the Apostolic succession. Once this succession is broken, as happened with the Protestants, these powers are lost.

● **How was the Apostolic succession interrupted amongst Protestants?**

The Apostolic succession was interrupted amongst Protestants because they ceased to believe in it (denying that orders was a sacrament instituted by our Lord Jesus Christ) and so ceased intending to transmit it. In fact, they abandoned the liturgical rites by which it was conferred.

● **Was the Apostolic succession also interrupted by the Anglicans?**

Some Anglicans today believe in the priesthood and claim that it has been preserved. However, the ritual adopted by Anglicanism during the 1550's considerably modified the rites of ordination to the point that they no longer expressed the specific grace they were supposed to confer. Such ordinations were thus invalid, and Rome denounced them as such at the time.

● **Didn't the Anglicans correct their ordination rite?**

Even supposing that these modifications were adequate, they nonetheless occurred too late, after the extinction of the hierarchy. *Nemo dat quod non habet*, as the adage says (no one can give what he does not have), and by that time the Anglicans were without the priesthood.

● **Is the Anglicans' lack of priesthood absolutely sure?**

The nullity of Anglican ordinations having been contested during the nineteenth century, Pope Leo XIII commanded an inquiry, which also concluded their invalidity. On September 13, 1896, he published the letter *Apostolicae Curae*, which definitively settled the question.[9]

● Are these truths under attack nowadays?

The reigning ecumenical climate in place since Vatican II has led to scandalous attacks on these elementary truths. In the spring of 1977, 124 clergymen of the Diocese of Rottenburg wrote a letter to their Protestant "colleagues" (men and women) of the Evangelical Church of Wurtemberg in which they recognized them as "ecclesiastics having the same powers and the same responsibility." It is clear that these "theologians" no longer had the Catholic conception of priesthood.

● What conception of priesthood did these clergymen of Rottenburg have?

The Rottenburg signatories declared:

> [The Church] abandoned a theory of sacrifice that might give the impression that Christ's sacrifice on the cross had to be offered anew or renewed for the sake of our reconciliation with God....At bottom, we think that today we have an intelligent practice of the Supper based upon Scripture, which could have existed before the Reformers.

● What does this declaration manifest?

We see the link uniting the priesthood to the holy sacrifice of the Mass: whoever abandons the sacrifice for the sake of the Protestant Supper can no longer have a correct idea of the priesthood, nor see any difference between Catholic "presidents" and Protestant pastors.

● Were the Rottenburg signatories sanctioned by the hierarchy?

The "theologians" of Rottenburg proclaimed the heresies indicated above. The bishop merely remarked that they had minimized Catholic doctrine, but took no corrective measures.[10]

● Who else has attacked these truths?

The scandal is even greater when these truths are attacked by the pope himself, but this is what Pope John Paul II did several times by exercising liturgical functions in the company of Protestant ministers

---

[9] Dz. 1963-66. At the time, some Anglican bishops tried to have themselves reordained by schismatic (but real) bishops in order to "recuperate" an Apostolic succession, which, by the very fact they sought to regain it, they recognized as having been lost. The general rule nonetheless remains that enounced by Leo XIII, and so we should consider every Anglican ordination *a priori* invalid without formal proof that it is otherwise in a particular case.

[10] See Rudolf Kraemer-Badoni, *Revolution in der Kirche: Lefebvre und Rom* (Munich: Herbig, 1980), p. 91.

clothed with priestly or episcopal garb. Memorably, on May 29, 1982, he gave a blessing at the same time as "Monsignor" Runcie, Anglican Archbishop of Canterbury, wearing his pontifical insignia. As for Cardinal Ratzinger, on February 3, 1998, at Hamburg, he presided at "ecumenical Vespers" together with a Protestant "bishop" wearing a stole.

76) Can a woman be ordained priest?

Only a baptized man can validly receive priestly ordination. This is clear from Holy Scripture, Tradition, and the Church's magisterium. Because the Church has no power over the essential conditions of the sacraments, it cannot authorize the ordination of women. Such an action would be invalid.

● How do we know that only men can be validly ordained priest?

It is an undeniable fact, established by Holy Scripture, that Christ called only men to be His apostles. The Church cannot alter this choice.

● Cannot the fact that Christ chose only men be explained by respect for the conventions of the time?

Jesus Christ, who is God and who founded a Church destined to last until the end of the world, could not let Himself be subject to the conventions of an age. In fact, He always showed Himself to be perfectly free in regard to social conventions and did not hesitate to contravene them on several occasions (concerning the Sabbath, the forgiveness of sins, the attitude towards public sinners, *etc.*). Had He wished to establish women apostles, nothing would have stopped Him. The single fact that the most Blessed Virgin Mary was never considered to be a "priest" suffices to prove that there cannot be priestesses in the Church founded by Jesus Christ.

● Does Holy Scripture explicitly forbid the establishment of "women priests."

St. Paul wrote to the Corinthians:

...as also I teach in all the churches of the saints. Let women keep silence in the churches: for it is not permitted them to speak, but to be subject, as also the law saith. But if they would learn any thing, let them ask their husbands at home. For it is a shame for a woman to speak in the church. Or did the word of God come out from you? Or came it only unto you? If any seem to be a prophet, or spiritual, let him know the things that I write to you, that they are the commandments of the Lord. (I Cor. 14:33-37)

Women, then, are not authorized to speak nor to officiate during religious ceremonies. St. Paul expressly justifies his exhortation by the general practice of the Church ("in all the churches of the saints"), by the law of the Old Testament ("as also the law saith"), by propriety ("it is a shame for a woman"), and above all by the commandment of the Lord.

- **What does the Church's Tradition have to say on the matter?**

There is a unanimous consensus in Church Tradition on this subject. Tertullian (d. ca. 220) wrote: "It is forbidden to women to speak in church. They do not have the right to preach, to baptize, to offer sacrifice, to seek a masculine office and even less the priestly service."[11]

- **Has there really never been ordination of women in the Church?**

When, during the fourth century, women were actually ordained in the sect of the Collyridians, St. Epiphanius (d. 403) reacted vigorously:

> In an illicit and blasphemous ceremony they ordain women and by them offer a sacrifice in the name of Mary. This means that this whole affair is blasphemous and impious; it is an alteration of the message of the Holy Ghost; in fact, the whole affair is diabolical and the work of the impure spirit....[12]
>
> Nowhere has a woman fulfilled the office of priest.[13]

Indeed, there have never been priestesses in the Catholic Church.

- **If not priestesses, were there deaconesses in the Church?**

Deaconesses, which existed for a certain time, did not fulfill the liturgical functions of a deacon; they were employed solely to perform the anointing with oil of women before baptism and to care for sick women. According to the Apostolic Constitutions: "A deaconess does not bless, nor perform anything belonging to the office of presbyters or deacons, but only is to keep the doors, and to minister to the presbyters in the baptizing of women, on account of decency."[14]

---

[11] Tertullian, *De Virginibus Velandis*, 9, 1.
[12] St. Epiphanius, *Adversus Haereses*, 78, 13, *PG* 42, 736.
[13] *Ibid.*, 79, 2, *PG* 42, 744.
[14] Apostolic Constitutions, VIII, xxviii, 6 [online at www.newadvent.org/fathers/].

- **Are there any recent documents on the impossibility of the ordination of women?**

Incorporating the teaching of different synods, the Code of Canon Law states the principle: "A baptized male (*vir*) alone receives sacred ordination validly."[15] In his Apostolic Letter *Ordinatio Sacerdotalis* of May 22, 1994, Pope John Paul II also restated the traditional doctrine:

> Wherefore, in order that all doubt may be removed regarding a matter of great importance, a matter which pertains to the Church's divine constitution itself, in virtue of my ministry of confirming the brethren (cf. Lk. 22:32) I declare that the Church has no authority whatsoever to confer priestly ordination on women and that this judgment is to be definitively held by all the Church's faithful.[16]

- **What is the authority of this teaching?**

Like all the popes after Vatican II, John Paul II was loath to engage his authority infallibly. Despite certain appearances, he did not do so here. He recalled the traditional doctrine, but by invoking the authority of the ordinary magisterium of the Church instead of personally exercising the charism of infallible teaching with which he was endowed as pope.

- **Is this teaching then fallible or infallible?**

The teaching of the Church on the impossibility of the ordination of women is indeed infallible, but its infallible character comes from the fact that this truth has always been the object of its ordinary magisterium and not from Pope John Paul II's document.[17]

77) What is the fundamental reason why women cannot be priests?

The fundamental reason why women cannot become priests is rooted in the order of creation. The relation between man and woman reflects the order of creation. Man is the symbol of God, and woman, that of creation. Consequently, woman by her very nature is not capable of being the authorized representative of God.

- **Isn't such a position discriminatory against women?**

It is not a question of establishing *a priori* principles (like discrimination or non-discrimination), but of observing reality and of acting in

---

[15] 1917 Code, Canon 968, 1 (1983 Code, Canon 1024).
[16] "On Reserving Priestly Ordination to Men Alone."
[17] On the ordinary and universal magisterium of the Church, see Question 19 of this catechism.

conformity with it. Only rank ideologues refuse to admit the differences that exist between the sexes.

● How do the differences between man and woman have a bearing on divine worship?

To the unbiased observer, it is clear that man has a more active, enterprising, and commanding nature. His part is to act upon the world and to transform it. That is why his role is to govern and direct society. Woman's nature, on the contrary, is more passive and receptive. Her domain is firstly the close circle of family and children; her lot is more to be directed than to direct. That is why St. Paul says: "The husband is the head of the wife" (Eph. 5:23). This is also why, in Sacred Scripture, God is represented with the traits of a man.

● God transcends the distinction of sex: He is in Himself neither male nor female. Could He not also be represented under the traits of a woman?

In fact, in Holy Scripture, God is represented with masculine traits. He is the Father and Spouse of the Chosen People. Praying "Our Mother," as is done in some places, goes against Revelation and blasphemously parodies the Gospel. All the religions that believe in a creator God conceive a masculine idea of Him, at least as regards the principal deity. Female deities are found, on the contrary, in pantheistic religions that discern no essential difference between God and the world. It is not by chance that, becoming incarnate, God became a man, and not a woman.

● Does the fact that Jesus Christ is man imply that priests must be men?

Since the fall of the first Adam, who, as head of the human race, dragged it down in his wake, Jesus Christ is the only mediator between God and men, the only Pontiff, the only High-Priest. The priests of the New Testament are only instruments He has chosen to continue His work, and whom He associates with His priesthood. From the fact that in order to be "the new Adam" the Word of God became incarnate in a male nature, only men can share in His priesthood.

● What does contemporary woman's clamoring to be ordained reveal?

The polemics surrounding the ordination of women reveals the false idea of priesthood that holds sway today. If the priest is considered to be merely a social leader presiding over the local assemblies of the People of God, consoling the afflicted and fostering the religious sentiment of the faithful, there seems to be no good reason why a woman could not fulfill this role. But a priest is something else entirely: an *alter Christus* (another Christ).

78) Can't the Church be accused of keeping women in a state of inferiority?

Women were kept in a state of inferiority in pagan societies. This is still the case today among the Jews and the Muslims. Christianity, on the contrary, has given woman her nobility: she enjoys the same dignity as man, of whom she is–especially in marriage–the companion and not the servant. But this recognition does not exclude that she is different from him and has other duties to fulfill.

- **But has it not been said that man symbolizes the Creator, and woman, the creature?**

Here it is a question, as the word indicates, of a simple symbol. By his nature, man is just as much a creature as woman and so must, like her, learn obedience and submission.

- **How did the Church render to woman her dignity?**

The Catholic Church honors woman beyond all measure in the person of Mary, virgin and Mother of God. She venerates her as the queen of all saints, elevated above every creature–apostles, bishops, popes, and even every rank of angels. The honor paid to Mary naturally overflowed to all women–in the measure that they resemble Mary.

- **In this vein, what in particular should be said about the honor paid to the Blessed Virgin?**

Mary's principal title of glory, the one that allows her to be honored above every creature, is specifically *feminine*: she is the *mother* of God (and, subsequently, the mother of all men in that they are called to be incorporated in her Son Jesus Christ). Unlike the "feminists," the Church exalts woman in that which specifies her feminine nature, and not by denying it. On the other hand, Mary is not a priest. Pope Innocent III wrote a letter on this subject to the Bishop of Burgos: "Though the Virgin Mary is above all the Apostles taken together, the Lord entrusted the keys of the kingdom of heaven to them, and not to her."[18]

---

[18] Decretal *Nova quaedam*, X.

- **What should be said about contemporary feminism?**

In its so-called "women's liberation," contemporary feminism in reality manifests the utmost contempt of womanhood since it tries to fit it to the masculine model rather than to develop properly feminine values. Indeed, woman then does find herself at a disadvantage: a woman will always make a poor man!

79) Why does the Church require priests to be celibate?

As another Christ, the priest must belong entirely to God and to our Lord Jesus Christ. Since he goes to the altar every day to offer the sacrifice of divine love, he must also offer his heart to God in an undivided love. An additional reason is that the priest must be at the disposition of all souls, as the father and brother of all, which would not be possible if he had to take care of his own family. The Catholic priest thus perfectly resembles Jesus Christ, who was not married either, and who lived entirely in the love of His Father and of immortal souls.

- **Are there other reasons why priests should be celibate?**

Our Lord, who was a virgin, desired that both St. Joseph and our Lady, with whom He lived for thirty years, be virgins; that His precursor, St. John the Baptist, be a virgin; that the disciple whom He loved, St. John, also be a virgin. From this the rule can be drawn that to draw close to our Lord one must be a virgin. Now, the priest is the minister of the Holy Eucharist.

- **Isn't celibacy a great sacrifice for the priest?**

Celibacy is undoubtedly a sacrifice, but sacrifice is the law of natural life (nothing can be chosen without, by the very fact, renouncing something else) and still more so of supernatural life and fruitfulness. Just as Christ redeemed the world by His passion, so also the priest will not be able to do very much for the Church and the salvation of souls unless he lives a life of sacrifice. Our age, so inclined to see in human love and sexuality the only joy of life, has for this very reason a great need of the example of priests and religious, who remind people of higher values and ideals.

80) Isn't celibacy an inhuman constraint against nature?

According to the teaching of the New Testament, celibacy lived for God is a lofty ideal. Christ said that in addition to those who are incapable of marrying, there are those who abstain from marriage for the kingdom of heaven (Mt. 19:12). "He that can take, let him take it."

- **Yet isn't marriage an image of the union between the soul and God?**

Marriage is an image of the love that should exist between God (or Christ) and the soul. But it is, precisely, only an image, and not the reality. That is why marriage is ended by death. In heaven there will be no more marriage (Mt. 22:30); then everyone will live in the love of God only, which for consecrated souls is already the only love. Celibacy is thus an anticipation of what life will be in eternity.

- **But doesn't marriage respond profoundly to the needs of human nature?**

Human nature also gives man understanding and free will which allow him to dominate his passions and sometimes to fight against them for the sake of a higher ideal. But man can (and often *must*) renounce the satisfaction of his sensible passions for a greater good. If he does not do so, he sinks to the level of the animal.

- **Why is the absolute celibacy of priests not found outside the Catholic Church?**

When young men renounce the happiness of founding a family so as to give themselves totally to God, they give a beautiful proof of the Church's vitality and of the enthusiasm the Faith can communicate. If the communities that separated from the Church abandoned celibacy very quickly, it is because they were unable to communicate this strength to their adherents.

81) Wouldn't the suppression of celibacy help remedy the shortage of priests?

The suppression of celibacy might lead in the short-term to an increase in the number of ordinations, but the problem would not thereby be resolved; one would have only capitulated before it. Many would be ordained who were not truly called by God, or who would not avail themselves sufficiently of the means to respond to His call. Rather, we should ask why there used to be enough men ready to make the sacrifice of celibacy, while this is no longer the case today.

- **Doesn't celibacy remain, nevertheless, a barrier?**

Celibacy is a very useful barrier to those who are not called. Without it, many men would tend towards the priesthood for futile reasons: a sure job enjoying a good reputation; a social promotion (this is the case in many Third World countries), *etc.* For the greater good of the Church and of the faithful, these people are kept far from the priesthood, at least for the most part, by the obligation of celibacy.

82) Is celibacy of apostolic origin?

Celibacy is of apostolic origin (this is at least very probable); it was consequently the rule in the Church from the start. In the beginning of the Church, married men could become priests and bishops, but they had to abstain from marriage after their ordination; if they could still live with their spouse, it was only as brother and sister.

• Doesn't St. Paul speak explicitly of the bishop's wife?

When St. Paul cites amongst the qualities required to become bishop or deacon the fact of being "the husband of one wife" (I Tim. 3:2; 3:12), this does not mean that deacons and bishops could continue to live in marriage after their ordination. It means rather that the fact of being remarried was considered as the sign of an inability to live in continence. One who still feels the need to remarry after the death of his first spouse does not seem to be able to live in celibacy. This prescription can have no other meaning, for if the churchman could continue to exercise the marriage right, a second marriage could not be an impediment to ordination.

• Did the Fathers of the Church address this question?

One Father of the Church, St. Epiphanius of Salamis (ca. 315–403), testifies: "Priests are chosen firstly from among virgin men, or else from among monks; but if persons apt to fulfill this service are not found among monks, priests are customarily chosen from among those who live in continence with their spouse or who, after one marriage, have become widowers."[19]

• Was this rule observed everywhere?

The same Father of the Church laments that this rule is not observed everywhere, and makes this comment: "In several places, priests, deacons and subdeacons are still begetting children. I answer that this is not in accordance with the rule, but it happens because of the heedlessness of men."[20]

---

[19] *Expositio Fidei,* 21; *PG* 42, 824.
[20] *Adversus Hæreses,* 54, 9; *PG* 41, 1024.

- **Don't the laws concerning ecclesiastical celibacy date from the fourth century?**

  The first *explicit* laws that we know of on the celibacy of clerics indeed were promulgated in the fourth century. It should be noted, however, that they were not presented as a novelty, but as a reminder of the ancient discipline. The Fathers of the African Council of 390 referred explicitly to the apostolic tradition when they taught anew the obligation of celibacy.[21]

- **Then why do some authors date priestly celibacy from the twelfth century?**

  The assertion that celibacy was an invention of the twelfth century contains only one element of truth: In 1139 the second Lateran Council decided that marriages contracted by clerics having already received major orders would no longer be only *illicit*, but henceforth also *invalid*. (Previously, the marriage of a priest or deacon was gravely sinful but nonetheless valid.)

83) Why are priests of the Catholic Eastern Rites allowed to be married?

The Church in the East, in a council held in the seventh century at Constantinople (the Council *in Trullo* of 691), made concessions to a widespread practice: It allowed priests to continue to live in a marriage concluded before their ordination. This Council kept the ancient discipline of celibacy for bishops only. Subsequently, this rule was then tolerated by popes for priests of the Eastern Churches who returned to unity with Rome.

- **The Oriental usage is then only a tolerance?**

  The Oriental usage is only a tolerance, and it marks a break with the primitive ideal. The Eastern-Rite Churches have, however, kept some vestiges of this ideal: The deacon or priest may continue to live in a marriage contracted *before* his ordination, but he cannot contract a marriage. If his wife dies, he must then observe celibacy. Most of the time, bishops are selected from among monks, for these are always celibate. Were a married man to become bishop, however, he would have to separate from his wife.

---

[21] See further the excellent book by Fr. Christian Cochini, S.J., *Origines apostoliques du célibat sacerdotal* (Paris-Namur: Lethielleux, 1981).

● What do the faithful think of these married priests?

The faithful of the Eastern Churches often consider married priests as inferior to priest-monks. They feel more or less that the celibate priest perfectly realizes the ideal of priesthood, and they prefer to go to confession to them.

IX

THE SACRAMENTS

84) What is a sacrament?

A sacrament is a visible sign instituted by Christ to give us His grace.

- **Why would Christ give grace by means of visible signs?**

   Jesus Christ linked the giving of (invisible) grace to visible signs because He took into account human nature. Everything man knows comes through his five senses. Man stands in need of perceptible, outward signs even for grasping and communicating spiritual realities.

- **Are the sacraments symbols of grace?**

   The sacraments are symbols, but not only symbols; for they really effect in the soul what they show by outward signs.

- **Can you give an example of this sacramental efficacy?**

   In baptism, the water poured on the forehead signifies that the soul is purified from sin. But at the same time, baptism effects this purification of the soul by giving it sanctifying grace. It makes of a person a child of God.

- **How many sacraments did Jesus Christ institute?**

   Jesus Christ instituted seven sacraments: baptism, confirmation, the holy Eucharist, penance, extreme unction, holy orders, and marriage.

85) Are the sacraments understood differently nowadays?

In modern catechesis the sacraments are rarely considered as efficient causes of grace. They are made to be signs that manifest redemption and the fact that we are once again pleasing to God. One no longer know for sure if they really transmit the grace of redemption or whether they merely recall what has already been worked in us. According to this conception, baptism, for example, does not have the effect of delivering us from original sin and making us children of God: It is only a sign that God has pardoned us our sins in Christ Jesus and is once again favorable towards us. Thus baptism is no longer necessary for transmitting the grace of redemption since all men are *already* saved (the theory of universal salvation).

- **Who were the first to deny the efficacy of the sacraments?**

The Protestants were the first to deny the efficacy of the sacraments. In general, they considered them to be means of expressing and fortifying faith only. The modernists, condemned by St. Pius X at the beginning of the twentieth century, upheld a similar theory. They considered the sacraments to be but an expression of faith and a means of sustaining it.

- **Do modern theologians also deny the efficacy of the sacraments?**

What Rahner says of the sacraments does not seem much different, although the language is more complicated:

> When the Church, faced with an existentially decisive human situation, totally commits herself by proclaiming herself the primordial sacrament and the principal and victorious answer of God for the world and for every man, this is what in Christian language we call the sacraments.[1]

Speaking of confession, the same Rahner writes:

> This word of pardon [of God in Jesus Christ] is again promised by the Church to everyone in a special manner each time someone—remaining a sinner even after baptism and capable of falling again into grave faults—confesses his great fault and misery to the Church before its representative; or else, in certain circumstances, brings them before God and his Christ in the collective confession of a community [here he is speaking of penance services]. When this word of divine pardon has been pronounced by an authorized representative of the Church after a baptized person's confes-

---

[1] Karl Rahner, *Grundkurs des Glaubens* (Freiburg: Herder, 1976), p. 398.

sion, this action of the word of God, which effects the pardon, we call the administration of the sacrament of penance.[2]

● What is notable in these passages of Rahner's?

Here it is especially a question of commitment and promise. God in Jesus Christ has made a commitment of Himself towards the world, and this promise is renewed towards men by the Church. Whether something is really worked in man is not said. Moreover, in the quotation above, a penance service and confession are essentially placed on the same level. Finally, it seems that the priest does not forgive sins as a representative of the Church, but of Christ in whose name he pronounces the word of pardon.

● Has Rahner developed these same ideas elsewhere?

Rahner is not always easy to understand, but the same ideas are always to be found. We read, for example, under the word "sacrament" in the lexicon *Sacramentum Mundi* (of which Rahner is co-author):

> [The sacraments] are the real personal and concrete symbols of the personal life which stems eternally from God the Father, gives itself to man by God's Word and Spirit and is to be accepted by man personally in the Church and responded to gratefully. It is an exchange "between" God and man "by means of" the sacraments. By virtue of the Christ-event, all being and life must be analysed and understood in the light of faith in this event. This leads to the theologically fundamental truth that all the reality of created being–"natural" and "supernatural"–is ipso facto constituted as coming from the Father through the Word of God and as ordained to the Father in the Holy Spirit. Since, therefore, it exists through the Word and in the Word, it is itself–by participation–word, and as such each creature "symbolizes" and "proclaims" both itself and others (persons and things) in various particular ways, ultimately symbolizing and proclaiming God himself....The Christ-event means the mystery of redemption, and this presupposes creation, the grace of original justice and sin, all within the horizon of salvation-history.[3]

● What does this passage mean?

Under the verbiage we find the idea that the sacraments are symbols by means of which men should recognize and experience that they are once again pleasing to God. As for knowing whether the sacraments really effect this return to grace with God is not specified. But it is rather doubtful since the sacraments are but intermediaries among others.

---

[2] *Ibid.*
[3] *Encyclopedia of Theology: The Concise* Sacramentum Mundi (New York: Seabury Press, 1975), pp. 1481-82.

86) Are the sacraments community celebrations?

Certainly, Christianity has a communitarian character. The Christians, members of the Mystical Body of Christ, are for this reason intimately united with one another. From the fact that the sacraments graft us into the Body of Christ and unite us ever more intimately with it, they also maintain communion among Christians. But the principal effect is firstly union with Christ, from which flows the union of Christians.

This order is often inverted nowadays. The sacraments are considered first of all as community celebrations that, as communitarian, favor the union of men with God. They will say, for instance, that the principal effect of baptism is the reception of the baptized into the parish community, which is false.

- **Are these new theories very widespread?**

We read these surprising words from the pen of Cardinal Ratzinger: "The concept of sacraments as the means of a grace that I receive like a supernatural medicine in order, as it were, to ensure only my own private eternal health is the supreme misunderstanding of what a sacrament truly is."[4]

- **In what is this sentence of [then] Cardinal Ratzinger surprising?**

This sentence is surprising because the sacraments are well and good supernatural remedies destined for our healing and spiritual health, even if it is not under this caricatured form. But mockery is always the easiest way to present something in a bad light when solid arguments are lacking.

- **Has Cardinal Ratzinger a false conception of the sacraments?**

Cardinal Ratzinger emphasizes the communitarian character of the sacraments, as the following quotations show:

> But union with him [God] is, accordingly, inseparable from and a consequence of our own unity....Grace is always the beginning of union. As a liturgical event, a sacrament is always the work of a community; it is, as it were, the Christian way of celebrating, the warranty of a joy that issues from the community and from the fullness of power that is vested in it.[5]

---

[4] Joseph Ratzinger, *Principles of Catholic Theology* (1982; Ignatius Press, 1987), p. 49.
[5] *Ibid.*, pp. 49-50, 51.

- **Are these passages questionable?**

The accent is falsely displaced, for the result is made the main element. The union of Christians with one another and the joy of faith and salvation, *etc.*, are the consequences and not the essence of the grace that unites souls to God.

87) May the Church suppress or add sacraments?

The seven sacraments were instituted by Jesus Christ Himself. The Church thus has no power either to suppress any of the seven or to add new ones. It is bound by the order of Christ.

- **Were sacraments suppressed or added after Vatican II?**

Without having been explicitly suppressed, one might say that the sacrament of confession is, in practice, moribund in many parts of the Church. Also, without presenting it explicitly as a sacrament, some people introduced into the Church the Pentecostal rite of the effusion of the Spirit (or the "baptism in the Spirit"), which is given by imposition of hands and strangely resembles an eighth sacrament.

- **Isn't the sacrament of penance administered in the form of penance services nowadays?**

The penance service which, in many places, pretends to replace confession is not identical to the sacrament. This ceremony does not have the power to remit sins, in particular mortal sins.

- **Why can't the collective absolutions given during penance services remit mortal sins?**

The Council of Trent solemnly defined that it is necessary to avow in detail mortal sins committed after baptism to be able to receive absolution for them, and that this obligation comes from God Himself (the Church thus cannot change it): "If anyone says that in the sacrament of penance it is not necessary by divine law for the remission of sins to confess each and all mortal sins...let him be anathema."[6]

- **Can't absolution ever be given collectively (without individual confession)?**

Collective absolution is only possible in cases of grave necessity. Those who receive it only receive the remission of their sins insofar

---

[6] Council of Trent, Session 14, Canon 7 (Dz. 917).

as they would be ready and willing to confess their sins to a priest individually if they could (and, for this reason, they remain bound to do so should they escape the danger that justified the collective absolution).

- **What are the cases of grave necessity justifying collective absolution?**

The cases of grave necessity justifying collective absolution mainly involve imminent danger of death (onboard a sinking ship, for example, or on a battlefield). During World War II, taking into account the upheavals of the time (deportation or prisoners without access to priests), the Sacred Penitentiary allowed the giving of collective absolution to crowds who, without it being their fault, risked otherwise going for a long time (and hence dying) without the sacraments.[7]

- **Aren't present-day penance services simply an extension of this permission given in 1944?**

Collective absolutions can only be valid in the case of grave and urgent necessity in which individual confession is really impossible. Only necessity can, in effect, dispense a divine commandment. It is glaringly obvious that contemporary penance services do not come under the state of necessity. In the note of March 25, 1944, mentioned above, the Sacred Penitentiary moreover recalled the teaching already given by Innocent XI in 1679: even a great crowd of faithful (during a feast, for example) is not sufficient cause for giving absolution to penitents who had not confessed individually, nor even to those half of whom had confessed.[8]

- **Whence comes this necessity of confessing one's sins to obtain their pardon?**

To prevent men from treating sin lightly and to enable them to receive appropriate counsel, our Lord Jesus Christ established priests as judges and physicians of souls (Jn. 20:22-23). To obtain absolution, it is necessary to come and manifest to them the state of one's soul.[9]

---

[7] Note of the Sacred Penitentiary of March 25, 1944, *AAS*, 1944, p. 156.
[8] Decree of March 2, 1679 (Dz. 1209).
[9] St. Thomas Aquinas, Supple. Q. 6, Art. 1.

- **Aren't the penance services at least able to forgive venial sins, while those who have committed mortal sins could be invited to confess them individually to a priest?**

Such an invitation to confess especially serious sins in private would necessarily have a discouraging effect. After such an announcement, who would still have the courage to go and kneel in a confessional, thereby displaying in the eyes of everyone that he had committed particularly heavy faults?

- **What are the consequences of these new penance services?**

One may well fear that numerous Catholics stay in a state of mortal sin and run the risk of being eternally lost.

- **Whence comes this general disaffection for confession?**

The general disaffection for confession comes in large part from the fact that today Catholics no longer have a sense of sin.

- **Why do Catholics not have a sense of sin any more?**

Catholics no longer have a sense of sin because quite often their priests and bishops no longer have it themselves. Instead of denouncing the gravity of offenses against God, preaching penance, and encouraging flight from dangerous occasions, they reduce everything to a human level (only offenses against human dignity count), neglect Divine justice, minimize the consequences of sin, and forget the necessity of making reparation.

- **Can you give an example of the way in which some priests and bishops destroy the sense of sin?**

During a meeting of the Deanery Council at Wangen, in the Allgäu (October 17, 1983), Canon Hubert Bour gave a conference on the theme "Sin and Forgiveness." He asserted notably: "The notion of mortal sin has been greatly abused; mere bagatelles have been made into mortal sins. Mortal sin is not the normal case. To a question about the frequency of mortal sin, a well-known theologian answered that perhaps one a day was committed in Paris and one from time to time in our diocese."[10]

- **Is the sacrament of penance expressly attacked?**

In the same conference, Canon Bour declared that the call to penance and conversion did not play a "central role" in Jesus' teaching; that Jesus did not "expressly institute the sacrament of penance,

---

[10] Report on the Meeting of the Deanery Council of Wangen of November 22, 1983.

even if two passages of the New Testament led to that belief"; that the passage of St. John's Gospel traditionally understood as instituting the sacrament of penance ("Whose sins you shall forgive they are forgiven them..."–Jn. 20:23) referred rather to baptism.

- **What is the Church's teaching on these points?**

   Here are the condemnations levied by the Council of Trent:

   Can. 1. If anyone says that in the Catholic Church penance is not truly and properly a sacrament instituted by Christ our Lord to reconcile the faithful, as often as they fall into sin after baptism: let him be anathema.

   Can. 2. If anyone, confusing the sacraments, says that baptism itself is the sacrament of penance, as though these two sacraments are not distinct, and that therefore penance is not rightly called "a second plank after shipwreck": let him be anathema.

   Can. 3. If anyone says that those words of the Lord Savior: "Receive ye the Holy Ghost; whose sins you shall forgive, they are forgiven them; and whose sins ye shall retain, they are retained" [Jn. 20:22 ff.], are not to be understood of the power of remitting and retaining sins in the sacrament of penance...: let him be anathema.

- **What is the rite known as "the baptism in the Spirit"?**

   The rite of "baptism in the Spirit"[11] was originally the distinctive mark of a Protestant sect called the Pentecostalists. It is a laying on of hands for the purpose of giving a palpable experience of the Holy Spirit and a participation of the charismatic gifts of the first Christians, especially speaking in tongues.

- **What is the origin of this Pentecostal rite?**

   Pentecostalism was born during the night of December 31, 1900, to January 1, 1901, in Topeka, Kansas.[12] In the hope of regaining the charisms of the Apostles (especially speaking in tongues), the Methodist pastor Charles Parham (1873-1929) laid hands on a girl named Agnes Ozman.[13] She immediately began to speak an unknown language, which a Czech recognized the next day as his mother tongue. The experience continued on the following days, and Pastor

---

[11] The Pentecostalists cite the words of John the Baptist: "I have baptized you with water; but he shall baptize you with the Holy Ghost" (Mk. 1:8). But in reality St. John the Baptist was speaking here of the *sacrament* of baptism that our Lord was going to institute and which, as distinct from St. John's baptism–a baptism of repentance–was to give the Holy Spirit. The difference between these two baptisms is clearly stated in the Acts of the Apostles (19:3-6).

[12] It was also in the United States that spiritualism was born, in 1847, when the Fox family girls in the village of Hyderville (in New York State) tried to make contact with the poltergeist that haunted their house. Ten years later, spiritualism counted more than ten million adepts.

[13] Agnes Ozman had requested this laying on of hands herself based on the Acts of the Apostles (8:17-19; 9:17; 19:6).

Parham set out to preach his discovery. Arrested later on a morals charge (he was accused of sodomy), Pastor Parham was eclipsed by some of his disciples, like William Seymour (1873-1929).[14]

- **How did the new Pentecostal rite spread?**

The "Pentecostalists" were at first rejected even by the Protestants (they were called "shakers" because of their contortions or "rollers" because some of them rolled on the ground during their services). They established their own chapels and organized themselves in very restricted groups. It was only during the 1930's in Europe, and in the 1950's in the United States, that their rite was taken outside of strictly Pentecostal churches to penetrate all Christian denominations. Pastor David du Plessis (1905-87) was the main architect of this "ecumenical" propagation of "the baptism in the Spirit." At the end of the twentieth century, there were about 100 million Pentecostalists worldwide.

- **Are there precedents for the Pentecostal phenomenon?**

The rite properly called "baptism in the Spirit" is new, but heretical sects have regularly experienced analogous phenomena throughout history. At the end of the seventeenth century, a wave of illuminism shook the Protestant Camisards of the South of France: people claimed they felt the Holy Spirit, they spoke in tongues and wept copiously. The same eccentricities occurred in 1731, at Paris, in the St-Médard Cemetery on the tomb of a Jansenist deacon: frenetic convulsions gripped entire crowds, ecstasies, speaking in unknown languages, "prophecies," *etc.*

- **How can this type of phenomena be explained?**

These strange phenomena can partly be explained by natural causes (uncontrolled nervousness, morbid psychic exaltation, hallucinations), but it is likely that the devil often intervenes. The first sign of diabolical possession indicated by the traditional Ritual for exorcisms is the person's speaking in languages never before studied.[15]

---

[14] Bothered by the personality of Charles Parham, who was a member of the Ku Klux Klan, some Pentecostalists today prefer to trace their movement to Seymour's preaching in Los Angeles, April 9, 1906. That evening, the audience received the "baptism in the Spirit" and began to speak in tongues, to laugh, to cry, to sing, to clap their hands and stamp their feet so vehemently that the old house where they were meeting collapsed. Another Pentecostal illumination (analogous to the first, but independent) occurred in Great Britain in 1904 and considerably influenced French Protestantism. But "Catholic" charismatism, even in France, is linked to American Pentecostalism. See Arnaud de Lassus, *Le Renouveau charismatique aujourd'hui*, Supplement to *Action Familiale et Scolaire*, No. 162, pp. 48, 61-65, 135.

[15] *Rituale Romanum*, tit. XI, c. 1, §3: "*Signa autem obsidentis dæmonis sunt : ignota lingua loqui pluribus verbis....*"

- **Can people who call on the name of Christ with such fervor really be manipulated by the devil?**

  Our Lord Himself said:

  > Beware of false prophets....Not every one that saith to me, Lord, Lord, shall enter into the kingdom of heaven: but he that doth the will of my Father who is in heaven, he shall enter into the kingdom of heaven. Many will say to me in that day: Lord, Lord, have not we prophesied in thy name and cast out devils in thy name and done many miracles in thy name? And then will I profess unto them: I never knew you. Depart from me, you that work iniquity. (Mt. 7:15, 21-23)

- **How did the Pentecostal rite penetrate into the Catholic Church?**

  The Pentecostal rite of baptism in the Spirit was spread in the Catholic Church by so-called Catholic "charismatics." The "Charismatic Renewal" can be defined as "the Catholic branch of the Pentecostal current."[16]

- **What is the origin of "Catholic" charismatism?**

  "Catholic" charismatism was born in the United States in Pittsburgh, Pennsylvania, on February 20, 1967, the day on which two Catholic students at Duquesne University received the laying on of hands in a prayer group led by a Protestant minister and began to speak in tongues. They then used the same rite to transmit to other Catholics the powers thus received. On February 18, 1972, an engineer returning to France from the United States transmitted the baptism in the Spirit to Pierre Goursat, who founded the Emmanuel Community (the main French charismatic community) in 1973.[17]

- **What was the effect of the Pentecostal rite on the first Catholics who received it?**

  The laying on of hands produced the same effects in the Catholic students of Duquesne University as it did in Protestants. One of them recounted: "I was so joyful that all I could do was laugh as I lay on the floor." Another testified: "The sense of the presence and love of God was so strong that I can remember staying sitting in the chapel for a half hour just laughing out of joy over the love of God." And a

---

[16] This is the definition given by the journal *Tychique* (review of the Charismatic community "Chemin Neuf" [New Pathway] in its July 1984 issue (No. 50).

[17] The founders of other French Charismatic communities received the "baptism in the Spirit" either directly from Protestants (Gérard Croissant, called "Brother Ephraim," founder of the Community of the Beatitudes), or through the intermediary of American Charismatics (Laurent Fabre, founder of New Pathway, received it from an American Jesuit.)

third: "When hands were laid upon me, immediately it felt as if my whole chest were trying to rise into my head. My lips started trembling, and my brain started turning flips. Then I started grinning; I couldn't help it."[18]

● What do these reactions show?

These unseemly reactions reveal diabolical intervention. Whereas the Holy Ghost makes order and discretion reign, the evil spirit, even when disguised as an angel of light, generally betrays himself by some grotesquery.[19]

● Can the devil then inflame souls with the love of God?

The devil cannot inflame souls with the love of God, but he can *give this impression* to those who desire too strongly to *feel* the action of grace:

> [T]he devil hath power to feign some false light or sounds, sweet smells in their noses, wonderful tastes in their mouths, and many quaint heats and burnings in their bodily breasts or in their bowels, in their backs and in their reins and in their members.
>
> And yet in this fantasy they think that they have a restful contemplation of their God without any hindrance of vain thoughts; and surely so have they in a manner, for they be so filled with falsehood that vanity cannot disturb them. And why? Because he, that same fiend that would minister vain thoughts to them if they were in a good way–he, that same, is the chief worker in this work. And know thou right well that he would not hinder himself. The thought of God will he not put from them, for fear that he should be held suspect.[20]

---

[18] Testimonies quoted in the work by Kevin and Dorothy Ranaghan, *Catholic Pentecostals* (Paramus, N.J.: Paulist Press, 1969), pp. 28, 64, 67.

[19] The fouteenth-century English mystic who wrote *The Cloud of Unknowing* (one of the basic texts of Carthusian novices) wrote:

> Many wonderful gestures follow them that be deceived in this false work. Some be evermore smiling and laughing at every other word that they speak, as they were giddy girls or silly jesting jugglers lacking behaviour. Better far were a modest countenance, with sober and demure bearing of body and honest mirth in manner.
>
> I say not that all these unseemly gestures be great sins in themselves, nor yet that all those that do them be great sinners themselves. But I say that if these unseemly and disordered gestures be governors of that man that doth them, insomuch that he cannot leave them when he will: I say then that they be *tokens*....And this is the only reason why I set so many of these deceits here in this writing: for why, that a ghostly worker shall prove his work by them. [English version: tr. Father Augustine Baker, O.S.B. (London: Burns, Oates and Washbourne, 1924), Ch. 53.]

[20] *The Cloud of Unknowing*, Chapter 52. The same author explains:

> They conceive a false heat wrought by the fiend, their ghostly enemy, caused by their pride and their fleshliness and curiosity of wit. And yet, peradventure, they ween that it is the fire of love gotten and kindled by the grace and the goodness of the Holy Ghost....This deceit of false feeling, and of false knowing following thereon, hath diverse and wonderful variations, according to the diversity of states and the subtle conditions of them that be deceived. (Ch. 45)

- **Are similar warnings to be found in the writings of the saints?**

  St. Vincent Ferrer, in his *Treatise on the Spiritual Life*, teaches:

  > The first remedy against the spiritual temptations which the devil plants in the hearts of many persons in these unhappy times, is to have no desire to procure by prayer, meditation, or any other good work, what are called revelations, or spiritual experiences, beyond what happens in the ordinary course of things; such a desire of things which surpass the common order can have no other root or foundation but pride, presumption, a vain curiosity in what regards the things of God, and, in short, an exceedingly weak faith. It is to punish this evil desire that God abandons the soul, and permits it to fall into the illusions and temptations of the devil, who seduces it, and represents to it false visions and delusive revelations. Here we have the source of most of the spiritual temptations that prevail at the present time; temptations which the spirit of evil roots in the souls of those who may be called the precursors of Antichrist....[21]

- **Does this passage of St. Vincent apply to Pentecostalism and Charismatism?**

  It was precisely so that she could "speak in tongues" that Agnes Ozman asked Pastor Parham to lay hands on her. It was also to benefit from these extraordinary "charisms" manifested by the Pentecostals that the Catholics at Duquesne asked for the same laying on of hands.

- **Doesn't the Charismatic Renewal accomplish some good, bringing back to the practice of Catholicism a certain number of souls and nurturing the piety of others?**

  The devil in his perspicacity knows how to lose a few to gain many. This is the teaching of Blessed Marie of the Incarnation:

  > Ecstasies, visions, and revelations are not a sure argument for the presence or assistance of God in a soul. How many have we seen who have been deceived by these sorts of visions? Even though they were the cause of the conversion or even the salvation of a few souls, it is nonetheless a strategy of the evil Spirit, who is content to lose a few to gain many.[22]

---

[21] St. Vincent Ferrer, "Treatise on the Spiritual Life," in Rev. Fr. Andrew Pradel, O.P., *Saint Vincent Ferrer of the Order of Preachers: His Life, Spiritual Teaching, and Practical Devotion*, tr. from the French by the Rev. Fr. T. A. Dixon, O.P. (London: R. Washbourne, 1875), p. 181 [available online through Google/books].

[22] Blessed Marie of the Incarnation (Madame Acarie), quoted by Lassus, *Le renouveau charismatique aujourd'hui*, p. 154. Blessed Jordan of Saxony (1190-1236) had to exorcise a certain Brother Bernard. Possessed by the devil, he preached in such a penetrating manner, with such a touching accent, such a pious air, and such profound words that he brought everyone who heard him to tears. Once the possession was discovered, however, he switched tone and pronounced only obscenities. When the Blessed asked him "Where are your beautiful speeches?" he answered: "Since my ruse has been discovered, I want to show myself as I am." (Jordan of Saxony, O.P., *Libellus de principiis ordinis praedicatorum*, §110-119.)

● What advantage can the devil find in these displays of piety?

Pentecostalism not only revived and revitalized a moribund Protestantism, which risked leaving the Catholic Church an open field, but today it is allowing him to progressively take hold of Latin America[23]; the devil finds obvious advantages. Likewise, "Catholic" Charismatism perpetuates within the bosom of the Church the errors that are destroying it.

● Isn't the Charismatic movement against the post-conciliar desacralization of the Church?

It is precisely because it reacts against certain excesses that the Charismatic movement attracts Catholics troubled by the crisis, but only to bring them round to the conciliar errors! (in the same way that Pentecostalism brought back to Protestantism those who fled its excessive rigidity in droves).

● Can you provide an example?

The Emmanuel Catholic Charismatic Community has reintroduced in many places adoration of the Blessed Sacrament, the Rosary, confession, *etc*. These "conservative" devotions have rallied very many disoriented Catholics. But this conservatism merely serves to conserve...the conciliar novelties! Who would deny that the sentimental scenes that the Charismatics know how to stage so well are the principal crutch still holding up the new liturgy?

● What is the link between Vatican II and the Charismatic movement?

Vatican II is fully responsible for the introduction of the Pentecostal rite within Catholicism. Not only because John XXIII desired a "new Pentecost,"[24] or because the Pentecostal pastor David du Plessis—who had worked so effectively to infiltrate the "baptism in the Spirit" into all the Protestant confessions—was invited to the Council as an observer (he was influential in introducing several passages on the charisms into the conciliar documents)[25] but it was especially the Vatican II decree on

---

[23] See above, Question 1.
[24] John XXIII, Apostolic Constitution *Humane Salutis* officially convening the Second Vatican Council (December 25,1961).
[25] The Constitution *Lumen Gentium* (on the Church), §12:
It is not only through the sacraments and the ministries of the Church that the Holy Spirit sanctifies and leads the people of God and enriches it with virtues, but, "allotting his gifts to everyone according as He wills," He distributes special graces among the faithful of every rank. By these gifts He makes them fit and ready to undertake the various tasks and offices which contribute toward the renewal and building up of the Church, according to the words of the Apostle: "The manifestation of the Spirit is given to everyone for profit." These

ecumenism, *Unitatis Redintegratio*, that led the Catholics of Duquesne University to receive "the baptism in the Spirit."

● How could this decree lead Catholics to "the baptism in the Spirit"?

Speaking about the communities separated from the Catholic Church, the Decree *Unitatis Redintegratio* states that "the Spirit of Christ has not refrained from using them as means of salvation."[26] It also says that "whatever is wrought by the grace of the Holy Spirit in the hearts of our separated brethren can contribute to our own edification."[27] These passages convinced the Catholics of Duquesne University to ask the Protestants for the imposition of hands on February 20, 1967.[28]

● How does Charismatism promote the errors of Vatican II?

Like Vatican II, the Charismatic movement contributes to the upholding of a false ecumenism (Charismatism springs from ecumenism), to the confusion of the orders of nature and grace in every domain, to the weakening of the hierarchical authority willed by God, and to the forgetting of the ascetical side of the spiritual life.

● How does Charismatism contribute to confusing nature and grace?

The desire to *feel* the action of grace (inherently intangible) is to expose oneself to the danger of confusing faith and religious sentiment (as the modernists do[29]), as well as divine inspiration and imagination, the theological virtue of hope and optimism, the life of grace and psychological well-being. Psychology, as it so happens, occupies an important place in Charismatic communities.[30]

---

charisms, whether they be the more outstanding or the more simple and widely diffused, are to be received with thanksgiving and consolation for they are perfectly suited to and useful for the needs of the Church.

[26] The Decree *Unitatis Redintegratio* (on Ecumenism), §3, in *The Documents of Vatican II*, Walter M. Abbott, S.J., editor (New York: The America Press, 1966), p. 346. See above Question 47.

[27] *Ibid.*, §4, p. 349.

[28] "As Catholics, they had been reassured by the Council, which had stated: 'Whatever is wrought by the grace of the Holy Spirit in the hearts of our separated brethren can contribute to our own edification.' After studying the matter, they decided to ask a group of Pentecostalists to pray for them and over them." Mario Panciera in *Présence Chrétienne*, No. 12 (April 1989), cited in the *Courrier de Rome* (*SiSiNoNo*), No. 111 (February 1990), p. 2.

[29] The confusion between faith and the religious sentiment is the fundamental error of modernism condemned by St. Pius X. See above, Question 11.

[30] The members of the Well of Jacob community conduct P.H.R. sessions (Personality and Human Relations) in the spirit of the American psychologist Carl Rogers, who played an important role in the elaboration of the techniques of group dynamics (Lassus, *Le renouveau*

● What can be said, in the last analysis, about the rite of the baptism in the Spirit?

The Charismatics themselves do not quite know how to explain the rite of the baptism in the Spirit. It cannot be a sacrament since Jesus Christ instituted only seven. Thus they see it as a means of conversion, a reactivation of the sacraments of baptism and confirmation, or else a religious experience. But none of these explanations can account for the *efficacy* of a rite that seems to act of itself like a sacrament.

● Can the baptism in the Spirit really be compared to a sacrament?

By linking spiritual effects to a specific rite, the baptism in the Spirit resembles the sacraments. But the latter transmit a grace that is not sensible (they leave us in the order of faith), while the other rite claims to make the action of God felt. Thus it can be defined as a caricature of a sacrament that transmits, not the grace of God, but a perceptible illusion of this grace. We know that the devil has the power to create this illusion in those who seek to experience physically the divine action.

● Should the Charismatics be considered as possessed by the devil?

Those who receive the baptism in the Spirit are not for that reason possessed by the devil, nor even necessarily guilty of mortal sin (because of a certain ignorance of what they are doing). But they open themselves nonetheless to a diabolical influence that establishes them in an illusion, risks falsifying their spiritual life and blinding them to the crisis in the Church and to their own personal duty. Some give up the Christian life when, years later, the mirages vanish.

● Should the healings and prodigies worked by Charismatics be attributed to the devil?

The devil cannot work miracles strictly speaking (which manifest an absolute power over nature), but he can produce prodigies (which use the laws of nature ingeniously). Undeniable miracles are not to be found among the Charismatics. They themselves acknowledge that a good number of healings that happen during their gatherings do not

---

charismatique, pp. 69-70). The New Pathway community, which recruits heavily among health professionals, proposes a medicine integrated with spirituality. The Beatitudes community is also heavily involved in psychotherapy. It is paradoxical that to perpetuate itself a movement that identifies itself as "charismatic" should need to specialize in human psychology, which the charisms of the Holy Spirit, on the contrary, should be able to move effortlessly and alone.

last.[31] Besides, these outpourings in unknown languages during some Charismatic meetings have been identified as blasphemies by people knowing the languages who happen to be present.

88) Can the Church change the rite of the sacraments?

The Church cannot touch the essential part of the sacraments (that is, that which is absolutely necessary for their validity). It can modify the accidental rites, but this must be done for the purpose of more clearly expressing the essence of the sacraments and of facilitating their worthy reception.

• Why can't the Church touch the essential part of the sacraments?

Pius XII explained:

For these Sacraments instituted by Christ Our Lord, the Church in the course of the centuries never substituted other Sacraments, nor could she do so, since, as the Council of Trent teaches (Conc. Trid., Sess. VII, can. 1, *De Sacram, in genere*), the seven Sacraments of the New Law were all instituted by Jesus Christ Our Lord, and the Church has no power over "the substance of the Sacraments," that is, over those things which, as is proved from the sources of divine revelation, Christ the Lord Himself established to be kept as sacramental signs.[32]

• For what purpose may the Church modify accidental rites?

The Council of Trent declares:

This power has always been in the Church, that in the administration of the sacraments, preserving their substance, she may determine or change whatever she may judge to be more expedient for the benefit of those who receive them or for the veneration of the sacraments, according to the variety of circumstances, times, and places.[33]

---

[31] One of them explained it thus: "We sometimes see someone begin to be cured but then relapse several days later; that person preferred being sick and helped by others to a healthy autonomy, or else refused to make the efforts to persevere and progress towards complete health, physical, psychic, or spiritual." (Yves Jehanno, *L'Enjeu du renouveau charismatique* [Paris: Fayard, 1988], p. 93.) It could not be more clearly shown that it is a question not of miracles but of simple prodigies (which help nature to produce an effect, but do not have power over it).
[32] Pius XII, *Sacramentum Ordinis*, §1.
[33] Council of Trent, Session XXI, cap. 2; Dz. 931.

• What are the sacraments the rites of which have been changed since Vatican II?

All the sacraments were changed following Vatican II. There are a new rite of Ordination (1968),[34] a new Mass (1969),[35] a new rite of Baptism (1969),[36] a new rite of Marriage (1969),[37] a new rite of Confirmation (1971),[38] a new rite of Extreme Unction (1972),[39] and a new rite of Penance (1973),[40] as indeed there are a new Breviary (1970),[41] a new calendar (1969),[42] new holy oils (1970),[43] a new Code of Canon Law (1983),[44] a new Way of the Cross (1991),[45] a new Catechism (1992),[46] a new rite of Exorcism (1998),[47] a new Martyrology (2001),[48] and a new Rosary (2002),[49] not to mention the "new Evangelization"[50] or, in France, the new Our Father, the new Creed (the expression "consubstantial with the Father" was replaced by "of the same nature as the Father"),[51] the new "Rejoice, O Virgin Mary," *etc*. Vatican II has made all things new, as if to found a new religion.

---

[34] Apostolic Constitution *Pontificalis Romani* of June 18, 1968. The forms of priestly ordination and episcopal consecration were modified.
[35] The *Novus Ordo Missae* was promulgated April 3, 1969.
[36] May 15, 1969; *AAS*, LXI, 548. For the baptism of adults, January 6, 1972; *AAS*, LXIV, 252.
[37] March 1969. But a new rite of marriage was also published in 1990 by John Paul II.
[38] Apostolic Constitution *Divinae Consortium Naturae* of August 15, 1971; Decree of August 22, 1971, *AAS*, LXIV, 77.
[39] Apostolic Constitution of November 30, 1972; Decree of December 7, 1972, *AAS*, LXV, 275.
[40] Decree of December 2, 1973, *AAS*, LXVI, 172.
[41] Apostolic Constitution *Laudis Canticum*, November 1, 1970; Decree of April 11, 1971, *AAS*, LXIII, 712.
[42] Motu Proprio *Mysterii Paschalis* of February 14, 1969.
[43] Decree of December 3, 1970, *AAS*, LXIII, 711.
[44] Apostolic Constitution *Sacrae Disciplinae Leges* of January 25, 1983.
[45] Inaugurated by John Paul II in 1991, this new Way of the Cross has fifteen Stations instead of fourteen, several of which were changed. It was used for the Jubilee in the year 2000.
[46] Apostolic Constitution *Fidei Depositum* of October 11, 1992.
[47] See *DC*, No. 2198, pp. 159-160.
[48] Published on June 29, 2001, this new Martyrology includes the names of 6,538 saints and blessed, of whom 1,717 (almost a third) were proclaimed such by John Paul II himself.
[49] Encyclical *Rosarium Virginis Mariae* of October 16, 2002.
[50] Launching the "new Evangelization" on March 3, 1983 (in an address to the Latin American Episcopal Council), John Paul II explained that it should be *new* not only in its fervor, but also "in its methods and expression" (*DC*, No. 1850 (1983), 438). The World Youth Days are a typical instance of this "new Evangelization."
[51] In July 1965, the philosopher Etienne Gilson published in the *France Catholique* an article provocatively titled "Am I Schismatic?" in which he challenged this bad translation. The article created a stir, but nothing was changed. He returned to the subject in 1967:
> The new Symbol fails to affirm the unity of the Trinity. It does not deny it, certainly, but neither does it teach it, and by imposing this omission on the faithful it prevents them from continuing to profess it as they had always done since the Council of Nicaea. For if the Son is of the same nature as the Father, He is God like Him, but if He is not of the same substance or of the same being as the Father, He might be a second God, just as the Holy Ghost might be a third....For [Judaism and Islam], Christianity is polytheistic. Until now the Christian could deny the accusation, since the three divine persons are but one and the same God; he can no longer do so if he is French, for if the three persons have in common their nature

89) Do the new rites better express the substance of the sacraments?

Far from making the sacramental action more readily understandable and facilitating its worthy reception, the new rites do the opposite: they relativize the truths of faith, make commonplace the sacred mysteries, and weaken the respect due to the sacraments.

- **Do the deficiencies of the new rites affect all the sacraments?**

The deficiencies of the new rites affect not only all the sacraments (more or less), but also other ceremonies such as funerals and exorcisms (which are not sacraments, but sacramentals).[52] So as not to be over long in our discussion, we shall limit our examination to four examples: the new rites of baptism, extreme unction, exorcism, and burial.[53]

- **What modifications were made by the new ritual of baptism?**

The new rite minimizes those elements that call to mind the supernatural effects of the sacrament; it suppresses several of the preparatory ceremonies, notably the triple exorcism that authoritatively wrests the candidate from the influence of the devil.

- **Why does baptism need preparatory ceremonies?**

"Whoever purposes to do a work wisely, first removes the obstacles to his work; hence it is written (Jeremiah 4:3): 'Break up anew your fallow ground and sow not upon thorns.'"[54] Great transformations require great preparations. That is why the catechumens of the first centuries were not only instructed in the Creed, but also subjected to a period of probation, examinations, and a series of rites and exorcisms

---

only and not their substance or being, each of them is God like the other two. Just as a father and son are two men of the same nature, the Father and the Son are two Gods....The object of the Symbol is not to make the mystery understandable, it is to define it. It is not defined by saying that the Son is of the same nature as the Father, for this is true of every son. What would be an unfathomable mystery would be a son who was not of the same nature as his father. By affirming that they are, nothing is being said.... (Etienne Gilson, *La société de masse et sa culture* [Paris: Vrin, 1967], pp. 128-129)

[52] Unlike the *sacraments* (instituted by our Lord Jesus Christ), the *sacramentals* have been instituted by the Church. They do not cause grace directly themselves, but they favor its reception.

[53] For an examination of the Holy Eucharist (attacked by Communion in the hand, the reduction of marks of adoration, the shortening of the Eucharistic fast, *etc.*), see Chapter 7 on the New Mass.

[54] St. Thomas Aquinas, *ST*, III, Q. 71, Art. 2.

over the course of their advancement.[55] All of that was incorporated into the traditional ritual of baptism.[56]

- ### Are the preparatory ceremonies of baptism effective in themselves or do they merely signify what the baptism properly does?

Several of the preparatory ceremonies of baptism, especially the exorcisms, are efficacious in themselves, distinct from baptism properly so called. Thus, says St. Thomas, they ought to be administered to those who were baptized in haste and therefore could not receive them.[57]

- ### What is the specific effect of the preparatory ceremonies of baptism?

The preparatory ceremonies remove the obstacles to receiving the full effects of baptism: an external obstacle—the devil, who possesses a certain power over nature; and an internal obstacle—the resistance offered to the realities of salvation by a disordered sensibility (the senses are, as it were, closed to the supernatural).[58]

- ### What ceremonies remove these obstacles?

The exsufflation (with the command: "Depart from him, unclean spirit, and give place to the Holy Ghost, the Consoler") and the two other solemn exorcisms, which command the devil not only to go out of but to depart from the baptized person to be, effectively remove the evil spirits.[59] The imposition of salt (on the tongue), of saliva (on the nostrils and ears—the *"Ephpheta"*), the imposition of hands (on the head), and the signs of the cross (on the forehead and breast) contribute to making the person receptive to the mysteries of salvation.

---

[55] Cf. Dom Bernard Marechaux, O.S.B., *Le baptême*.

[56] This is precisely what the innovators sought to destroy: Annibale Bugnini boasted that "for the first time in the history of Catholic liturgy," a rite for the baptism of infants had been prepared that was not "an abridged form of adult baptism" (*DC* 1544 [1969], 676). It was a matter of applying the conciliar constitution on the liturgy, which requested that the rite for the baptism of infants be adapted "to circumstance that those to be baptized are, in fact, infants" (*Sacrosanctum Concilium*, §67).

[57] *ST*, III, Q. 71, Art. 3.

[58] *Ibid.*

[59] The anointing (done *before* the baptism on the breast and between the shoulders with the oil of catechumens) is also a ceremony for fight. The catechumen is anointed in the manner of boxers in order to be prepared for the fight against the devil (whereas the anointing made on the head *after* the baptism with the holy chrism expresses the consecration of the Christian: "christ" = *anointed*). See St. Thomas, *ST*, III, Q. 66, Art. 10, ad 2. In the new ritual, the anointing of catechumens is no longer made between the shoulders but on the breast only.

- **What ceremonies did the new ritual of baptism suppress?**

In the new ritual, the priest does not wear the violet stole to meet the candidate at the church door. It omits the exsufflation, the two additional exorcisms, and the blessing of the salt. It no longer renews the gesture of the Lord in healing the deaf-mute with His saliva and telling him "*Ephpheta.*"

- **What does the priest's wearing of a violet stole at the entrance of the church signify?**

This welcome manifests that the unbaptized cannot enter the house of God without being purified of his sins. But in our age of ecumenism and universal salvation, no one wants to hear of this.

- **What does the blessing of the salt signify?**

The salt, symbol of wisdom, is to protect our nature from the corruption of sin, while at the same time imparting a taste of the supernatural realities. But this symbolism demands the spirit of faith. The innovators have thus eliminated it.

- **What does the *Ephpheta* accompanying the imposition of saliva signify?**

Ephpheta means "Be opened." This ceremony helps to perceive "the good odor of Jesus Christ" and to open the ears of the soul to the teaching of the faith (teaching that comes from hearing, says St. Paul,[60] that is, by an exterior teaching). But for the modernists, the truths of faith, on the contrary, come from the depths of the consciousness.

- **What other changes did the rite of baptism undergo in the new ritual?**

Instead of addressing the future baptized through the godparents, (N., what do you ask of the Church of God?; N., do you renounce Satan?; N., do you wish to be baptized?), the new ritual addresses the questions to the parents (What do you ask for N. of the Church of God?).

- **Isn't this manner of speaking to the parents more in conformity with reality?**

Though the newborn makes no act of his own will in receiving baptism, the orientation of his will is changed by the sacrament. His soul acquires the moral dispositions of someone who would have

---

[60] *Fides ex auditu* (Rom. 10:17).

voluntarily turned away from sin to adhere to Jesus Christ. In this sense, everything the godparents say in his name is realized in the infant's soul (just as it had really contracted the state of someone who had turned away from God yet without personally committing the act of original sin). This is the mysterious and supernatural change that the Church manifests by having the godparents speak in the baptized person's name. The new ritual abandons this profoundly supernatural vision for a purely superficial one.

- **Can you give a last example of changes made to the rite of baptism?**

In the traditional rite the priest makes the sign of the cross on the child's forehead and breast, saying: "Receive the mark of the cross on your + forehead and within your + heart. Embrace the faith with its divine teachings. So live that you will indeed be a temple of God." In the new rite, the sign of the cross is made on the forehead only, and the priest declaims: "N., the Christian community welcomes you with great joy. In its name, I mark you with the cross which is the sign of the Christ, our Savior. And you, parents, will mark him after me with the same sign."

- **What does this last example show?**

This last example shows the same tendency to weaken the expression of the supernatural realities the sacrament produces in the soul to emphasize the superficial aspects of the ceremony (here: the joy of the community welcoming a new member).

- **Was the rite of extreme unction also altered?**

In the traditional rite of extreme unction, the five senses are anointed by the priest, who at the same time prays that God deign to forgive the sins committed by these senses: "Through this holy unction and of His most tender mercy, may the Lord pardon thee whatsoever sins thou hast committed by sight [hearing, speech, *etc.*]." This symbolic action was ruined in the new rite.

- **How does the new rite of extreme unction spoil this symbolism?**

In the new rite, only the forehead and hands are anointed; the sacramental words only mention sin in general.

- **What other changes were made to extreme unction in the new Ritual?**

    The new Ritual also tends to make of extreme unction a group celebration. There are directions for the "common celebration of extreme unction for a large assembly."

- **Is this communal celebration of extreme unction blameworthy?**

    Such communal celebrations encourage the administering of this sacrament without distinction between the healthy and the sick during gatherings of the elderly, whereas only someone seriously sick can validly receive the sacrament.

- **What can be said of the new exorcisms?**

    The reformed Rite of Exorcism was first published provisionally [*ad interim*] in 1990, then definitively in 1998. It was one of the last areas affected by the liturgical reform.

- **Why did the innovators tackle exorcisms so late?**

    The innovators tackled exorcism so late because it was the least of their concerns (in general, the devil's influence is minimized or passed over in silence throughout the new liturgy). The German episcopate even declared that it was pointless to publish a new Ritual of exorcisms since henceforth exorcisms shouldn't be performed at all![61]

- **Are the new exorcism prayers bad?**

    Fr. Gabriel Amorth, the chief exorcist of the Diocese of Rome and honorary president of the International Association of Exorcists, frankly accused the new exorcism prayers of being ineffectual: "Efficacious prayers, prayers that had been in existence for twelve centuries, were suppressed and replaced by new ineffective prayers....We exorcists have all tried out the new prayers in the New Ritual *ad interim* and we have come to realize that they are absolutely ineffectual."

- **How can the ineffectiveness of the new exorcism prayers be explained?**

    Fr. Amorth stated that "this influence [of "the world beyond"] has had a hand in many of the liturgical reforms." He also denounced the incompetence of the two commissions that drafted the new Ritual: "None of the members of these commissions had ever performed an

---

[61] A fact reported by Fr. Gabriel Amorth, interviewed in *30 Days,* June 2000 (posted online at www.freerepublic.com/focus/f-religion/1320032/posts). The subsequent statements by Fr. Amorth are quoted from this interview.

exorcism, had ever been present at an exorcism and ever possessed the slightest idea of what an exorcism is. Here lies the error, the original sin of this Ritual. Not one of those who collaborated on it was an exorcism specialist."

● Isn't it excessive to accuse the authors of the new Ritual of incompetence?

Fr. Amorth proves their incompetence by the facts: "Point 15 treats of evil spells and how one should behave when dealing with them.... The Roman Ritual used to explain how one should confront it. The New Ritual on the other hand categorically declares that it is absolutely forbidden to perform exorcisms in such cases. Absurd. Evil spells are by far the most frequent causes of possessions and evil procured through the demon: at least 90 percent of cases. It is as good as telling exorcists they can no longer perform exorcisms."

● Are there other facts proving this incompetence?

Fr. Amorth continued: "Point 16 solemnly declares that one should not carry out exorcisms if one is not certain of the presence of the devil. This is a masterstroke of incompetence: the certainty that the devil is present in someone can only be obtained by carrying out an exorcism."

● Did the exorcists' protests have any result?

The exorcists' protests obtained one thing only: the insertion of a Notification from the Congregation for Divine Worship stating that exorcists are not obliged to use the new Ritual and that, should they wish to do so, they may ask their bishop for authorization to use the old one. In this case, the bishop must in turn ask for authorization from the Congregation which, as the Notification states, "willingly accords it."

● Are there similar deficiencies to be found in the new Ritual for Exorcists?

Fr. Amorth reported, concerning the new Benedictionary[62]: "I have read its 1,200 pages minutely. Well! any reference to the fact the Lord must protect us against Satan, that the angels protect us from the attacks of the demon, has been systematically suppressed. All the prayers for the blessing of homes and schools have been suppressed. Everything should be blessed and protected, but today there is no longer any protection against the demon. There no longer exists any defense or any prayers against him."

---

[62] Promulgated on May 31, 1984, *AAS*, LXXVI, 1085-1086.

- **What are the consequences of these modifications and suppressions?**

The consequences of these changes are visible everywhere: the influence of the devil is making itself felt more and more in our societies.

- **What can be said, very briefly, about the new funeral rite?**

The new funeral rite no longer says anything about the soul, the gravity of judgment, the possibility of damnation or purgatory. It gives the impression that the deceased is assuredly saved and already with God.

- **Does the new funeral rite leave out the existence of sin?**

Like all the other new rites, the funeral rite leaves much latitude in the choice of prayers; the celebrant may make mention of sin and guilt, or he may omit it. As for the word "soul," it no longer appears in any prayer. During an era when the existence of the human soul is often denied, its mention would be, to the contrary, quite necessary.

90) Are the sacraments celebrated according to the new rites valid?

The sacraments administered according to the new rites can in principle be valid. However, a doubt exists about the validity of confirmation and extreme unction administered without olive oil. In a certain number of other cases, bad translations of the sacramental form can also cause doubts about the validity of the sacraments.

- **Why must confirmation and extreme unction be administered with olive oil?**

Just as the word wine in the primary meaning of the term designates the fermented juice of grapes—even if it is employed secondarily to designate wine from palm, rice, *etc.*—so the word oil (*oleum*) in Antiquity designated in first place, in the proper sense, the liquid obtained from the pressing of olives. Thus, just as only wine from grapes and bread from wheat constitute the valid matter of the Eucharist, likewise olive oil is the valid matter of confirmation and extreme unction. Such was the traditional and common opinion of theologians.[63]

---

[63] Concerning extreme unction, St. Thomas Aquinas teaches: "On the contrary, oil is appointed (James 5:14) as the matter of this sacrament. Now, properly speaking, oil is none but olive oil. Therefore this is the matter of this sacrament."(Suppl., Q. 29, Art. 4).

● Is this opinion based solely upon a philological reason?

This opinion is not based primarily on philology, but on the fact that, just as Christ used wheaten bread and grape wine during the Last Supper, so also the anointings that He recommended to the Apostles could only be anointings with olive oil. It would never have occurred to the Apostles to use anything else than oil taken in the proper sense—in the noble sense of the term. The use of another kind of oil renders the validity of the sacrament at least doubtful.

● Are there other arguments in favor of olive oil?

It may be observed that on the same Holy Thursday on which He instituted the priesthood—the day also when He took bread and wine to institute the Eucharist—our Lord watered the Garden of Olives with His sweat and blood in proximity to an olive press as if to sanctify the matter of which the holy oils would be made. In fact, it is also on Holy Thursday each year that the bishops consecrate the holy oils during the chrismal Mass.

● When and how did the use in the sacraments of oils other than olive oil originate?

On December 3, 1970, a decree of the Congregation of Rites authorized the utilization of other vegetable oils in the administration of the sacraments.[64]

● How did the Congregation of Rites explain this change?

The Congregation of Rites offered no explanation of how something that had always been considered as probably invalid had suddenly become possible.

● Was there, then, no explanation forthcoming for this change of oil?

No doctrinal explanation for this change was given. The decree only invoked a practical reason, which Paul VI adopted two years later in the Apostolic Constitution *Sacram Unctionem Infirmorum*:

> ...since olive oil, which hitherto had been prescribed for the valid administration of the sacrament, is unobtainable or difficult to obtain in some parts of the world, we decreed, at the request of numerous bishops, that in the future, according to the circumstances, oil of another sort could

---

[64] *Ordo Benedicendi Olea et Conficiendi Chrisma*, nos. 3-4. The 1983 Code of Canon Law (Can. 847) says: "In administering the sacraments in which holy oils must be used, the minister must use oils pressed from olives or other plants and, ...consecrated or blessed recently by a bishop...."

also be used, provided it were obtained from plants, inasmuch as this more closely resembles the matter indicated in Holy Scripture.[65]

● Doesn't this explanation resolve the question?

This practical explanation tends rather to increase the problem, for it is evident that it has never been as easy as today to obtain olive oil in every corner of the globe.[66] Now, if till the present, in spite of much greater transportation difficulties, the Church always refused to change the matter of the sacrament, it is because she had good reasons.

● Isn't the change in the form of certain sacraments —for example, the new form for consecrating bishops—a reason for doubting their validity?

Some have argued that the change in the formula for episcopal consecration invalidated new consecrations from 1968 on. But in reality, the new Ritual uses a form close to that of certain Eastern Rites. Thus its validity cannot be seriously challenged even if this dismembering of the Roman rite is deplorable.[67]

● Are there other reasons for doubting the validity of the new sacraments?

The presence of correct matter and form are not sufficient to assure the valid confection of a sacrament. The minister must also intend to give the sacrament as the Church wishes to give it.

● Then a priest who does not believe in the efficacy of the sacraments is incapable of validly administering the sacraments?

The problem does not lie in the faith of the minister, but in his intention. A priest who has lost the faith can still validly administer the sacraments if he wants to be, at least in this regard, a minister of the Church (if he has the general intention of doing what the Church does). If, on the contrary, he knowingly refuses to be an instrument of Christ and the Church, the sacrament is not valid.

---

[65] November 30, 1972.
[66] In the thirteenth century, St. Thomas had already answered the argument according to which olive oil is not available everywhere: "Though olive oil is not produced everywhere, yet it can easily be transported from one place to another" (Suppl., Q. 29, Art. 4, ad 3).
[67] See on this subject the study of Fr. Pierre-Marie, O.P., *Sont-ils évêques?* [Are They Bishops?] (Editions du Sel, n.d.). A two-part English version was published in the Dec. 2005 and Jan. 2006 issues of *The Angelus*.

- **Is it really thinkable that there are priests who administer the sacraments while knowingly refusing to do what the Church does?**

    Numerous are the priests today who, during their years of study, were deliberately indoctrinated against the Catholic notion of sacrament (mocked as magic and sleight of hand). It cannot be excluded that, in the administration of the sacraments, they quite consciously refuse to effect a sign that gives grace, desiring merely to preside over a community celebration and to fulfill a social function.

91) Should one receive the sacraments in the new rites?

Because of the defects presented above, one should not receive the sacraments in the new rites, but only in the traditional rites, which alone are worthy and certainly valid. Receiving the sacraments under a form that is even slightly doubtful is not allowed. An exception should be made, however, for the last rites, when in case of emergency it is impossible to summon in time a priest faithful to Tradition.

X

Archbishop Lefebvre and the Society of St. Pius X

92) What is the Society of St. Pius X?

The Priestly Society of Saint Pius X is a congregation of priests founded by Archbishop Marcel Lefebvre. It was officially erected in the diocese of Fribourg, Switzerland, on November 1, 1970, by the diocesan bishop, the Most Reverend François Charrière. On February 18, 1971, the Society received a letter of praise from the Prefect of the Congregation for the Clergy at Rome, Cardinal Wright. The Society, thus, was recognized by the competent authorities; it is a work of the Church.

- **How big is the Society of St. Pius X at this time?**

As of [2009], the Society numbers 509 priests regularly ministering in 63 countries on all the continents, and seminarians and Brothers. It is aided by two auxiliary congregations of nuns (the Sisters of the Society of St. Pius X and the Oblates of the Society of St. Pius X). Some thirty friendly congregations work with it towards the same end.

- **What are some of the friendly congregations that work with the Society of St. Pius X?**

Among the friendly congregations of men working with the Society of St. Pius X one can name the Benedictine monks of France, Brazil, Germany, and the United States; the Capuchins of Morgon, the Dominicans of Avrillé, and the religious of the Society of the Transfiguration at Merigny, in France. On the feminine side, there are the Benedictine nuns in France and Germany; the Poor Clares of Morgon,

France; six traditional Carmels; the cloistered Dominican nuns of Avrillé; the Little Sisters of St. Francis in France and the Franciscan Sisters of Christ the King in the United States; the teaching Dominican Sisters of the congregations of Fanjeaux, Brignoles, and Wanganui; the Sisters of the Transfiguration at Merigny and the Little Handmaids of St. John the Baptist at Rafflay, France; and the Consoling Sisters of the Sacred Heart and the Disciples of the Cenacle in Italy. Other traditional religious communities exist in other parts of the world.

93) What ends does the Society of St. Pius X pursue?

The primary and principle end of the Society is the formation of good priests and their sanctification. In the present crisis of faith, it also has the mission of keeping whole and inviolate the Catholic Faith.

• Is there a link between these two ends?

A true reform of the Church can only come about by a reform of the priesthood. Only good and holy priests will be able to reignite in the hearts of the faithful the love of God and enthusiasm for the Faith. It was the catastrophic state of official seminaries that pushed Archbishop Lefebvre to found the Society. In almost every official seminary, fundamental truths of faith are denied and spiritual formation is deficient. Sometimes they teach rebellion against the teachings of the Church and incite the seminarians to sin.

94) Was the suppression of the Society of Saint Pius X valid?

It was Bishop Pierre Mamie (successor of Bishop Charrière as bishop of Fribourg) who signed the May 6, 1975, decree of suppression of the Society of Saint Pius X shortly after Archbishop Lefebvre had had discussions with Cardinals Garrone, Wright, and Tabera. Archbishop Lefebvre always contested the validity of this suppression both for reasons of legal procedure and of justice (for, in reality, the Society was peremptorily suppressed because of its fidelity to the Catholic Faith and to the traditional Mass).

• Why did Archbishop Lefebvre contest the legal proceeding that ended in the suppression of the Society?

According to canon law, a bishop can no longer suppress a religious congregation (or a clerical society of common life) once it has been erected officially in his diocese; only Rome can do this.[1] Now, the Society of St. Pius X was officially erected by Bishop Charrière in 1970. Archbishop Lefebvre judged that his successor no longer had the right to suppress it. Only Rome, and not the diocesan bishop, could do so.

- **Is this legal argument absolutely decisive?**

Archbishop Lefebvre always considered this legal argument to be decisive—especially since the Vatican never responded.[2] However, the Archbishop's resistance was not based essentially on quibbles of legal procedure, but on fundamental reasons touching on faith and morals. Thus, even if one should grant that the suppression of the Society of St. Pius X was legal (which some still maintain to this day[3]), these reasons stand, and the suppression does not become just simply because it is legal. For a judgment can very well respect the formalities of law yet be profoundly unjust and immoral.

- **Can the suppression of the Society of St. Pius X be considered as unjust and immoral?**

The suppression of the Society of St. Pius X was unjust and immoral not only because of the injustices and the lies by which it was brought about (the bishops of France waged a campaign against what they decried as the "wildcat seminary of Ecône" even though the seminary was perfectly in order!), but especially because of the *purpose* for which it was done: the imposition of the New (ecumenical) Mass and the errors of Vatican II. They had to prevent priests from receiving and in turn transmitting Catholic theology and the Mass. This purpose being totally illegitimate and contrary to the common good of the Church, so was the suppression of Ecône.

95) Was the suspension inflicted on Archbishop Lefebvre valid?

On July 22, 1976, Archbishop Lefebvre was struck with a suspension *a divinis*. This suspension was as invalid as the suppression of the Society of St. Pius X, for Archbishop Lefebvre was never summoned

---

[1] Canon 493 of the 1917 Code establishes this rule for religious congregations (*"supprimi nequit nisi a Sancta Sede"*). Canon 674 extends this rule to societies of common life without vows, which is what the Society of St. Pius X is.
[2] The tribunal of the Apostolic Signatura refused to examine the case brought before it by Archbishop Lefebvre.
[3] The debate bears upon the precise statute under which the Society of Saint Pius X was instituted at Fribourg (society of common life or a simple *pia unio*). On this subject, see the life of Archbishop Lefebvre by Bernard Tissier de Mallerais (*Marcel Lefebvre: A Biography* [2002; Angelus Press, 2004], p. 481) and the article by Canonicus in *Le Courrier de Rome*, No. 286 [476], pp. 3-6.

before the competent tribunal, and the only reason for his suspension was his attachment to the Tradition of the Church. *"Sine culpa nulla poena"*–if there is no guilt, the penalty is null and void.

- **What is a suspension "*a divinis*"?**

The suspension *a divinis* is a penalty depriving clerics of their right to exercise the functions of holy orders. If the suspension had been valid, Archbishop Lefebvre would no longer have had the right to celebrate Mass nor administer the sacraments.

96) Shouldn't he have obeyed anyway?

The pope and the bishops have received their authority from Christ for the protection and defense of the Faith. The general rule is, of course, to obey them. But should they happen to use their authority against the very purpose for which it was conferred on them–that is to say, by wishing to impose acts sinful or inimical to the Faith–then their subordinates have not only the right but even the duty to resist them: "We ought to obey God rather than men" (Acts 5:29).

- **Is it really permissible to disobey authorities of the Church for the sole reason that one judges their orders to be unjust?**

A simple personal injustice or a measure that one deems imprudent cannot justify a refusal to obey. But it is quite something else when the order given goes directly against the divine law; that is to say, when faith or morals are at stake. In this case, "obedience" would not be a virtue, but a vice. It would be in reality disobedience–while the apparent "disobedience" would prove to be the true obedience (obedience to God rather than men).

- **Is this teaching in conformity with the popes' teaching?**

Leo XIII wrote in the Encyclical *Diuturnum Illud*:

The one only reason which men have for not obeying is when anything is demanded of them which is openly repugnant to the natural or the divine law, for it is equally unlawful to command to do anything in which the law of nature or the will of God is violated. If, therefore, it should happen to any one to be compelled to prefer one or the other, viz., to disregard either the commands of God or those of rulers, he must obey Jesus Christ, who commands us to "give to Caesar the things that are Caesar's, and to God the things that are God's" [Mt. 22:21], and must reply courageously after the example of the Apostles: "We ought to obey God rather than men"[Acts 5:29]. And yet there is no reason why those who so behave themselves should be accused of refusing obedience; for, if the will of rulers is opposed to the will and the laws of God, they themselves exceed the bounds of their own power and pervert justice; nor can their authority then be valid, which, when there is no justice, is null.[4]

- **Don't these words of the Pope concern only the civil authority?**

Leo XIII's words were written in regard to the civil authority, but they express a principle. They hold in general for any and all authority.

97) Is it lawful to resist the pope?

When the pope abuses his mandate and causes the Church serious harm, one has not only the right but even the duty to resist him.

- **Are there examples in Church history of such resistance to the pope?**

At the very beginning of the Church, St. Paul stood up against St. Peter who, out of fear of displeasing the Judeo-Christians, no longer wished to dine with the converted pagans. This was a serious decision because it risked causing a split and might favor the false opinion that the practice of the Jewish law was incumbent on Christians. St. Paul declared: "But when Cephas [Peter] came to Antioch, I withstood him to his face, because he was deserving of blame" (Gal. 2:11).

- **What do the Doctors of the Church have to say about such resistance to the pope?**

St. Thomas commented on St. Paul's resistance:

> It must be observed, however, that if the faith were endangered, a subject ought to rebuke his prelate even publicly. Hence Paul, who was Peter's subject, rebuked him in public, on account of the imminent danger of scandal concerning faith, and, as the gloss of Augustine says on Galatians 2:11, "Peter gave an example to superiors, that if at any time they should happen to stray from the straight path, they should not disdain to be reproved by their subjects."[5]

- **Do other theologians teach the same thing?**

John de Torquemada (1388-1468) explicitly states that it is not out of the question that a pope might "command something contrary to natural or divine law."[6] In support of his assertion, he cites Pope Innocent III (1198-1216), who stated that one ought to obey the pope in all things, provided that he not rise up against the general discipline

---

[4] Leo XIII, Encyclical *Diuturnum Illud*, June 29, 1881, §15.
[5] St. Thomas Aquinas, *ST*, II-II, Q. 33, Art. 4.
[6] Juan de Torquemada, O.P., *Summa de Ecclesia*, Part I, Bk. IV, c. 11.

of the Church, in which case one should not follow him, unless there were a sound reason for doing so. He reiterates that one should withstand a pope if he "should wish to undertake something contrary to the constitution of the universal Church, such as, for example, deposing all the bishops or something else of this kind which would introduce disorder into the Church."[7]

- **Can you cite other examples?**

Thomas Cajetan (1469-1534), the great commentator of St. Thomas, wrote in a work devoted to the defense of the papacy:

> It is necessary to stand up to a pope who would rend the Church.... Otherwise, why should it be said that authority was given to build up and not to destroy (II Cor. 13:10)? Against a bad usage of authority, one will employ the appropriate means: by refusing obedience in what is evil, by not seeking to please, *by not keeping silent*, by rebuking, by inviting the authorities to make the necessary reproaches following the example of St. Paul and in accordance with his precept.[8]

- **Is this teaching on resistance against the pope particular to the Dominicans?**

Francis Suarez (1548-1617), who is considered to be the greatest Jesuit theologian, taught: "Should the pope prescribe something against good morals, he should not be obeyed. Should he undertake something that is obviously against justice or the common good, it is licit to resist him."[9] The same Suarez teaches elsewhere that the pope would become schismatic "were he to wish to excommunicate the whole Church or were he to seek to change all the liturgical ceremonies that rest on apostolic traditions."[10]

- **Did St. Robert Bellarmine mention resisting the pope?**

St. Robert Bellarmine (1542-1621) also teaches that it is licit to resist a pope who would harm the Church:

> Just as it is licit to resist a pope who attacks the body, so also is it licit to resist him if he attacks souls or disturbs the civil order or, above all, if he tries to destroy the Church. I say that it is licit to resist him by not doing what he orders and by impeding the execution of his will.[11]

---

[7] *Ibid.*, Bk. II, c. 106.
[8] Thomas Cajetan, O.P., *De Comparatione Auctoritatis Papae et Concilii* (Angelicum, 1936), No. 412 [emphasis added]. Francis de Vitoria, O.P., teaches the same: "If the pope, by his orders and his acts, destroys the Church, one may resist him and prevent the execution of what he commands" (*Obras* [BAC, 1960], pp. 486-87).
[9] F. Suarez, S.J., *Opera Omnia* (Paris, 1856), X, 321 (*Tractatus de Fide Dogmatica*, disp. 10, sect. 6, n. 16).
[10] F. Suarez, S.J., *Tractatus de Caritate*, disp. 12, sect. 1, n. 2.
[11] St. Robert Bellarmine, S.J., *De Romano Pontifice*, II, 29.

● But is it not defined that submission to the Roman Pontiff is necessary for salvation?

Just as membership in the Church (at least by desire[12]) is necessary for salvation, so is submission to the pope (the submission which is precisely one of the conditions for belonging to the Church). This truth was defined by Boniface VIII in his Bull *Unam Sanctam*.[13] But this submission obviously does not imply an unlimited obedience. Cajetan explains in his commentary on the *Summa Theologica*:

> If someone, for a reasonable motive, holds the person of the pope in suspicion and refuses his presence and even his jurisdiction, he does not commit the delict of schism, nor any other whatsoever, *provided that he be ready to accept the pope were he not held in suspicion.* It goes without saying that one has the right to avoid what is harmful and to ward off dangers. In fact, it may happen that the pope could govern tyrannically, and that is all the easier as he is the more powerful and does not fear any punishment from anyone on earth.[14]

● Haven't certain saints declared that holiness is incompatible with dissent against the pope?

Some saints may have advanced this pious exaggeration, but in any case that remains their personal opinion, which is contradicted, as we have seen, by many other saints. What is true is that in the matter of submission to the pope, complete, filial, and trusting obedience is the normal rule. But the reality of the rule does not mean there are never exceptions. Now, there is currently in the Church a quite exceptional crisis.

● Can the Society of Saint Pius X and allied communities consider themselves to be subject to the pope?

The virtue of obedience is a summit between two opposite vices: insubmission and servility. In the current crisis, true obedience consists neither in accepting the prevailing errors under the pretext that they

---

[12] Three conditions are necessary for really and truly belonging to the Church: baptism, faith, and submission to legitimate authority. But those who are not *really* members of the Church can, if really necessary, be saved by a supernatural desire to belong to the Church; they are then said to be members *in voto* (by the wish, by the desire). This desire, inspired in the soul by the Holy Ghost, can be *explicit* (in a catechumen who is preparing for baptism, for example) or *implicit* (in someone who does not know the Catholic Church). A person having what is called "baptism of desire" (that is to say, a truly supernatural desire for baptism) is thus a member of the Church, not in fact (*in re*) but by intention (*in voto*). Sometimes it is said (in a manner of speaking) that such a person belongs to the *soul* of the Church without being in its body.

[13] "Furthermore, we declare, say, define, and proclaim to every human creature that they by necessity for salvation are entirely subject to the Roman Pontiff" (Dz. 469).

[14] Thomas Cajetan, O.P., *Commentarium in II-II*, 39, 1.

are favored by the popes (which would be servility), nor in refusing the authority of the popes under the pretext that they are bad (the attitude of those called "sedevacantists"). True obedience consists in accepting the authority of the pope as pope, in praying for him, and respecting his person while actively resisting the bad orientations he wishes to impart to the Church. Such is the attitude of the Society of Saint Pius X and allied congregations, who can therefore say that they are indeed in a state of submission to the pope.

98) Didn't the episcopal consecrations of 1988 cause a schism?

Schism is the rejection in principle of the pope's authority, and not a simple act of disobedience. But the Society of St. Pius X acknowledges the authority of the pope, and its priests pray for him at every Mass. The episcopal consecrations, which exteriorly constituted an act of disobedience, did not give rise to any schism. Besides, the reasons given above fully justify this apparent disobedience to the pope.

- **Isn't it contradictory to protest one's recognition of the pope's authority while resisting him?**

A man might say to his father "You are not doing right" without telling him "You are no longer my father, I don't want to have anything more to do with you." These are two very different attitudes. Schism corresponds only to the second.

- **Doesn't the fact of consecrating bishops without papal mandate automatically produce a schism?**

An episcopal consecration without papal mandate does not of itself produce a schism. Cardinal Castillo Lara, doctor of Canon Law and president of the Pontifical Commission for the Authentic Interpretation of Legislative Texts, explained it thus in 1988: "The act of consecrating a bishop without papal mandate is not in itself a schismatic act."[15]

- **Can you cite another authority?**

Count Neri Capponi, professor emeritus of Canon Law at the University of Florence, also declared that an episcopal consecration against the pope's will does not constitute a schism by itself:

> He must do something more. For instance, had he set up a hierarchy of his own, then it would have been a schismatic act. The fact is that Archbishop Lefebvre said "I am creating bishops in order that my priestly

---

[15] *La Repubblica*, October 7, 1988.

order can continue. They do not take the place of other bishops. I am not creating a parallel church." Therefore this act was not, *per se*, schismatic.[16]

- **Even if it is not *per se* schismatic, isn't the consecration of bishops without Rome's permission always a delict, and doesn't it always incur *ipso facto* the penalty of excommunication?**

In the Latin Church, the pope has reserved for himself the decision to consecrate bishops since roughly the eleventh century. To fight against the schism of the Chinese "Patriotic Church" in the twentieth century, Pope Pius XII made the decision to impose excommunication on the consecration of bishops without papal mandate. This law was incorporated in Canon 1982 of the 1983 Code of Canon Law. On July 1, 1988, the Vatican invoked this canon to declare that Archbishop Marcel Lefebvre and the four bishops consecrated by him were excommunicated. They always contested this excommunication, which was lifted by Benedict XVI on January 24, 2009.

- **How could Archbishop Lefebvre have considered an excommunication expressly provided for in the Code of Canon Law as null and void?**

Church laws (and notably the one reserving to the pope decisions regarding episcopal consecrations) may admit of exceptions in extraordinary cases of extreme necessity. For in the Church, the supreme law is the salvation of souls.[17]

- **Is it certain that a case of necessity can thus suspend the application of a law?**

The principle by which a case of necessity may suspend the application of a positive law is simple common sense. When a house on a one-way street is burning, the firefighters do not worry too much about the traffic regulation! The end takes precedence over the means. The application of a law is suspended when it would go directly against its end (here: the protection of human life).

---

[16] *Latin Mass* Magazine, May-June 1993.
[17] *Suprema lex, salus animarum.* The 1983 Code of Canon Law even cites this adage in its concluding canon (1752).

- **Does the principle of state of necessity also apply for religious laws?**

  The natural law can never admit of exception (it forbids things bad *by nature*, which can therefore never become good); positive laws–even religious–can, on the contrary, admit of exceptions as Holy Scripture shows.

- **Are there cases of necessity dispensing from the fulfillment of the law in Holy Scripture?**

  The principle of case of necessity appears several times in Holy Scripture. Compelled by need, the Machabees decided to use their swords on the Sabbath day rather than allow themselves to be killed without fighting back (I Mac. 2:23-41). The Lord also invokes this principle against the princes of the priests seeking to catch him in a fault; he even cites it as self-evident (Lk. 14:5; Mac. 2:24-27): "Which of you shall have an ass or an ox fall into a pit and will not immediately draw him out, on the Sabbath day?"

- **Is the principle of case of necessity affirmed by theologians?**

  The principle of case of necessity is notably set forth by St. Thomas Aquinas, who cites the traditional adage: "Necessity has no law."[18]

- **Did the crisis currently affecting the Church really necessitate the consecration of bishops without the pope's authorization?**

  Every member of the Church has the right to receive from it the doctrine and the sacraments necessary for salvation. If the normal hierarchy (pastor, bishop, *etc.*) do not fulfill their duty, the faithful find themselves in a state of necessity that allows them to have recourse to any Catholic priest (because of the necessity, this priest then receives from the Church what is called jurisdiction of suppliance, or supplied jurisdiction, in order to minister to the faithful). In the current crisis, supplied jurisdiction empowers traditional priests to baptize, hear the confessions of, marry, *etc.*, Catholics who otherwise would not depend on them. But since the crisis was continuing unabated, and since bishops are necessary for confecting the sacraments of holy orders and confirmation, Archbishop Lefebvre found himself in the necessity of consecrating Catholic bishops to respond to the needs of souls.

---

[18] *Necessitas legem non habet. ST*, III, Q. 80, Art. 8.

- **Did Archbishop Lefebvre avoid the penalty of excommunication even though he consecrated bishops?**

Canon 1323, §4, of the 1983 Code of Canon Law (which substantially incorporates Canon 2205, §2, of the traditional Code), foresees that "[they] are not subject to a penalty when they have violated a law or precept": ..."a person who acted coerced by grave fear, even if only relatively grave, or due to necessity or grave inconvenience...." Obviously, such was the case of Archbishop Lefebvre.

- **If Archbishop Lefebvre were mistaken in his judgment that a state of necessity existed, would his excommunication be valid?**

The 1983 Code of Canon Law exempts from the penalty of excommunication not only one who actually finds himself in a real state of necessity, but also one who thinks he is in such a state without this conviction being the result of a fault on his part (Canon 1323, §7). Consequently, even should one refuse to acknowledge the real existence of the necessity, it would still be indisputable that Archbishop Lefebvre *thought* he was in such a state, and that, according to the new Code (in force at the time of the consecrations), he would not incur any penalty.[19]

- **Did the official authorities accept this argument of necessity developed by Archbishop Lefebvre?**

The official authorities never *publicly* recognized the soundness of Archbishop Lefebvre's argumentation. However, they often evinced *in private* that they scarcely believed in the reality of this excommunication. That is why Pope Benedict XVI finally withdrew it officially on January 24, 2009.

- **By lifting the excommunications of 1988, did Benedict XVI do Archbishop Lefebvre justice?**

The lifting of the excommunications was, unfortunately, but a half-measure: it allowed the four bishops consecrated by Archbishop Lefebvre to be no longer considered excommunicated, but it did not show clearly that this excommunication was always null, and it did not justify Archbishop Lefebvre's heroic act of June 30, 1988. The time for a full rehabilitation is yet to come.

---

[19] For a more in-depth discussion of this argument, see *Sel de la Terre*, No. 24, pp. 50-67. On the legitimacy of the episcopal consecrations of 1988, see the study by Fr. Mura in Nos. 4, 5, 7, and 8 of *Sel de la Terre* as well as the pamphlet by Fr. François Pivert, *Schism or Not?* (1988; Angelus Press, 1995).

99) Does the Society of St. Pius X have a false notion of Tradition?

Today the SSPX is often reproached with having a too static concept of Tradition. Conciliar Rome holds up the "living Tradition,"[20]–the adjective *living* intended to suggest that Tradition can move, like every living thing. But this is precisely the modernist error of historicism: doctrinal truth can never be reached definitively, but is perceived and expressed differently over the course of several centuries. This error was condemned by Popes St. Pius X and Pius XII.

- **Is the error of historicism really and truly present at Rome today?**

Archbishop Lefebvre often reported that when he would be speaking with Cardinal Ratzinger or other Roman personalities and would quote some condemnation issued by Pius IX or some dogmatic definition of the Council of Trent, he would hear his interlocutor reply: "But Monsignor, we are no longer living at the time of Pius IX; we are not in the era of the Council of Trent…"

- **Isn't it normal for traditions to evolve over time?**

Tradition (with a capital *T*) ought to be distinguished from traditions. The first is immutable, while the latter can undergo a certain change.

- **What is Tradition?**

Tradition (with a capital *T*), is the Apostolic Tradition, that is to say, the deposit of faith confided once and for all to the Apostles and which the Magisterium [the Church's Teaching Authority] must transmit and protect till the end of the world.[21]

- **Is Tradition absolutely immutable?**

The deposit revealed by God and transmitted by Tradition is absolutely immutable since Revelation closed with the death of the

---

[20] For example, John Paul II in his Motu Proprio *Ecclesia Dei* of July 2, 1988 (excommunicating Archbishop Lefebvre) denounced "the root" of the traditionalist resistance, which is "an incomplete and contradictory notion of Tradition." He explained that this notion is *incomplete* "because it does not take sufficiently into account the living character of Tradition, which, as the Second Vatican Council clearly taught, 'comes from the apostles and progresses in the Church with the help of the Holy Spirit' (DS 4822)." This notion would, moreover, be *contradictory* in that it is opposed to the universal magisterium of the Church (on this last point, see Questions 19 and 31 of the Catechism).

[21] See above, Question 8.

last Apostle.[22] But this immutable deposit is expressed more and more precisely by the Magisterium, which inventories and classifies it at the same time that it transmits and defends it.

● Then the Church's teaching does evolve?

Rather than speaking of *evolution* (a very ambiguous word), one should speak of *development.* Also, it should be understood that this development is *homogeneous,* that is, without mutation: it is simply the unfolding of what was included from the beginning, which a kind of compression prevented from being fully visible.[23]

● Might one not then correctly say that Tradition is living?

Tradition is living in the sense that the revealed deposit left by the Apostles is not only transmitted as a dead letter in writings, but also by *living* persons who have the authority to defend it, to show its significance, and to make it lived by faith (which is the function of the Magisterium). But it remains nonetheless that this deposit is itself *immutable*; truth does not change, and nothing that has once been defined by the Magisterium can then be modified. The expression "living Tradition," often understood as a moving, evolving Tradition, is thus today particularly dangerous.

● What are the Church traditions that coexist with immutable Tradition?

All the pious practices, the rules of institutes of religious life, methods of apostolate, liturgical or legal laws and customs that are transmitted in the Church without having been directly instituted by God at the time of the Apostles are ecclesiastical traditions, distinct from Tradition in the strict sense.

● Can all these ecclesiastical traditions be changed?

Ecclesiastical traditions are not as immutable as revealed Tradition, and, in fact, they slowly evolved over time. But they are the inheritance of the saints and the expression of the wisdom of the Church (which is guided by the Holy Ghost). It would thus be impious and very imprudent to disturb them without a proportionate reason.

---

[22] See the 21st condemned proposition of St. Pius X's Decree *Lamentabili* (Dz. 2021).
[23] See above, Question 12, as well as Bishop Tissier de Mallerais's "La Tradition vivante et combattante," *Sel de la Terre,* No. 30, pp. 16-32.

- **But haven't the "traditionalists" got an excessive and too rigid attachment to ecclesiastical traditions which, after all, are human?**

    Such a rigid and exaggerated "traditionalism," which would freeze all exterior forms and refuse any adaptation to contemporary needs, may indeed exist (it can be found among some Eastern schismatics called "Orthodox"). But this was not the attitude of St. Pius X nor of Archbishop Lefebvre, who knew how to intimately unite fidelity to the Church's past and adaptation to the needs of the day. After all, the anti-modernist battle waged by the both of them (and still being waged today by those called "traditionalists") was not essentially over human traditions by over revealed Tradition, the object of the virtue of faith. The traditionalist resistance is not first and foremost a question of Latin or cassocks or liturgical rubrics; it is well and truly a matter of faith.

- **How did St. Pius X reconcile fidelity to the past with adaptation to present needs?**

    Pope St. Pius X, who so severely condemned modernism, was at the same time a great reforming pope: he reformed the Breviary and Church music; he was the first to prepare a clear and complete Code of Canon Law; and by his two decrees on Communion, he dispelled the final influences of Jansenism. And this is only the list of his major reforms. No pontificate since the Council of Trent had promoted so many reforms as St. Pius X! But these were good reforms, inspired by a truly supernatural zeal, without any contempt for the past, and only aiming at creating the best conditions for the Church's action in the modern world for the sake of the salvation of souls.

- **Can Archbishop Lefebvre be compared to St. Pius X on this point?**

    Archbishop Lefebvre acted exactly like St. Pius X. He cleaved to Tradition with a capital T (which transmits the deposit of faith to us) and loved the Church's past as much as he knew how to be enterprising and innovative in his pastoral methods. His biography furnishes numerous examples of this.[24]

- **Where does the expression "living Tradition" used against the "traditionalists" nowadays come from?**

    The expression "living Tradition" comes from a document of Vatican II (*Dei Verbum* 12) and it mentions evolving tradition. From the

---

[24] See Bernard Tissier de Mallerais, *Marcel Lefebvre* (2002; Kansas City: Angelus Press, 2004), in particular pp. 183-86.

modernist viewpoint, the role of the magisterium is not to safeguard the deposit of Revelation, but to ensure ecclesial "communion" (in space and time). Fidelity to Tradition does not mean first of all fidelity to a deposit handed down from the Apostles, but rather docility to what the pope, guarantor of unity, says *today*.

- **Is this new notion of "living Tradition" to be found in the teaching of Benedict XVI?**

The notion of "living Tradition" is omnipresent in Pope Benedict XVI's teaching. In an allocution of April 26, 2006, for example, he defines the nature of Tradition: "The Church's apostolic Tradition consists in this transmission of the goods of salvation which, through the power of the Spirit makes the Christian community the permanent actualization of the original communion." He explains: "Tradition is the communion of the faithful around their legitimate Pastors down through history, a communion that the Holy Spirit nurtures, assuring the connection between the experience of the apostolic faith, lived in the original community of the disciples, and the actual experience of Christ in his Church."[25]

- **What is notable in this definition of Tradition?**

Under the pretext of emphasizing the *living* character of Tradition ("Tradition is the living river that links us to the origins, the living river in which the origins are ever present," the Pope also says), the essential *content* of this Tradition is left aside: revealed truth, which is immutable.

- **How should we respond to this new notion of "living Tradition"?**

It suffices to answer with St. Paul: "But though we, or an angel from heaven, preach a gospel to you besides that which we have preached to you, let him be anathema" (Gal. 1:8).

100) Wouldn't it have been possible to continue to go along with Rome?

Simple common sense shows, and experience confirms, that it is currently impossible to fully live and defend the Catholic Faith while being approved by Conciliar Rome. Following upon the episcopal consecrations of 1988, Rome conceded the celebration of the former liturgy to a few communities, but in return these were obliged to recognize the New Mass as a fully legitimate rite and to refrain from any criticism of Vatican II. In particular, they had to accept (or at

---

[25] General Audience, Wednesday, 26 April 2006.

least not criticize) religious freedom and ecumenism. Such a silence constitutes *per se* culpable complicity.

- **Which are the communities that obtained permission to use the traditional liturgy in exchange for their silence about the errors of Vatican II?**

The communities having been authorized the use of the traditional liturgy in exchange for their silence about the errors of Vatican II are in particular the Fraternity of St. Peter (issuing from a split with the Society of St. Pius X in 1988), the Institute of Christ the King (founded by Fr. Wach at Gricigliano, near Florence), the Benedictine abbey of Le Barroux (brought round in 1988), the Fraternity of St. Vincent Ferrer at Chéméré (which abruptly went from sedevacantism to the conciliar cause while Archbishop Lefebvre was dealing with Rome in 1987), the Institute of Opus Mariae (Fr. Vladimir), the Society of St. John Marie Vianney of Campos, Brazil (governed by Msgr. Rifan and brought round in 2002), and finally, most recently, the Redemptorists of Papa Stronsay. These communities are generally designated by the name "*Ecclesia Dei* communities."

- **Why do all these communities have the common name "*Ecclesia Dei* community."**

These communities are designated by the generic name "*Ecclesia Dei* communities" because most of them are under the Commission of the same name founded at Rome at the time of the 1988 episcopal consecrations for rallying those who left the Society of St. Pius X.

- **Where does the name "*Ecclesia Dei*" come from?**

The words "*Ecclesia Dei*" designate the document by which Archbishop Lefebvre was excommunicated. One might say that all these communities were established as a result of this excommunication and benefit from Archbishop Lefebvre's heroic act of June 30, 1988. If the founder of Ecône had not first announced (May 29, 1987) and then performed (June 30, 1988) these episcopal consecrations, Conciliar Rome would never have granted the traditional liturgy to all these communities.

- **Why was Conciliar Rome so bothered by these episcopal consecrations?**

Conciliar Rome was bothered by these episcopal consecrations because they assured the survival of Tradition. Until then, it might have been thought that the traditionalist reaction would eventually die out once there were no more traditional bishops to ordain traditional priests. Since Archbishop Lefebvre was quite old, it was only a matter of time, and Conciliar Rome's entire strategy consisted in trying to gain time. The consecrations of 1988 reversed the situation. Even though they left Archbishop Lefebvre, the *Ecclesia Dei* communities benefited from it. Rome in effect granted them the use of the traditional liturgy in order to detach them from Archbishop Lefebvre.

- **Do the *Ecclesia Dei* communities acknowledge that their prosperity is due to the consecrations of 1988?**

Since they are tolerated only insofar as they are publicly separated from him, the *Ecclesia Dei* communities generally avoid acknowledging their debt to Archbishop Lefebvre. Some laymen enjoy a greater freedom of speech. In 2006, the editor of the *Remnant,* a newspaper of the *Ecclesia Dei* community in the United States, publicly recognized that the Society of St. Pius X was like the counterweight that enabled the *Ecclesia Dei* communities to exist and to develop. Consequently, and very logically, he declared that he did not wish an agreement between Conciliar Rome and the Society of St. Pius X for the time being, for this displacement of the counterweight might weaken the whole traditionalist movement.

- **Aren't all these tactical considerations too human?**

It is characteristic of Vatican II to have replaced the courageous profession of the Catholic Faith with tactics, diplomacy, and dialogue (the documents on religious freedom and ecumenism are the clearest manifestation of this). Opposite, Archbishop Lefebvre was always motivated by considerations of faith. He only resorted to the consecrations of 1988 in order to continue transmitting the Catholic faith and sacraments. While keeping the same attitude, it is not out of place to note that the faith of Ecône's founder, who refused to get bogged down in human calculations, ultimately proved to be much more astute than all the maneuvers of the Vatican's diplomats.

- **Can the episcopal consecrations of 1988 then be considered to be a great victory of Catholic Tradition?**

Yes, the episcopal consecrations of 1988 constitute a great victory for the Church. They saved the traditional Mass. The slow but real progress of the Mass within the Church is an incontestable fruit of the consecrations.

- **If the victory was won, what prevents the Society from being reconciled with the Roman authorities today?**

The consecrations of 1988 contributed to saving Catholic Tradition not only by assuring the transmission of the sacrament of holy orders, and thus of the traditional Mass and sacraments, but also by protecting a small part of the Church's flock against the conciliar errors. Now, these conciliar errors continue to ravage the Church, and they reign even at Rome. To continue to be protected against them effectively, it is therefore necessary to keep a distance from the Roman authorities. The definitive victory is yet to come.

- **Wouldn't it be possible to continue resisting the conciliar errors without being outside the normal chain of command of legitimate Church authorities?**

During an epidemic, the most basic prudence imposes the strict separation of the sick from the healthy. A certain communication remains indispensable (for taking care of the sick), but it is limited as much as possible and surrounded with painstaking precautions. The same holds for the situation today: it is impossible to frequent the conciliar authorities on a regular basis without exposing oneself to contracting their errors. The example of the *Ecclesia Dei* communities furnishes the striking proof.

- **Have the members of the *Ecclesia Dei* communities really accepted the errors of Vatican II or have they only kept quiet about them?**

Without pretending to judge the internal forum or possible exceptions, it seems that most of the members of the *Ecclesia Dei* communities have ended, unfortunately, by adhering to the conciliar errors. They began by keeping a prudential silence. Then they had to give more and more tokens of unity. Unawares, they were subjected to the psychological pressure of liberalism, all the more effective the less compulsory it seems. They ended by refraining from thinking otherwise than they spoke and acted. ("One must live the way one thinks or end up thinking the way one lives," as Paul Bourget said.) In short, they were completely caught in the machinery into which they imprudently put a finger.

- **Is acceptance of the conciliar errors common to all the *Ecclesia Dei* communities?**

There are undoubtedly nuances, but, in general, all the *Ecclesia Dei* communities today accept the conciliar errors. When making its peace with Conciliar Rome in July 1988, Le Barroux publicly imposed a condition: "That no doctrinal or liturgical counterpart be required of us, and that silence not be imposed on our *antimodernist preaching.*"[26] But by the following October, one monk had observed "a certain relativizing of the critique of *Dignitatis Humanae* and Assisi" within the abbey.[27] In fact, Le Barroux was even to go so far as to try to justify the errors of Vatican II publicly.[28] The Fraternity of St. Peter, which at first claimed to be continuing exactly what the Society of St. Pius X was doing (except for the episcopal consecrations) has similarly slid.

• But do the *Ecclesia Dei* communities stand firm as regards the liturgy?

Far from resisting firmly, the *Ecclesia Dei* communities have all more or less accepted the new liturgy: Dom Gerard (the father abbot of Le Barroux)[29] had to concelebrate the New Mass with the Pope (on April 27, 1995). Fr. Wach (superior of the Institute of Christ the King) had already done as much (on December 21, 1991[30]). Bishop Rifan has also concelebrated the New Mass (on September 8, 2004). The Fraternity of St. Peter had to accept the principle of concelebrating the Holy Thursday chrismal Mass with the bishops of the dioceses where it is established (Rocca di Papa meeting, February 8-12, 2000[31]). The Fraternity of St. Vincent Ferrer is a little more reserved: they "only" recommend attending the Holy Thursday chrismal Mass in choir and receiving Communion[32] (but even this is a liturgical participation and therefore an acceptance of the New Mass).

---

[26] "Green Light for Le Barroux Monastery: Dom Gerard's Declaration," [French] *Présent*, August 18, 1988.
[27] Letter of Fr. Joseph Vannier (former subprior of Le Barroux) to Dom Gerard, *Fideliter*, January-February 1989, p. 14.
[28] From 1993, Le Barroux attempted to justify the new Catechism of the Catholic Church (cf. *Sel de la Terre*, No. 9, pp. 175-88, on this bad try); Fr. Basil (of the same abbey) set himself to justifying the religious freedom taught by Vatican II in a "monumental" study of 2,960 pages (see *Sel de la Terre*, No. 30, pp. 202-7). He recognized that other authors who had so far tried to reconcile *Dignitatis Humanae* with Tradition (Fr. Lucien, Fr. Harrison, Fr. Margerie, Fr. de Saint-Laumer, *etc.*) had not succeeded, but he thought he had found the solution. For several years, Fr. Basil's thesis was presented in *Ecclesia Dei* circles as *the* proof that it is possible to reconcile Vatican II with Tradition. Unfortunately, another monk of Le Barroux, Fr. Jehan, published a dissertation in canon law in 2004 proving that Fr. Basil's thesis suffered from a "fatal" flaw: it radically falsified the teaching of St. Thomas Aquinas on "Law" (see *Sel de la Terre*, No. 56, pp. 180-7). Instead of preaching Christ the King, the "rallied" devote themselves to defending Vatican II in contradictory writings that only add to the general confusion.
[29] He entered eternity February 28, 2008. R.I.P.–*Ed.*
[30] Photograph in *Sel de la Terre*, No. 21, p. 182.
[31] On this important meeting at Rocca di Papa, cf. Jonathan White's account in *Sel de la Terre*, No. 41, pp. 226-33.
[32] *Sedes Sapientiae*, No. 68, pp. 3-30. Cf. *Sel de la Terre*, No. 32, pp. 217-19.

- **Surely the *Ecclesia Dei* communities at least gain a wider field of apostolate in exchange for these compromises?**

The situation varies quite a bit from country to country (and in France, from diocese to diocese), but most of the bishops restrict the activities of the *Ecclesia Dei* communities. Even those bishops who are not too hostile towards them hesitate to welcome them since they fear the reactions of their clergy or the activist laity. Rome for its part fears the reactions of the bishops. The situation of the *Ecclesia Dei* communities would be precarious in the extreme were it not for the Society of St. Pius X's counterweight.

- **Finally, what does this situation reveal?**

The situation of the *Ecclesia Dei* communities, which are gradually being constrained to abandon traditional doctrine yet which are only accepted in various dioceses with many restrictions, clearly confirms the existence of "the state of necessity" invoked by Archbishop Lefebvre to justify the consecrations of 1988. Now as then, for those who desire to defend the Catholic Faith to the bitter end, it is impossible to place themselves in the hands of authorities who contradict or relativize the Catholic Faith. That is why the "doctrinal discussions" called for by the Society of Saint Pius X must precede any practical solutions. But this situation will not last indefinitely, as Our Lord promised: "The gates of hell shall not prevail" (Mt. 16:18).